THE
COMPLETE FILMS
OF
LAURENCE OLIVIER

ALSO BY THE AUTHOR

Burt Lancaster
Bette Davis
Cary Grant
Barbara Stanwyck
The Films of Elizabeth Taylor (with Mark Ricci)
  (CITADEL)
Ida Lupino
The Great British Films (CITADEL)
The Films of Charles Bronson (CITADEL)
The Films of the Thirties (CITADEL)
The Films of the Twenties (CITADEL)
500 Best British and Foreign Films to Buy, Rent or
  Videotape (Editor)
More Films of the Thirties (CITADEL)

Six-portrait montage of Olivier in (clockwise from top): *Brideshead Revisited, Hamlet, Othello, Richard II,* and as himself in the early 1950s. Center shot is also from *Brideshead Revisited.*

The Complete Films of
LAURENCE OLIVIER

by

JERRY VERMILYE

A CITADEL PRESS BOOK
Published by Carol Publishing Group

For

<small>HARRYETTA PETERKA</small>

—In the Olivier tradition,
as brilliant and versatile a
performer as ever an actor or
director could hope to work with.

ACKNOWLEDGMENTS

The author wishes to express his gratitude to the following individuals and organizations for helping locate rare stills and videocassettes, and for giving so generously of their time to offer editorial assistance: The British Film Institute's National Film Archive, Laurie Britton, Jim Butler, Judy and Paul Caputo, John Cocchi, Christopher Paul Denis, Sherman R. Emery, Bob Finn, Bill Grayson, Alvin H. Marill, Mark Ricci and the Memory Shop, and Allan Turner.

And a vote of thanks to all of the anonymous still and portrait photographers whose artistry illustrates these pages, as well as to the companies which aired or distributed these films and plays: ABC-TV, CBS-TV, Columbia, Continental, Fox, General Film Distributors, Granada TV, Home Box Office, Metro-Goldwyn-Mayer, NBC-TV, Paramount, RKO Radio, Showtime, 20th Century-Fox, United Artists, Universal, Wardour, and Warner Bros.

A Citadel Press Book
Published by Carol Publishing Group
Citadel Press is a registered trademark of Carol Communications, Inc.

Editorial Offices: 600 Madison Avenue, New York, N.Y. 10022
Sales & Distribution Offices: 120 Enterprise Avenue, Secaucus, N.J. 07094
In Canada: Canadian Manda Group, P.O. Box 920, Station U,
  Toronto, Canada M8Z 5P9

Queries regarding rights and permissions should be addressed to Carol
  Publishing Group, 600 Madison Avenue, New York, N.Y. 10022

Carol Publishing Group books are available at special discounts for bulk purchases, for sales promotions, fund raising, or educational purposes. Special editions can be created to specifications. For details contact: Special Sales Department, Carol Publishing Group, 120 Enterprise Avenue, Secaucus, N.J. 07094

Designed by A. Christopher Simon

Manufactured in the United States of America

10 9 8 7 6 5 4 3 2 1

Library of Congress Cataloging-in-Publication Data

Vermilye, Jerry.
    The complete films of Laurence Olivier / by : Jerry Vermilye.
        p. cm.
      "A Citadel Press book."
      ISBN 0-8065-1302-0
      1. Olivier, Laurence, 1907-1989—Criticism and interpretation.
    I. Title.
    PN2598.O55V4   1992
    791.43'028'092—dc20
                                                92-9794
                                                CIP

CONTENTS

THE MAN

As a very young actress, I was once asked what it was like to act with him, and I remember saying: "You don't have to act, you just react."

Not true, of course. Finally you realise that you have to act with every fibre of your being and every ounce of your skill to stay on your feet; he was constantly challenging you to be better.

—JOAN PLOWRIGHT

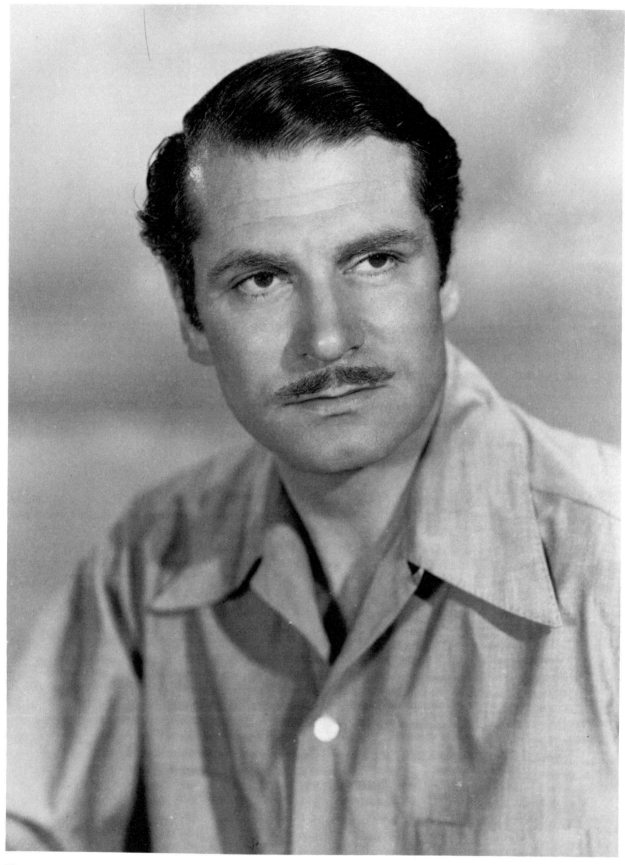

Portrait from the 1950s.

LAURENCE OLIVIER

Was he really, in his lifetime, the greatest living actor? Quite likely he was. It would be a hard title to disprove. Nevertheless, it would seem that Laurence Olivier did it all. Blessed in his prime with the sort of striking good looks that, coupled with an excellent speaking voice and physique, can assure an actor of longevity as a leading man of all the entertainment media, Laurence Olivier was not satisfied to ride to success on his surface attributes. Unimpressed by his own appearance (long-standing dissatisfaction with his nose moved him to sport a wide succession of false ones in many of his roles), the actor had no wish to ride to beckoning Hollywood fame in his youth as a second-string Ronald Colman, despite a remote resemblance to the older British actor. Instead, he realized the more fascinating challenges of so-called "character" acting and, by the early forties, this barely thirty-plus young movie star was already portraying middle-aged romantic roles in hit movies like *Rebecca* (1940) and *That Hamilton Woman* (1941), as well as such foreign-accented younger parts as the French-Canadian trapper of *49th Parallel* (1941) and the visiting Russian engineer of *The Demi-Paradise* (1943). In *Carrie* (1952), Olivier had his first *American* role, and in *The Beggar's Opera* (1953), he raised his own, untrained singing voice in a costume musical. At thirty-seven, with a thorough background in Shakespearean theatre, Olivier moved into territory where no predecessor had succeeded—not only starring in a major film version of the Bard's *Henry* V (1944) but *directing* it as well—and all of this accomplished under the most difficult and challenging of times, for Britain was, of course, embroiled in World War II.

An outwardly modest man of sound breeding and well-controlled temperament, Laurence Olivier was nevertheless forced to contend with the praise and acclaim attendant on a multitude of acting awards, apart from the signal honor of knighthood at forty, and a peer of the realm, earning the (unprecedented for an actor) title of *Lord* Olivier in 1970, aged sixty-three.

Despite three marriages—all to actresses—and four children, acting remained, if not his greatest love, his eternal mistress. And, when the tribulations of age, disease, and physical infirmity precluded the repetitive demands of stage performance, Olivier shifted his thespian commitments exclusively to films and television. There, despite a paucity of parts worthy of his talents, he continued to work, painful and debilitating illness notwithstanding. To inquisitive interviewers, he said he did it for the money—that he needed it to support his young, second family. But those who knew him best realized that it was the *work* that kept him going—that, absolutely refusing to retire, helped him reach the ripe age of eighty-two.

Most probably, Laurence Olivier's greatest acting accomplishments occurred in the living theatre. But, of course, those performances are dust, remaining only in the mortal memories of those who were present at the time. We have only the old theatrical programs and production photographs as evidence that such events ever happened. Otherwise, the wide spectrum of Olivier's incredible talent, range, and professional daring continues to be available for evaluation as long as the existence of film and video.

He was born in Dorking, Surrey, on May 22, 1907, the third child and second son of Agnes Crookenden Olivier and the Reverend Gerard Kerr Olivier, an Anglican clergyman. The family was of French Huguenot derivation, and they named the youngest child Laurence Kerr, after Laurent Olivier, a sixteenth-century ancestor whose name was the earliest recorded on the family tree. The actor later termed his family background "an atmosphere of genteel poverty—probably the most fertile ground for ambition there can be."

Known familiarly to his family as "Kim," young Laurence was far closer to his mother than his temperamental father, whose dramatic behavior in the pulpit was an early inspiration to the future actor. As the boy's sister Sybille later revealed, "Father didn't like Larry, and Larry was terrified of him. Mother adored Larry. He always amused her very much. He was a complete clown."

At nine, Larry joined his older brother Dickie at All Saints, a small, choir-oriented boarding school that housed fourteen boys in just two dormitories. Among them, Laurence Naismith, a fellow student who would later gain employment as a character actor, recalled Larry Olivier as "a natural actor, even as a boy—and he had great presence." But, Naismith also felt: "He was not altogether a nice boy, or at least so I thought then; a bit of a bully. Yet he did have this commanding presence."

When, the following year, the school presented Shakespeare's *Julius Caesar*, Larry was cast as First Citizen. But, at ten, his intensity proved him unworthy, in rehearsal, of so trivial a part, and he was instead promoted to the important role of Brutus, with Larry's brother Dickie playing the title role. The play's director, school precentor Geoffrey Heald, was suitably impressed with Larry's apparent aptitude for stage movement and speaking verse. This amateur stage debut was witnessed by a number of theatrical professionals, including the famed actress Ellen Terry, who was sufficiently moved to write in her diary, "The small boy who played Brutus is already a great actor."

The school subsequently cast Larry Olivier as Maria in *Twelfth Night*, where he did so well as a "leading lady" that he went on to make his greatest impact in his next— and last—All Saints production, *The Taming of the Shrew*, in which the boy had the female lead of Katharina, opposite Geoffrey Heald's Petruchio. This time the returning Ellen Terry declared that she had seldom seen Kate played better by a *woman*. An Olivier family friend, Sybil Thorndike, then on the verge of stardom at thirty-five, well remembered that production, later commenting, "His shrew was really wonderful—the best Katharina I ever saw. . . . You know, some people are born with technical ability. And Larry was. He didn't have to work hard at technical things, because he knew it all from the start, instinctively."

In 1920, when the boy was still at All Saints, his mother died at forty-eight of a brain tumor. Many years later, the adult Olivier admitted in an interview, "I often think, and say, that perhaps I've never got over it."

In the autumn of 1921, fourteen-year-old Larry became a boarder at St. Edward's school (familiarly known as "Teddie's") in Oxford where he was, to his chagrin, cast as Puck in a production of *A Midsummer Night's Dream*—a role he threw himself into with such fervor

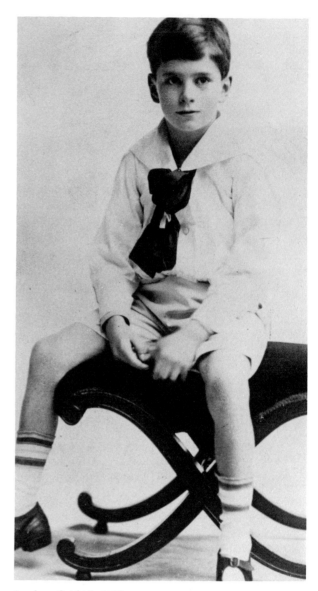

As a boy of eight in 1915.

that the boy found himself faced with something he'd never experienced before—popularity with his peers.

From St. Edward's, the young Olivier went on to professional study at Elsie Fogerty's Central School of Speech Training and Dramatic Art in London. He later gave Miss Fogerty credit for instilling in him a self-conscious emotional block about his appearance when, putting her finger atop his nose, she informed the boy, "You have weakness . . . *here*." As Olivier later rationalized the problem, "It lasted until I discovered the protective shelter of nose putty and enjoyed a pleasurable sense of relief and relaxation when some character part called for a sculptural addition to my face." During the Christmas school holidays, he found his first professional theatrical employment, as second assistant stage manager at the theatre in Letchworth's St. Christopher's School, where he also served as general understudy in a children's play called *Through the Crack*. And during Easter, he doubled as assistant stage manager and played Lennox in *Macbeth*.

While still a student at the Central School, the seventeen-year-old aspiring actor "turned immediately and with grim determination to the necessity of finding work," making the traditional rounds of every theatrical agent in central London. His first appearance on a West End stage on November 30, 1924, was as the Suliot Officer in *Byron* by Alice Law. He received bottom-of-the-cast billing as "Lawrence Olivier," but it was a beginning—brought to pass because the play's producer and star was one of his Central School instructors, Henry Oscar. Later that season, young "Lawrence" had more to say and do by doubling as Master Snare and Thomas of Clarence in *King Henry IV, Part II*—his first London bout with Shakespeare, although not one of the critics took any notice.

Directly after his year as a London drama student, he appeared that summer at the Brighton Hippodrome,

where he participated in *Unfailing Instinct* (which served as a curtain-raiser for *The Ghost Train*) and, because of a clumsy entrance, fell into the footlights and drew one critic's attention—and his first professional notice: "Mr. Laurence Olivier made a good deal out of a rather small part."

That October, the novice actor gained his first sustained employment with the Lena Ashwell Players, a company that paid miserable wages to tour the London suburbs in a series of one-night stands. Their often having to change makeup in restrooms earned them the sobriquet "The Lavatory Players." Olivier portrayed Flavius in *Julius Caesar*, but was fired for his onstage penchant for lapsing into hysterical laughter at the slightest provocation.

A period of subsequent unemployment eventually ended with the aid of family friends Sybil Thorndike and her husband, Lewis Casson. With Casson and his producing partner Bronson Albery preparing *Henry VIII* for the West End, Larry was made supernumerary and general understudy, as well as one of two assistant stage managers, for the princely reimbursement of £3 per

Standing at left as a girl in *Twelfth Night* (1917), with Fabia Drake, John Freebairn-Smith, Jack Sutters, and Fred Oxley at All Saints choir school.

With Freda Clark in *The Farmer's Wife* (1926).

As *Uncle Vanya*
(1927).

week. A few months later, for the same management, he played a servant (with several lines) in Shelley's *The Cenci*, again doubling as A. S. M. Olivier later recalled, "I was a marvelous Assistant Stage Manager. I ought to have stayed an A. S. M. all my life."

In March of 1926, Larry Olivier auditioned for—and was accepted into—the Birmingham Rep, which was about to perform *The Marvellous History of Saint Bernard* in London. In it, with his surname misspelled "Ollivier" in the program, he had the small role of a minstrel. Soon thereafter, in that company, he first made the acquaintance of actor Ralph Richardson; their mutual dislike was immediate, and was only exacerbated by Olivier's fancied crush on Richardson's actress-wife, Muriel Hewitt. With the Birmingham Rep's touring division, Olivier then spent six months as Richard Coaker, the lovesick young farmer, in *The Farmer's Wife*, and was asked to remain in Birmingham as the company's leading juvenile. In the one-act comedy *Something to Talk About*, he sported a monocle as a young aristocrat. More important roles followed, including Jack Borthwick in *The Silver Box*, Tony Lumpkin in *She Stoops to Conquer*, Parolles in a modern-dress version of *All's Well That Ends Well*, and the title role in *Uncle Vanya*.

It was now 1926, the year Ronald Colman starred in a Hollywood-made silent-screen version of *Beau Geste*, and after Olivier saw the film, his colleagues noticed the novice actor combing his hair in the Colman style and experimenting with a pencilled-on Colmanesque mustache. (Olivier later admitted that he spent the next few years trying to *be* another Colman.)

When the Birmingham Rep's Barry Jackson developed a package of five plays to transfer to London for an experimental season at the start of 1928, he opened with Elmer Rice's expressionistic *The Adding Machine*. Olivier worked hard on this American drama, determined to make the most of his small part. Reviewing the play in *The Observer*, St. John Ervine wrote, "Mr. Laurence Olivier, as the young man who accompanies Judy O'Grady into the graveyard, gave a very good performance indeed—the best, I think, in the play. He had little to do, but he *acted*."

In the company's subsequent modern-dress *Macbeth*, Olivier played Malcolm in a gray flannel suit. An ill-conceived, and often poorly acted offering, it was later recalled by actress Jessica Tandy, who was then making her debut with the Birmingham Rep: "Not a very inspired production until Larry appeared. The scene in exile with Macduff was electrifying, and one left the theatre with an exhilarating feeling of having seen the beginnings of an actor of enormous potential."

There followed a revival of Shaw's *Back to Methuselah*, with Olivier as Martellus, and then he was given his

As Tony Lumpkin in *She Stoops to Conquer* (1927).

With Dorothy Turner in *Aren't Women Wonderful?* (1927).

With Edmund Willard, Jack Hawkins, and Robert Irvine in *Beau Geste* (1929). Olivier is lying down at the right.

big break—the title role—and his first lead on the London stage—in Tennyson's 1876 verse drama *Harold*, about England's last Saxon king. The twenty-year-old actor's performance was received with more praise than was the play; again, St. John Ervine was impressed, and wrote prophetically: "The good performance he gave in *Macbeth*, added to the good performance he gives in *Harold*, makes me believe that when romantic and poetic drama return to their proper place in the theatre, Mr. Olivier will be ready to occupy the position of a distinguished romantic actor."

The Birmingham/London season came to a popular close with their modern-dress *Taming of the Shrew*, in which Olivier had little to do, though prominently visible throughout the play—and by now sporting his own homegrown Ronald Colman mustache!

Having turned twenty-one, Laurence Olivier now displayed maturity and self-assurance, as well as striking good looks, and when he went into the West End production of *Bird in Hand*, replacing Patrick Susands as Gerald Arnwood, the squire's son lovesick over an innkeeper's daughter, he found himself attracted as well to the dark-haired twenty-year-old actress cast opposite him. Her stage name, at that time, was Jill Esmond Moore, and when the smitten Olivier proposed marriage, she suggested that they first get to know one another better.

The young Olivier then took a chance with an untried World War I play, R.C. Sherriff's *Journey's End*, which was to be directed by an unimportant actor named James Whale, who wanted him for the pivotal role of Capt. Dennis Stanhope. It was an enterprise which would involve three weeks of rehearsal and minuscule pay for a two-performance engagement! Among his colleagues were three young actors at the start of long, notable careers of their own: Maurice Evans, George Zucco, and Melville Cooper. *Journey's End* had its first performance at the Apollo Theatre on December 9, 1928. But it was the following one which drew the London critics, whose enthusiastic reactions stirred much talk of financial backing, though the professional consensus was that war plays had no commercial value. And, while his fellow cast members refrained from accepting other work as they awaited the fate of *Journey's End*, the role of Stanhope proved an important stepping-stone for Laurence Olivier; it convinced producer Basil Dean that the West End's youthful answer to Hollywood's Ronald Colman would be right for the Colman role in Dean's ambitious staging of *Beau Geste*. In turn, the little-known Colin Clive replaced Olivier (and became an overnight star) at the Savoy Theatre in *Journey's End*, where it scored a huge and long-running success. Meanwhile, the original Stanhope became part of a spectacular production that would include a pitched Foreign Legion military battle, while employing a cast of 120, among whom were Madeleine Carroll, Robin Ervine, and Marie Lohr. Essentially cinematic in its material, *Beau Geste* proved far too long and unwieldy for either the reviewers or London audiences, closing in little over a month. Adding insult to injury, critic James Agate, who had had nothing but praise for Olivier's Stanhope, dismissed the actor's performance as Beau, instead singling out eighteen-year-old Jack Hawkins (who played his brother John) as "a young actor with a future."

Olivier continued to work in leading West End roles, but in brief runs of unsuccessful plays (*The Circle of Chalk, Paris Bound, The Stranger Within*) until, in mid-1929, he was offered the opportunity of playing in the New York production of a London hit called *Murder on the Second Floor*. Apart from the lure of legendary Broadway—and his first trip to the United States—was the prospect of proximity to Jill Esmond, who was enjoying a successful run there in *Bird in Hand*. And so he sailed for New York, where he received a warm reception from Jill—and a cool one in his play, which folded in five weeks.

Back in London, Olivier had a good dramatic role in *The Last Enemy* that drew critical praise, but only added another flop to his burgeoning resumé. There followed an especially fallow period, during which he accepted a few weeks' work in each of two motion pictures, the Anglo-German *The Temporary Widow*, opposite Lilian Harvey, and *Too Many Crooks*, a forgettable little "Quota quickie," designed to fulfill the British Quota Act, providing low-budget British films to balance the flood of Hollywood imports.

Jill Esmond returned from New York in the spring of 1930, and when her engagement to Laurence Olivier was formally announced, she became the object of more attention from the press than did he, for her career was then in high gear. As for Olivier, having established himself as a West End leading man, he was naturally loath to accept supporting roles—even the important one then being proffered by Noël Coward, boorish Victor Prynne in Coward's *Private Lives*. The play was designed as a comedic vehicle for Coward and Gertrude Lawrence, and it took all of Coward's powers of persuasion to make him accept it. As the actor-playwright later recalled, "Poor Larry never really enjoyed playing it very much. But really, curiously enough, it did him a lot of good."

And, indeed, Olivier's memoirs suggest that he actually enjoyed the experience, especially the backstage (and occasional *onstage*) laughs engendered by working with the irrepressible Noël and "Gertie." By then, Larry and Jill Esmond were Mr. and Mrs. Olivier, having made a

A late-twenties portrait.

With Noel Coward in *Private Lives* (1930).

Arriving in Hollywood with Jill Esmond (1931).

About to leave Broadway for Hollywood in 1931.

big-scale event of it on July 25, 1930, at All Saints, Marylebone.

Private Lives was, of course, a major hit of the London season, garnering glowing reviews for its leads but scant notice for Olivier and Adrianne Allen, as the secondary couple. In the London *Times*, Ivor Brown observed that "both look too intelligent for the pair of dear, good boobies who are the victims of the capricious couple; but both have high talent and can assume a blankness, though they have it not." As Coward himself later wrote, "Larry managed, with determination and much personal charm, to invest the wooden Victor with enough reality to make him plausible."

Before crossing the Atlantic once again to play Victor in the New York *Private Lives*—opposite a blond-wigged Jill (replacing the now-pregnant Adrianne Allen)—Olivier spent daylight hours filming *Potiphar's Wife*, while continuing onstage at night. Opposite Nora Swinburne's wealthy aristocrat, he played her handsome chauffeur in this sex drama which won him modest praise, while drawing criticism for the movie's "immoral" premise. In its eventual American release, *Potiphar's Wife*—perhaps designed to attract the prurient—became *Her Strange Desire*.

During the run of *Private Lives*, Noël Coward not only proved a valuable role-model for playing modern comedy, but also used psychology to cure the younger actor of his penchant for onstage giggling, whenever anything struck him as amusing. And, as Olivier told Kenneth Tynan in a 1967 BBC-TV interview: "He taxed me with his sharpness and his brilliance. He used to point out when I was talking nonsense, which nobody else had ever done before. He gave me a sense of balance of right and wrong. Noël was a tremendous influence. He made me a little bit more sensible than I had been up till then, I think."

Broadway was then a rich hunting ground for acting talent for Hollywood, and both Oliviers were tested by a number of film studios while playing *Private Lives* in New York. Oddly enough, the general consensus seemed to be that Jill Esmond (then most impressive in her just-released film debut in Alfred Hitchcock's *The Skin Game*) had a more promising movie future than Laurence Olivier. Paramount considered signing them both, but didn't. Instead, RKO got them, with $700-a-week contracts.

Ironically, RKO began by loaning Jill out to Paramount to play Ruth Chatterton's daughter in *Once a Lady*—at the same time Esmond's actress-mother Eva Moore was in Hollywood playing character roles in MGM's *But the Flesh Is Weak* and Universal's *The Old Dark House*. His studio hoped to exploit Olivier's likeness to Ronald Colman, casting him opposite the tem-

pestuous French import Lily Damita in *Friends and Lovers*, an unlikely and forgettable triangle romance which also starred Adolphe Menjou and Erich von Stroheim. This trivial programmer did little to convince the young British actor that Hollywood was the place for him and his wife. As it was, they were, for the most part, collecting their paychecks for doing nothing except await further acting assignments. Then while Larry was loaned to Fox for *The Yellow Ticket* and played opposite Ann Harding in RKO's *Westward Passage*, Jill had high hopes of getting the coveted daughter role opposite John Barrymore in *A Bill of Divorcement*. Its producer, David O. Selznick, seemed enthusiastic about her, and Jill knew it could mean genuine motion-picture stardom. But instead, RKO settled on a New York actress named Katharine Hepburn, and the Oliviers sailed back to England, where an offer awaited him to costar with Gloria Swanson in her first self-produced British picture, *Perfect Understanding*. He replaced her then-husband, Michael Farmer, who was demoted to a small part. The film's utter failure ended Swanson's producing career and sent her back to Hollywood.

Understandably unhappy with motion pictures, despite the money involved, Olivier returned to the London stage as the young schoolmaster in Keith Winter's *The Rats of Norway*, which opened in April 1933. It was not a leading role, but he liked the script's dramatic elements, and was especially excited about working with Gladys Cooper and an old friend, Raymond Massey. An assured success, the play drew general acclaim that included Olivier, although he was chastised by *The Observer*'s critic for his "frequent inaudibility." With a long run thus assured, the Oliviers leased a fashionable house in London's Chelsea district—only to be met by new offers from Hollywood. Especially tempting was the one from MGM, which wanted him in the movie capital two weeks later. The offer was one no up-and-coming actor could afford to refuse—the chance to costar with Greta Garbo in *Queen Christina*. He held out for $1,500 a week (Metro had originally offered forty weeks work for only $40,000), as well as first-class return transportation. The studio not only agreed, but also promised him another important movie, should the Garbo project fail to materialize. Olivier continued to haggle with Metro over further details, basically not relishing a return to Los Angeles.

Finally, with Louis Hayward replacing him in *The Rats of Norway*, the actor sailed for America that July, accompanied by his wife. MGM was preparing to start shooting the bedroom scene at the country inn where Olivier's character, the Spanish envoy to the seventeenth-century Swedish court, first meets the queen (disguised as a boy), shares a night with her, and inspires such ardor that she is subsequently ready to abdicate for him.

But Olivier found no on-set rapport with the notoriously aloof Garbo. Their rehearsals produced no response from the Swedish star, no warmth to meet his own anxious enthusiasm. As he later recalled: "I went into my role giving everything that I had, but at the touch of my hand Garbo became frigid. I could feel the sudden tautness of her, her eyes as stony and expressionless as if she were marble. I worked on the film for about two weeks."

Although Garbo herself never offered any explanation of what happened, the consequence was that Olivier was released from the film and replaced by Garbo's former lover and silent-film costar, John Gilbert. And, although the studio wanted to test him for the male lead, opposite Norma Shearer, in *Romeo and Juliet*, the English actor dismissed that idea with the statement that he didn't consider Shakespeare suitable material for motion pictures!

He and Jill then left Hollywood, vacationing in Hawaii, where MGM wired him the offer of a year's $1,500-a-week *contract* (with a forty-week guarantee)—which Olivier ignored. Instead, he and his wife returned to Broadway to act together in Mordaunt Shairp's *The Green Bay Tree*, a daring drama about a homosexual relationship. This became a difficult and challenging experience because of its producer-director, the legendary acid-mouthed egocentric Jed Harris. The play's eventual success (it opened in October of 1933) may have been as much attributable to the negative energy generated by Olivier's hatred of Harris as to the excellence of play and cast. British-born James Dale, who portrayed the wealthy older man in the relationship, recalled, "It was one of the most unhappy experiences for both of us." And yet Olivier received rave reviews—the best he had yet had. In *The New York Times*, Brooks Atkinson thought Dale and Olivier acted "like bolts of lightning," continuing, "Olivier's Julian is an extraordinary study in the decomposition of a character. His ability to carry a character through from casual beginnings to a defeated conclusion, catching all the shades of meaning as he goes, is acting of the highest quality."

James Dale's candid comments on his colleague, however, reveal a young actor of uncertain discipline: "He was inclined to speak with his mouth shut and was very fidgety onstage. He was restless and active, which made it difficult for the others, who never knew what he was going to do. I had a long dinner scene with him, and it was the most terrible experience, because he would never do the same thing. Night after night, I never knew what he was going to do; I got the impression that he didn't know himself. But the audience liked it very much indeed. The character in *The Green Bay Tree* was a limp,

wet, lackadaisical, rather effeminate lad—the very last thing that Larry Olivier was, is, or ever will be. I understand that he didn't like himself in the part."

Olivier was overjoyed when he and Jill left the play in March 1934, to return home for his friend Noël Coward's London production of S. N. Behrman's American play *Biography*, opposite its original star, Ina Claire. Olivier received good notices, but Claire failed to duplicate her Broadway success in the central role, and the play suffered a brief run. Again, Olivier found success elusive, playing Bothwell opposite Gwen Ffrangcon-Davies in Gordon Daviot's short-lived *Queen of Scots*. Reluctantly, he then went into *Theatre Royal* (an understandably discreet Transatlantic title-change for the George S. Kaufman-Edna Ferber play *The Royal Family*). Reluctantly, because his engagement was only designed as a temporary pinch-hit for Brian Aherne, the British actor who was delayed in Hollywood, filming *What Every Woman Knows* with Helen Hayes. But, by the time of Aherne's belated arrival, Olivier had made that John Barrymore-like role so much his own that Aherne could only stand back in admiration. And then, not only did the play's elderly female star, Marie Tempest, refuse to participate in additional rehearsals with Aherne, but Katharine Cornell made Aherne an unrefusable offer to play Romeo opposite her Juliet in New York. His departure enabled Laurence Olivier to enjoy a personal triumph in the flamboyant, athletic role of Tony Cavendish. But this success was curtailed two months later when his onstage Fairbanksian acrobatics induced a broken ankle; Robert Douglas took over the part and completed the play's run.

Fortuitously, Olivier's next role confined him to a wheelchair in Keith Winter's *The Ringmaster*, an eight-performance 1935 flop, despite an impressive cast (including wife Jill) and first-night enthusiasm. His subsequent play, *Golden Arrow*—and his first as actor-manager—only lasted a week longer than *The Ringmaster*, though it served to inaugurate the career of twenty-year-old Greer Garson, who was given the female lead.

The spring of 1935 marked some important turning points for Laurence Olivier. A month prior to the opening of *Golden Arrow*, he had signed a long-term film contract with producer-director Alexander Korda's London Films Productions, joining a "star stable" that already included Charles Laughton, Ralph Richardson, Raymond Massey, and Merle Oberon. And he made the formal acquaintance of an enchanting young actress who had, he recalled, paid him an impulsive backstage visit during the run of *Theatre Royal*, simply to express her excitement over his performance. Her name was Vivien Leigh, and she was already a very married wife and mother who had just become the toast of the West End

With Edith Evans and John Gielgud in *Romeo and Juliet* (1935).

With James Dale in *The Green Bay Tree* (1933).

with her star-making performance in *The Mask of Virtue*, as a French gamine who passes as an innocent virgin.

Olivier also appeared in his first Korda movie, the spy drama *Moscow Nights* (U.S. title: *I Stand Condemned*), under Anthony Asquith's direction. Though no cinema landmark, *Moscow Nights* inspired *The Observer*'s reviewer to write: "The surprise of the picture is Laurence Olivier, who plays the young officer with as much wit and feeling as if the tomfool fellow were really a possible character."

That autumn of 1935, John Gielgud and his producing partner, Bronson Albery, offered Olivier the opportunity of sharing with Gielgud the roles of Romeo and Mercutio in their forthcoming *Romeo and Juliet*. Robert Donat, their first choice, had declined the offer, despite a cast that included Peggy Ashcroft as Juliet and Edith Evans as the Nurse. Encouraged by Gielgud's hit 1934 production of *Hamlet*, Olivier realized a renewed interest in Shakespeare, and entered into the hectic three-week rehearsal period with an enthusiasm that managed to override the intrinsic differences between his own realistic acting technique and Gielgud's more stylized, classically-oriented one. Their professional rivalry did not hurt the play's box-office potential. However, the harsh press criticism of Olivier's "poetry butchering" Romeo performance devastated the actor. In *Confessions of an Actor*, Olivier later recalled, "My Mercutio went down, I suppose, very well, but this could never be a compensation for me." Nor could a small role as an Italian aviation pioneer in *Conquest of the Air*, a Korda film destined to spend five years on the proverbial "shelf."

Prior to *Romeo and Juliet*, seven years had elapsed since Olivier's last previous experience with the Bard. But now he made up for lost time by accepting the coveted lead opposite Elisabeth Bergner in a movie version of *As You Like It*, being produced and directed by her husband, Paul Czinner. For thirteen weeks, the actor filmed by day, while playing Mercutio at night. Its mixed notices ("colorless" . . . "does not seem to be comfortable before the film camera") not only did little to convince Olivier that he had a future as a movie actor, but also underscored his conviction that Shakespeare was not for filming.

Convinced that his career was best centered on the stage, he then joined forces with his by-now friend and colleague, Ralph Richardson, to produce and team in *Bees on the Boatdeck*, an allegorical comedy which J.B. Priestley had been commissioned to write for them. It opened at London's Lyric Theatre in May 1936, and ran a mere four weeks, sending Olivier back to the Korda movie studios to resume a degree of solvency. The result was *Fire Over England*, prophetically casting him romantically opposite Vivien Leigh in a drama about Queen Elizabeth (played by Flora Robson) and the Spanish Armada. As Elizabeth's lady-in-waiting, Leigh would spend the next three-and-a-half months in close proximity to Olivier, cast as a swashbuckling naval officer. On their first day together at Denham Studios, his ironic response to her pleased greeting was "we shall probably end up fighting. People always get sick of each other when making a film."

Not a few weeks into shooting *Fire Over England*, the actor became a father when Jill Esmond gave birth to a son they named Simon Tarquin. But it was already too late for their marriage; on the set of their film, the love scenes between Leigh and Olivier were fast becoming a reality. And when they confided in their producer, Alexander Korda knowingly responded that he knew all about it—nor was their relationship any secret to the film's cast and crew.

With 1937's *Fire Over England*, directed by the American William K. Howard, Laurence Olivier finally had a noteworthy role in a motion picture whose popularity equaled its critical reception. And although the highest praise went to Robson's Virgin Queen, Leigh and Olivier also won notice as the love interest. One British reviewer thought the movie superior to "any historical drama yet made in this country."

Meanwhile, offscreen, Shakespeare consumed Olivier's theatrical interests. At the invitation of producer Tyrone Guthrie, he joined the Old Vic (formerly the Old Victoria Theatre), where so many of London's current and future stars solidified their classical careers. For Olivier, his Old Vic debut in *Hamlet* (for a change, being performed in its over-four-hour entirety) on January 5, 1937, proved the most traumatic opening night of his life. For want of adequate rehearsal time, the cast never had the benefit of a complete run-through. Nor was Olivier then considered much more than a popular and glamorous young stage and screen star who lacked a solid foundation in Shakespeare. His vital, athletic interpretation of the Danish prince couldn't hope to please conservative traditionalists, who undoubtedly preferred the intellectual sensitivity of John Gielgud's earlier production of the play. But, inspired by the adrenalin of professional terror, the naturalistic sincerity of Olivier's characterization that first night drew an ovation and a flood of critical analysis that marked an auspicious boost to his future as a serious artist.

At the Old Vic that 1937–38 season, the actor enjoyed a thorough immersion in the Shakespearean classic roles: Henry V, Iago, Sir Toby Belch, and Coriolanus. Offstage, the Leigh-Olivier romantic liaison became ever more serious. In the late spring of 1937, she joined him at the Old Vic as Ophelia in a production of *Hamlet* which visited Denmark to perform in the courtyard of Kronborg Castle, site of the play's legendary Elsinore. Unfortunately, stormy weather cancelled any possibility of the planned outdoor performances, and the company had to carry on in a makeshift "theatre" set up in the ballroom of Copenhagen's Marienlyst Hotel—where they scored an improvisatory triumph.

Upon returning to London, although still legally tied to their respective spouses (for whom they professed continued respect), Vivien Leigh and Laurence Olivier veered off on their own to share living quarters in Chelsea. And, before enjoying a holiday together in Venice, they portrayed unhappy lovers in a downbeat minor Korda film entitled *The First and the Last* which the producer thought so little of that he shelved it, with no further thought to its release. Much later, after its stars had gained international celebrity following their respective triumphs in *Gone With the Wind* and *Wuthering Heights*, it reached cinemas as *21 Days*. In the U.S., where its title was stretched to *21 Days Together*, Leigh and Laurence Olivier attended a New York City performance during World War II—only to leave the theater in dismay halfway through.

In late-thirties Britain, Korda next cast Olivier opposite Merle Oberon and Ralph Richardson in a Technicolor comedy, *The Divorce of Lady X*, while Leigh was loaned to MGM's British unit for the secondary (and more interesting) female lead in the Robert Taylor vehicle *A Yank at Oxford*, in which she was a pretty but conniving minx. She then did that performance one better in *St. Martin's*

With Rene Ray in *Bees on the Boatdeck* (1936).

As *Henry* V (1937).

As *Hamlet* (1937).

Lane (retitled *Sidewalks of London* in America), a decided preparatory step toward portraying Scarlett O'Hara, this time in the esteemed company of Charles Laughton and Rex Harrison.

At the Old Vic, Olivier took on a second Shakespearean season with *Macbeth*, the notorious "Scottish play" whose ill luck on this occasion included the fatal heart

With Jessica Tandy in *Henry V* (1937).

With Enid Bennett, Arthur Whatmore, Marda Vanne, and Alexander Knox in *The King of Nowhere* (1938).

With Sybil Thorndike in *Coriolanus* (1938).

attack, on the day before the play's opening, of the Old Vic's guiding force, sixty-three-year-old Lilian Baylis. With stylized makeup, settings, and direction, *Macbeth* failed to repeat the success of the previous season's *Hamlet*. Indeed, Olivier considered it an "utter disaster" in every way. This production, which featured Judith Anderson as Lady Macbeth, marked the occasion of the actor's 1937 television debut, when the BBC broadcast live excerpts from the play to those few individuals equipped to receive it. The experience did not increase Olivier's enthusiasm for that embryo medium—to which he wouldn't return for twenty-one years.

At thirty-one, amid the usual Old Vic season limited to works of the Bard of Avon, Olivier enjoyed an outstanding success in an unusual departure—a curious James Bridie comedy called *The King of Nowhere*, in which he was a contemporary actor, who, having escaped from a nursing home for the mentally ill, rises to head a neo-Fascist campaign to reform civilization—only to be returned to the asylum. With war clouds gathering over Munich, Old Vic audiences evinced little interest in Bridie's advanced political ideas. The Old Vic wisely returned to Shakespeare and *Coriolanus*.

Standing at right, with Esme Percy, Ernest Thesiger, Morland Graham, Edmund Gwenn, Alexander Field, George Benson, and Hermione Baddeley in a scene from *The Pickwick Papers*, as part of a special Command Performance matinee entitled "Here's to Our Enterprise" at London's Lyceum Theatre (1938).

By now, the West End's professional cognoscenti were beginning to note improvements in Laurence Olivier's acting, the obvious benefits of his devotion to two seasons of the Old Vic's classical repertoire. With the close of that company's 1937–38 season, he had won the full approval of London's more influential critics and the adulation of theatregoers. A matinee idol now for certain, he was on the verge of career changes that would keep him off the British stage for the next six years.

In June of 1938, Olivier and Leigh were vacationing in the south of France, when a Hollywood offer came their way regarding Samuel Goldwyn's production of *Wuthering Heights*. With Merle Oberon already set for the leading part of Cathy, it was proposed that the British actor costar as Heathcliff, while Vivien Leigh was suggested for the secondary role of Isabella. Olivier had no desire for a return to the American movie capital, nor did he wish to see Leigh return to supporting roles. He was soon busy filming again for Korda in a spy drama called *Q Planes* in Britain (and *Clouds Over Europe* in the U.S.), opposite Valerie Hobson and Ralph Richardson, with whom he confided; director William Wyler had even journeyed to London to persuade him to do the Goldwyn picture. By now Vivien (having read the screenplay) was interested in playing Isabella, and attempted to change Olivier's mind—especially because she thought he was giving up a wonderful role with the idea that it would keep them apart.

When he left Vivien for Hollywood, there had arisen

the possibility that Oberon might *not* do the film, thus opening her role for Leigh. But the rumors were only that; Merle stayed on the project, and Geraldine Fitzgerald was only too happy to be cast as Isabella. Almost from the start of filming, Olivier found *Wuthering Heights* problematical. He had difficulty with Wyler's demanding direction, he resented the kinder treatment accorded Oberon, and he upset producer Goldwyn, who hated his "stagey acting" and considered removing him from the movie altogether. Most of all, Olivier missed Vivien Leigh, and that temporary separation manifested itself in behavior—as the actor much later admitted in TV interviews—so high-handed that it prompted sarcastic, "vicious" treatment by Wyler. Olivier foolishly allowed his condescending sentiments to surface, declaring that the film medium was probably "too anemic to take great acting." The result was a down-to-earth off-the-set lecture from Wyler that Olivier always credited with making him begin to appreciate the motion picture as a valid creative medium, not only for "popular" subject matter, but also for that great English playwright Olivier then considered unfilmable—William Shakespeare. As the actor wrote in 1986 in *On Acting*: "What Willie Wyler was really trying to teach me was humility. I'll say it now—instead of at the end—as a homage to him: my stage successes have provided me with the greatest moments outside myself; my film successes the best moments within myself."

Separated from the actor for the first three weeks of his

filming *Wuthering Heights*, Vivien Leigh impulsively booked passage on the *Queen Mary* and left England to join him—even though it meant a mere five days in Hollywood before she would be obliged to return to begin Old Vic rehearsals for *A Midsummer Night's Dream*.

It was during that brief visit that she got the role countless actresses had coveted—Scarlett O'Hara in *Gone With the Wind*.

What she neglected to tell Olivier right away was that a seven-year Selznick contract went with the role of Scarlett—a revelation that initially infuriated the actor, who envisioned long separations between them. But Selznick managed to pacify Olivier, and, while Vivien began shooting what has become the world's all-time favorite motion picture, Olivier returned to Broadway for the male lead opposite Katharine Cornell in S. N. Behrman's *No Time for Comedy*. Almost simultaneously, that play became a hit that won raves for both its stars, and *Wuthering Heights* opened to outstanding notices, especially for Laurence Olivier. Without a doubt, it was he who created the film's greatest impact—an impact still felt more than half a century later, for his brooding, mercurial Heathcliff remains among the screen's great romantic performances.

During the pre-Broadway tour of *No Time for Comedy*, Olivier had received the saddening news of his father's

As Gaylord Esterbrook in *No Time for Comedy* (1939).

death at seventy. His son's career had proved a source of pride to the Reverend Olivier, no less so in that he recognized that a certain measure of his own theatricality in the pulpit had been passed on to his younger son. As Olivier later recalled: "I can remember him in later life, smirking a little and putting his thumbs into his waistcoat arm-hole, and saying, mock self-deprecatingly, 'Your father wasn't a bad actor.' "

And while Olivier was starring on Broadway, Vivien Leigh—missing him dreadfully and eager to complete *Gone With the Wind* so that they could be together—was driving herself mercilessly on a production with which she had become increasingly disenchanted, due to behind-the-scenes problems that would take a separate volume to recount. With the picture finally completed late that June, she fled to New York, and, with Francis Lederer replacing Olivier in his play, they sailed back to England and a Riviera vacation before he would have to return to Hollywood for Alfred Hitchcock's *Rebecca*. On August 9, 1939, when they left Britain, accompanied by Vivien's mother, to return to America's movie capital,

With Katharine Cornell in *No Time for Comedy* (1939).

London was on the verge of war. And, as he filmed Selznick's production of the Daphne du Maurier bestseller, Olivier became impatient for its completion, so that he might demonstrate his patriotism for the Mother country (his compatriot David Niven had already returned home and was in uniform). That December he interrupted shooting *Rebecca* to escort Leigh to the spectacular Atlanta premiere of *Gone With the Wind*. At thirty-two, Olivier suddenly found himself an acknowledged star in the company of an overnight, twenty-six-year-old superstar. Her only disappointment at that time was that Joan Fontaine—and not she, Vivien—was playing the female lead in *Rebecca*. It was shared by Olivier, whose emotions, if little consolation to costar Fontaine, at least helped color his moody role with the appropriate tone. *Rebecca* not only would take the 1940 Academy Award for Best Picture, but also garner nominations for both Fontaine and Olivier. And, of course, Vivien Leigh had become 1939's nominal Best Actress when *Gone With the Wind* brought her the Oscar, among its many other awards.

The two again entertained hopes of working together in a movie—MGM's planned adaptation of Jane Austen's classic *Pride and Prejudice*, but, while Olivier was judged perfect casting for the aristocratic, snobbish Darcy, Metro bosses preferred to see *her* as the tragic heroine of *Waterloo Bridge*. While Leigh and Olivier fought to team in one or the other of these two MGM projects, their energies were wasted: Robert Taylor was assigned to *Waterloo Bridge*, and Greer Garson was cast opposite him in *Pride and Prejudice*. As it developed, each of them was equally well cast in their respective films. But they were now more determined than ever to enjoy a *joint* acting venture, and, with the prospect of Olivier's becoming active in the British war effort, they decided they could wait no longer. As soon as their filming chores were done, they embarked on a risky stage venture, teaming in their own production of *Romeo and Juliet*. Financing the project with their entire savings of about $60,000, they were matched by Warner Bros., which hoped to secure Olivier's services for a movie on the life of Disraeli.

At the same time, their efforts to secure marital freedom from their respective spouses was finally producing results. By August of 1940, this would now be possible, although Jill Esmond was granted custody of Simon Tarquin, and Leigh Holman would have charge of Vivien's daughter Suzanne. Although far from subject to the tabloid scandals of more contemporary times, the adulterous Leigh-Olivier relationship could scarcely have been easy for those involved, although it has been recorded that their earlier spouses maintained congenial friendships with the pair already being referred to in theatrical circles as "The Oliviers."

No efforts were spared in making *Romeo and Juliet* a memorable event. Not only was Olivier starring, but he also directed, supervised all aspects of the production, and even wrote incidental music for entrances and exits. Motley was engaged to design an elaborate turntable set, and the supporting cast included Dame May Whitty as the Nurse, Alexander Knox as Friar Laurence, Edmond O'Brien as Mercutio, and a pre-Hollywood Cornel Wilde as Tybalt. Immense publicity heralded the San Francisco opening, which proved a sellout, due chiefly to the glamour of its starring duo. An equal success followed in Chicago, prior to the play's Broadway opening, an event as eagerly awaited as it was critically condemned. In *The New York Times*, Brooks Atkinson complained of difficulty in hearing the actors. And, while acknowledging the attractiveness of both stars, he noted, "They hardly act the parts at all, and Mr. Olivier in particular keeps throwing his part away." Atkinson went on to note: "The superficiality of his acting is difficult to understand. He is mannered and affected, avoiding directness in even simple episodes. As his own director, Mr. Olivier has never heard himself in the performance. This is just as well; he would be astonished if he did."

Explanations of *Romeo and Juliet*'s disastrous 1940 revival and its quick subsequent closing vary between possible critical resentment with Hollywood stars invading Broadway to the likelihood that Olivier's infatuation with both the play and Vivien Leigh had blinded him to the flaws in his production. Or perhaps he was not yet ready to produce, direct *and* star—all at one time.

At thirty-three, Olivier was now more eager than ever to serve Britain, hoping to join his old friend Ralph Richardson in the Fleet Air Arm. But the age limit for unqualified fliers was then twenty-eight, and Richardson discouraged him from applying.

Back in Hollywood, Leigh and Olivier replenished their coffers by finally costarring in *That Hamilton Woman* (called *Lady Hamilton* in the U.K.)—a film that Alexander Korda, then temporarily relocated in the U.S., was producing to rally Americans to the cause of Britain. In this handsome costume drama, the real-life lovers portrayed English history's illicit pair, Emma Hamilton and the ever-married Lord Horatio Nelson, war hero of the Napoleonic era. During its production, on August 30, 1940, Vivien Leigh formally became Mrs. Laurence Olivier.

Returning to Britain at the start of 1941, the actor applied for a commission in the Fleet Air Arm, and was made a second-line flier. Although not permitted to engage in combat, he found himself useful instead in radio broadcasts and in such propagandistic motion pictures as *The 49th Parallel* (U.S. title: *The Invaders*) and *The Demi-Paradise* (aka *Adventure for Two*). And while he acted in films, Vivien Leigh returned to the London

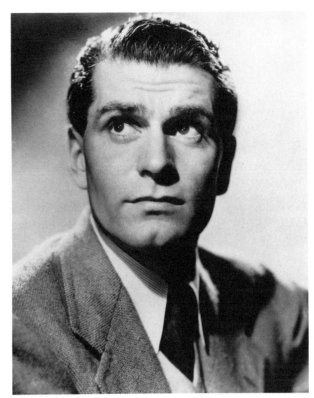

With Vivien Leigh in *Romeo and Juliet* (1940).

An early forties portrait.

As Hotspur in *Henry IV, Part I* (1946).

With Margaret Leighton in *Henry IV, Part I* (1946).

stage, at his urging, in Shaw's *The Doctor's Dilemma*, an immediate hit that ran a surprising 474 performances. In 1943, she spent the summer entertaining the troops in North Africa.

And, as Olivier neared the completion of his service to Britain, he began planning for what would become his greatest contribution to World War II propaganda, the Shakespearean masterpiece *Henry V*. Under the sponsorship of Filippo Del Giudice's Two Cities Films, the ambitious project became an imaginative reality, resplendent in Technicolor, yet filmed under difficult wartime conditions that render the splendid end-result all the more astonishing. The movie was planned as an *acting* vehicle for Olivier, who unsuccessfully sought William Wyler to direct it. And, with neither Carol Reed nor Terence Young available, the job fell to Olivier himself. Blending the real (outdoor battle scenes, filmed in Ireland) with stagey theatricality (obvious sets with painted backdrops), Olivier enlisted the help of many former stage colleagues, some of whom were not above taking virtual bit parts. The success of the film, completed in early 1944, is reflected in the special Academy Award given to Olivier "for his outstanding achievement as actor, producer and director in bringing *Henry V* to the screen." The Oscar was later presented in gratitude to Del Giudice for making the film possible. Olivier was also named Best Actor by the New York Film Critics.

Vivien Leigh, who had been a spectator throughout most of *Henry*'s filming, now returned to the screen as the young Egyptian queen in Shaw's *Caesar and Cleopatra*, opposite Claude Rains's Roman conqueror in the most expensive British motion picture then yet made. In the midsummer of 1944, only six weeks into production, Vivien suffered a miscarriage. She completed the movie, a less-than-pleasurable experience, and was then confined for a while to a sickbed. Subject to chest ailments since girlhood, the actress would become increasingly more vulnerable to illness, both physical and mental. Advised now by her doctors to take a lengthy rest, the willful actress instead chose to return to the stage, directed by her husband, as Sabina in Olivier's 1945 production of Thornton Wilder's *The Skin of Our Teeth*.

Following *Henry V*, it was later disclosed, Two Cities Films had paid Olivier £15,000 *not* to make another picture for eighteen months, while he helped publicize that production. Which did not prevent him for returning to the Old Vic in an impressive variety of classical character roles that allowed Olivier the pleasure of altering his face, voice, and personality in such plays as *Peer Gynt*, *Arms and the Man*, *Richard III*, *Uncle Vanya*, *Oedipus Rex*, and *The Critic*. Certain factions in the British theatrical community were now hailing Olivier as the greatest of living actors—a profound source of embar-

rassment to him. And he made plans to follow *Henry V* with a second Shakespearean picture, *Hamlet*.

In 1945, the Oliviers—now true "Royals" of the British theatre world, much as the Lunts were to Broadway—moved to a unique Buckinghamshire country estate named Notley Abbey, that had originated in the twelfth century with Augustinian monks. A rambling edifice on seventy-five acres near the Thames, it was purchased with his income from *Henry V*. As the actor wrote in *On Acting*: "At Notley I had an affair with the past. For me it had mesmeric power; I could easily drown in its atmosphere." And so, of course, Notley became the Mecca for all of their friends, who vied for coveted country-weekend invitations.

While *Henry V* had been resplendent in the magnificent hues of carefully coordinated Technicolor, *Hamlet* emerged a monochromatic masterpiece. Initially, Olivier was quoted as saying that this was due to his envisioning the latter as an "etching"; later, he revealed that *Hamlet* was shot in black and white because he was embroiled in a feud with the Technicolor people. However, it's difficult to believe Olivier's *Hamlet* would have been quite so effective in color. During *Hamlet*'s filming in July 1947, Olivier became one of forty-seven new Knights on the King's Birthday Honors List. Sir Laurence was then the youngest actor ever to be accorded that honor.

While he continued with *Hamlet*—again tripling as actor, producer, and director—Vivien was filming a remake of *Anna Karenina* that, aside from Ralph Richardson's comforting presence as her screen husband, was not a happy experience, due to petty on-set feuds involving miscast actors. The results were consistent with the two movies' behind-the-scenes atmosphere: *Anna Karenina* was neither a critical nor a financial success, while *Hamlet* won Academy Awards for 1948's Best Picture and Best Actor Laurence Olivier. It also remains the most popular and best known of all film versions of that play (although Franco Zeffirelli's 1990 production with Mel Gibson may someday challenge that position). At the time of *Hamlet*'s London premiere in May of 1948, with Britain's royal family in attendance, the Oliviers were in Australia with a company of players on an Old Vic tour with *The School for Scandal*, *The Skin of Our Teeth*, and *Richard III*. These plays would afford the couple their first onstage teaming since the disastrous American *Romeo and Juliet* eight years earlier, but it would mark the beginning of the end of their personal relationship. Olivier later wrote that he "lost" his wife in Australia, for it was there during that tour that she met and began a longstanding relationship with Peter Finch, a young actor whose talent and personality also impressed Olivier. Later on, curiously enough, Olivier would even sponsor Finch's career in Britain.

Taking a curtain call following an Old Vic performance of *The Critic* (1946).

Much has been written about Vivien Leigh's problems with health, both mental and physical, and it seems that manic depression was prominent among them. Also, her career during the 1940s had become increasingly subservient to her husband's. And, while he rode high on the prestige and acclaim of *Henry V* and *Hamlet*, her *Caesar and Cleopatra* and *Anna Karenina* offered scant competition, either in quality or popularity. It appears that, all through her life and career as Lady Olivier, Leigh strived to be as much accepted as an *actress* as her husband was an actor. The Australian tour had offered its greatest rewards for her in her performance of Sabina in *The Skin of Our Teeth*, but it was subsequently overshadowed by his successful *Hamlet* film. Nor was Vivien's self-confidence improved by watching Jean Simmons's beguiling performance in a role she herself might have played.

It was also during the Australian tour that Olivier received notification that his services—along with those of codirectors Ralph Richardson and John Burrell—would no longer be required by the Old Vic's Board of Governors. After five years, it appeared that they considered it time for a change. As the Old Vic aimed its sights on becoming Britain's National Theatre, the board deemed it advisable that its artistic leaders not be individuals "however able, who have other calls upon their time and talent." Like Richardson, who was in Hollywood filming *The Heiress* with Olivia de Havilland, Olivier was out of the country for a prolonged period, and thus unable to

With Alec Guinness in *King Lear* (1946).

Filming the "To be or not to be" soliloquy in *Hamlet* (1947).

With Vivien Leigh in Boston to receive a Master of Arts degree from Tufts University (1946).

On the set of *Hamlet*, receiving his *Henry V* Oscar from producer Hal Wallis and Ray Milland (1947).

With Vivien Leigh, following the completion of his *Hamlet* film (1947).

30

argue his case in person. However, Old Vic production standards were reported to have slipped in their absence, and press criticism was influential. Like their fellow touring actors, Leigh and Olivier both had taken considerable salary cuts to facilitate the Australian sojourn, and had also turned down such lucrative film offers as a *Cyrano de Bergerac* in Hollywood and an *Othello* in Britain, as well as a life of Shakespeare in which she would have appeared opposite him as Anne Hathaway.

Back in London, Olivier faced the release from Old Vic commitments as a career turn that might be beneficial, after all. Under the aegis of his Laurence Olivier Productions, he and Vivien might enter a new era of actor-manager partnership that would make the Oliviers Britain's answer to America's Alfred Lunt and Lynn Fontanne, in artistry as well as popularity. Convinced that Tennessee Williams's *A Streetcar Named Desire* was the perfect London stage vehicle for Leigh, Olivier sought the British rights to the long-running Broadway hit, while he and Vivien opened in the West End in *The School for Scandal*, *Richard III*, and *Antigone* at the New Theatre. By now, subtle changes were evident in their relationship, partially the result of sometimes-public squabbles on tour. Olivier reports in his memoirs that Leigh casually informed him early in that spring of 1949 that she no longer loved him . . . that her affection had become more like that of a *sister*. Yet it was decided that they would carry on as though nothing had changed, although as the actor later recorded, "occasional acts of incest were not discouraged."

In March, Olivier's production company presented Edith Evans in James Bridie's *Daphne Laureola*, with Peter Finch—recently arrived from Australia with his wife Tamara—cast as her young admirer. By now, Olivier was preparing *Streetcar* for Vivien, and seemed more apprehensive about London's acceptance of such steamy American realism than concerned about his wife's ability to portray the demanding role of Blanche DuBois, a Southern belle many poles apart from Scarlett O'Hara. Olivier himself directed the production, one he later called his "most painful undertaking yet," a comment motivated by the questionable necessity of Vivien's taking on a harrowing role that required an onstage mental breakdown every night. The effect of her opening-night performance was devastating, both to the actress and her audience, and the effort of re-creating Blanche eight times a week took its toll. As the actress was much later to admit, "It tipped me over into madness." And, despite Jessica Tandy's triumph as Broadway's original Blanche, Tennessee Williams himself would later admit that Vivien Leigh's performance had "everything that I intended, and much that I had never dreamed of." For Olivier, there was the satisfaction that his wife was winning acclaim at last, purely for her acting. But at what price?

Olivier began 1950 as an actor-manager, directing himself in the London premiere of *Venus Observed*, a play he had commissioned of playwright Christopher Fry. Originally, Leigh had been set to be his leading lady, but the success of her run in *A Streetcar Named Desire* ruled that out, and she was replaced by a newcomer named Heather Stannard. A costly undertaking, this eccentric comedy pleased critics and public sufficiently to enjoy a seven-month run, after which Olivier took on the production of a new play, *The Damascus Blade*, in which he directed John Mills and Peter Finch. The play closed before reaching London, a disaster attributable chiefly to its author, Bridget Boland.

Anxious to refill the family coffers, the Oliviers then accepted Hollywood offers that would have her repeating her *Streetcar* characterization for the screen, while Olivier played the married lover of Jennifer Jones in a movie version of Theodore Dreiser's novel *Sister Carrie*. Had not her husband been similarly engaged, Leigh would not likely have made the journey to re-create so draining a role—especially considering her unfamiliarity with the Methods of director Elia Kazan, who had brought the Williams play to Broadway in 1947. During their five months in Los Angeles, they were not infrequently the guests of such friends as Danny Kaye, Spencer Tracy, and Lauren Bacall and her husband Humphrey Bogart. *Carrie* (as his film was retitled before release) brought Olivier back in professional touch with William Wyler, who couldn't fail to note a marked change in his leading man's current attitude toward working in the movies. Together, they helped create a film that, while never very popular, is now considered by many as containing one of Olivier's finest performances, from his meticulous American accent to the subtle detail with which he portrays a transgression of upper-middle-class respectability to impoverished degradation.

Leigh's motion-picture Blanche would, of course, bring her a second Oscar, and, as they sailed for home among only five passengers on a small French freighter, they remained confident in their knowledge that Hollywood still viewed them as the ideal, stylish British show-business couple. And yet Olivier, in his memoirs, admitted even considering suicide before the end of that voyage.

Back in London, success eluded Olivier's production efforts to interest Londoners in Gian Carlo Menotti's opera *The Consul*, among other theatrical enterprises. But, during a period of enforced rest at Notley Abbey, the Oliviers devised a plan to star in an alternating program of Shakespeare's *Antony and Cleopatra* and Shaw's *Caesar and Cleopatra*, to be directed, not by Olivier (who sensed his limitations in terms of time and energy), but by Michael Benthall. The chief result was acclaim for Vivien ("A lass unparalleled" was the *Observer's* headline) but far less for her husband, whom critic Kenneth Tynan was so cruel as to suggest was "acting down" for the sake of Leigh, whom he dismissed as "a minor actress."

During this period, England's foremost theatrical couple granted a series of interviews to Felix Barker, who pictured their lives and careers in rosy hues when his work was published as their first joint biography, *The Oliviers.*

On a day off from his stage obligations, Olivier played a cameo role as a policeman who views inventor Robert Donat's new cinema invention in *The Magic Box.* Later that year of 1951, he and Vivien and their *Cleopatra* company accepted an invitation to take the joint venture to New York's Ziegfeld Theatre—ironically, the very scene of their *Romeo and Juliet* disaster eleven years earlier. This time, however, advance bookings passed the $300,000 mark, and audiences *wanted* to see them, regardless of what the critics might think. Not that the reviews were negative; indeed, they were raves, with *The New York Times* calling *Antony and Cleopatra* "the best production of this or any other Shakespeare play for twenty-five years." The two plays ran in tandem from December 20, 1951, until April 12, 1952, after which the couple accepted an invitation from Noël Coward to rest at his island retreat in Jamaica. By then, Vivien appeared in a state of nervous exhaustion, bordering on a breakdown. In New York, a visit to a psychiatrist had brought forth a mention of "manic depression," but nothing that either party was then willing to take seriously. However, her mood swings warned of a growing progression toward schizophrenia.

Ever anxious to surprise his public, Olivier now made plans to play a role in which he would *sing*—as the highwayman Macheath in a film version of John Gay's musical, *The Beggar's Opera.* In preparation for it, he had already begun taking music lessons in New York during the run of the *Cleopatra* plays. While the actor coproduced his movie with veteran filmmaker Herbert Wilcox, Peter Brook directed; and, although fellow cast-members like Dorothy Tutin and Daphne Anderson were vocally dubbed on the picture's soundtrack, Olivier's screen voice—like that of Stanley Holloway—was all his own. However, star and director did not see eye to eye on their interpretations of the work. As Wilcox later recalled, "Peter enjoyed a superiority complex that shone from his young blue eyes like highly polished brass buttons, insolently surveying and cocking a snoot at the conventional." Ultimately, Olivier acceded to Wilcox's request that he allow Brook to have the final word, lest

the film never be completed. The result was a personal failure that Olivier, for all his enthusiastic swashbuckling, was unable to carry off.

With neither *The Beggar's Opera* nor *Carrie* engendering any rave reviews or crowds at the box office, Olivier had cause for depression over the state of his career. Nor had he had a stage hit in four years. Hollywood producer Irving Asher had wanted both Oliviers for his film *Elephant Walk,* to be shot partially in Ceylon, but the actor was unimpressed with the script about a triangular love story involving a tea-planter's wife with his plantation manager. But, while Olivier remained tied to *The Beggar's Opera,* Leigh took advantage of the offer to star in the film with Dana Andrews and Peter Finch. In less than three weeks of filming, Vivien's undisciplined and irrational behavior disrupted location work to the extent that Asher contacted Olivier in desperation, begging him to come there and cope with her. Upon his arrival, the actor realized his presence there was useless. Not only was Vivien beyond reason, but it was abundantly clear that she and Finch were making no secret of their affair. Forced to return to London by his professional commitments, Olivier did so, while the *Elephant Walk* company moved on to Los Angeles, where, it was hoped, professional help could calm Leigh's behavior; as a "star investment," she was far too important to replace without an effort. But Hollywood was not the answer to her problems; on the set, she had trouble remembering her lines, was given to fits of inexplicable sobbing and was heard, through her closed dressing-room door, reciting, in the appropriate Southern accent, Blanche's demented lines from *A Streetcar Named Desire.* Summoned by his old friend David Niven, Olivier flew from London, only to find his wife staring blankly at him, informing him that she was "in love with . . . Peter Finch."

With the aid of friends like his then-manager Cecil Tennant and Danny Kaye, Olivier was able to get a sedated Leigh—whom Elizabeth Taylor had now replaced in *Elephant Walk*—back to England, where she was taken directly to the Netherne Hospital in Surrey, an institution that specialized in nervous conditions. With the press clamoring for pictures and details of the unfortunate situation, Olivier found it difficult to find privacy, even in Italy, where he sought refuge with friends. Electro-convulsive therapy was a part of Vivien's recuperation, and eventually Olivier was able to bring her home to Notley for a prescribed minimum of three months' convalescence. By mid-July, she was sufficiently recovered for the two of them to attend a performance of Shaw's *The Apple Cart,* in which their friend Noël Coward was appearing. But Vivien herself felt that only returning to work would affirm her recovery, and Olivier now entertained thoughts of including her in his plans for

With Vivien Leigh, Eileen Beldon, Terence Morgan, and Georgina Jumel in *The Skin of Our Teeth* (1948).

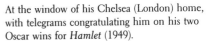
At the window of his Chelsea (London) home, with telegrams congratulating him on his two Oscar wins for *Hamlet* (1949).

Visiting with Spencer Tracy, Elizabeth Taylor, and Joan Bennett on the Hollywood set of *Father's Little Dividend* (1950).

a Coronation Year production. The result was *The Sleeping Prince*, a light comedy by Terence Rattigan, who termed it "a little nonsense for a great occasion." As it turned out, the June 1953 Coronation of Queen Elizabeth was well behind them by the time the Oliviers graced the West End stage that November in Rattigan's

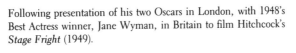
Following presentation of his two Oscars in London, with 1948's Best Actress winner, Jane Wyman, in Britain to film Hitchcock's *Stage Fright* (1949).

play about the Grand Duke of Carpathia's involvement with an American chorus girl. Olivier directed, and, it was later observed, deliberately lowered his own somewhat eccentric performance to help Vivien's. Their presence enabled the play to achieve 274 performances, curtailed only by their subsequent commitments. During the play's nine-month run, Olivier recorded a series of dramas for American radio, produced a pair of West End plays and, together with Vivien and Danny Kaye, participated in a charity benefit at the London Palladium in which they performed the Dietz-Schwartz "Triplets" number from the film of *The Band Wagon*.

Olivier now began planning to film his *Richard III*, a project which preoccupied him completely, once again in the joint capacity of actor-director, while Alexander Korda served as producer. Rethinking his concept of the character for the subtleties of the screen fascinated him. Production began in September of 1954 on location in Spain, with the film's climactic Battle of Bosworth Field, and finished a mere seventeen weeks later. Highly acclaimed in Britain, the film made entertainment history by having its American premiere on network television. NBC paid half a million dollars for the rights to show it once. And although most of its audience viewed the movie in black-and-white in those early-color days of 1956, it has been assessed that more people saw Olivier's performance that night than had witnessed *Richard III* in all of its British stage incarnations since its 1592 premiere!

In his late forties now, and goaded by some of his critics to look to his theatrical acting laurels, Olivier accepted an offer to perform at Stratford-on-Avon in the Royal Shakespeare Company's 1955 productions of *Macbeth* and *Titus Andronicus*, and after Vivien completed work on a film version of Terence Rattigan's play *The Deep Blue Sea*, she joined him there in a season to which was added *Twelfth Night*, playing Viola to his Malvolio. Their private lives were now very much altered from the earlier times; her various illnesses and lapses were kept private, and their public images were carefully maintained, as befitted so prominent and well-loved a show-business couple. Working under John Gielgud's direction in *Twelfth Night* brought Olivier into conflict with the ideas of his old Shakespearean rival, and the critical response was less than satisfactory. *Macbeth*, directed by Glen Byam Shaw, was far more successful, garnering high praise for the actor, but compensatory words for Vivien Leigh's Lady Macbeth. Nor did the pattern change much during the course of *Titus Andronicus*—their final joint acting venture. The criticism of Kenneth Tynan, in particular, appeared to have been fashioned by a wedge-driving Iago, so acidic was its content. After praising Olivier as "the greatest actor alive," he went on to add, "As Lavinia, Vivien Leigh received the news that she is about to be ravished on her husband's corpse with little more than the mild annoyance of one who would have preferred foam rubber."

Peter Finch's rented-room presence at Stratford couldn't have helped matters, but it afforded Vivien a sympathetic companion when her husband was too busy working in his roles to coddle her, and Olivier (who was not above a few dalliances of his own that season) later admitted feeling some relief in the knowledge that Finch helped relieve some of his own marital burden. For the most part, party-giving also became a source of desperate relief for Vivien, though acting colleague Anthony Quayle later recalled, "I could feel the awful tensions beneath the gaiety." Late in 1955, Leigh made two attempts to run away with Finch, the second of which was foiled by a fog that confined them to the VIP lounge at Heathrow Airport. Terence Rattigan, never one to toss away a good plot device, recycled the incident a few years later in his screenplay for *The VIPs*, in which Elizabeth Taylor attempts to run away from industrialist-husband Richard Burton with lover Louis Jourdan.

The Leigh-Finch liaison apparently reached its end after the younger actor confronted Olivier over drinks at Notley Abbey, and got into a session of darkly comical theatrical theorizing climaxed by an intervening Leigh, who demanded to know, "Which one of you is coming to bed with me?" According to the actress, it provoked all three of them to hysterical laughter. Vivien elected to spend that Christmas in Devon with her first husband, Leigh Holman, who would now assume the role of mentor and comforter in times of stress. The year 1956 did not begin well for the Oliviers. Following the sudden death of Alex Korda, their own plans to film *Macbeth* fell through for want of financial backing. But things improved with Noël Coward's offering Vivien his new comedy *South Sea Bubble*, while Olivier was asked to direct and costar with Marilyn Monroe in a film version of *The Sleeping Prince*, whose title would eventually be changed to the more commercial *The Prince and the Showgirl*.

Much has been written about Olivier's experiences working with Monroe—hardly a fruitful professional relationship, this "unholy alliance of Thespis and Aphrodite," as the actor's biographer Anthony Holden so succinctly put it. Both before and after the movie was made, Olivier found Monroe "enchanting" and "adorable"; amid production, accompanied by her ever-present coach and mentor, Paula Strasberg, the actress became a "monster." That performance, under Olivier's frustrated guidance, eventually brought Marilyn Monroe her only important acting award, Italy's David de Donatello statuette.

While performing in the successful *South Sea Bubble*

With Vivien Leigh in a formal portrait by London's Vivienne (1950).

and while her husband was busy coping with Monroe, Vivien Leigh found that, at the age of forty-two, she once again was pregnant. In August, the actress left her play to wait out the remainder of her time at Notley. But she couldn't refuse a charity-benefit invitation in which she performed with Olivier and John Mills, and it has been written that that brought on another miscarriage. After which she recuperated in Italy with Rex Harrison and his then-wife Lilli Palmer.

Early in 1957, there seemed a strong likelihood that both Oliviers might team with Spencer Tracy (who held great admiration for the British actor) in a movie version of Terence Rattigan's stage hit *Separate Tables*, in which Olivier might both star and direct. But talks eventually broke off over structural changes that would unite Rattigan's pair of connected one-act plays into a unified screenplay. And, when Burt Lancaster, the film's producer, decided that *he* wanted the role Tracy might have played, the Oliviers withdrew, to be replaced, in turn, by Rita Hayworth and David Niven.

Thus forsaking the $300,000 he might have realized from *Separate Tables*, Olivier now made what at first must have seemed a foolish career move. For less than £50 a week, he signed to act in a contemporary stage work by England's twenty-seven-year-old "angry young man," the antiestablishment playwright John Osborne. And yet, *The Entertainer*'s third-rate never-was of a music hall song-and-dance comedian, Archie Rice, would provide the actor with what both he and many of his critics would eventually consider his greatest contemporary role. In addition, in committing himself to that play, Olivier would put his faith—and his career—in the directorial hands of a young Osborne contemporary, Tony Richardson.

In a 1959 interview in London's *Daily Mail*, Olivier explained his identification with this role: "There must have been something of Archie in me all along. It's what I might so easily have become . . . because I'm always thinking that I've never had the opportunity to make people laugh as much as I would have liked. *I'd like to make them die with laughter.*"

Of *The Entertainer*, the *Daily Express*'s hard-to-please John Barber wrote: "Olivier is tremendous. Not because of that hilarious music hall act. It is the man backstage who counts. Olivier has it all. The puffed cheeks and uneasily refined accent. The gurgling, leering funny stories. And the too-hearty laugh that conceals the pang of shame. For there is more to this man than you think. 'Old Archie,' he boasts, 'is dead behind the eyes.' Then he hears his soldier son has been killed. And the man's agony shows naked. Before your eyes, you see how a body crumbles as the heart cracks within."

As the *Times*'s critic stated, "less expertly played, the part would fall all over the place in the last quarter of an hour." And, in fact, to have witnessed Nicol Williamson's vain efforts to make Archie Rice his own in a 1982 Off-Broadway revival of *The Entertainer* was to realize the impact of Olivier's contribution to the play.

After its limited, five-week London engagement, *The Entertainer* had to close so that the Oliviers could fulfill an agreement to take *Titus Andronicus* and a company of sixty on a 5,000-mile tour of European capitals, beginning in Paris and concluding back in London, where the *Times* lauded his Titus as one of the peaks of his career.

It was now mid-1957, and Olivier not only looked forward to a return booking in *The Entertainer*, but also was set to portray "Gentleman Johnny" Burgoyne in the Kirk Douglas-Burt Lancaster filming of Shaw's play, *The Devil's Disciple*. Added to which, under his sponsorship, the West End had a smash hit in Ray Lawlor's all-Australian play *The Summer of the Seventeenth Doll*.

The closing of *Titus Andronicus* on August 4, 1957, not only marked the unofficial end of "the Oliviers" as an acting team, but also brought their personal isolation into prominence when the actor spent his summer holiday touring Scotland (where he was still hoping to film *Macbeth*) with his twenty-year-old son Tarquin, while Vivien headed for Italy in the company of Leigh Holman and their daughter Suzanne. Britain's gossip columns now fairly reveled in their own particular brand of interpretations of the Olivier union, with rumors of a marital breakup persisting for the next several years. And, while Vivien would assure the press, "Larry and I are still very much in love," her husband's cryptic words were "I have no comment on something that does not exist."

Olivier continued to seek financial backing for *Macbeth*, although it seems doubtful that he would have involved Vivien in the project, so distant had even their *professional* relationship now grown. At length, her schizophrenic periods would result in their informal decision to separate, lest they do one another bodily harm. A public pretense was maintained for a time, but, with a heavy work schedule facing him, Olivier allowed their lives to become quite separate.

A turning point for the actor now occurred with a cast-change in *The Entertainer*, resulting in the replacement of Dorothy Tutin (as Archie's daughter Jean) by a newcomer named Joan Plowright. And, although she was herself married and twenty-two years Olivier's junior, their immediate rapport soon blossomed into a full-fledged love affair, continuing on the other side of the Atlantic when she joined Olivier on *The Entertainer*'s pre-Broadway tour, replacing Geraldine McEwan as Jean for the twelve-week New York engagement. Their relationship was put on temporary hiatus for the remainder of 1958 by his commitment to film *The Devil's Disciple*, a movie whose making was far from congenial for the actor. In fact, it was a picture that he always avoided

Assisted with his mustache by director William Wyler on the set of *Carrie* (1950).

About to board Mauretania with Vivien Leigh before sailing to New York for the two *Cleopatra* plays (1951).

At the Hollywood opening of the Sadler's Wells Ballet at the Shrine Auditorium with Mrs. Darryl F. Zanuck, Clifton Webb, and Vivien Leigh (1950).

seeing himself in, despite some excellent notices from the critics.

Olivier's failure to find backers for his *Macbeth* on either side of the ocean was cruelly underscored by a magazine poll of British moviegoers when a majority expressed indifference toward seeing *any* future film starring Laurence Olivier. And so he turned toward the

With Vivien Leigh in *The Sleeping Prince* (1953).

As Marc Antony in *Antony and Cleopatra* (1951).

With Vivien Leigh in *Antony and Cleopatra* (1951).

With Vivien Leigh in *Caesar and Cleopatra* (1951).

With Danny Kaye and Vivien Leigh, performing in a charity benefit at London's Palladium (1951).

With Claire Bloom and associate director Anthony Bushell on the film set of *Richard III* (1954).

With Vivien Leigh on vacation in Nice, where she recovered from a nervous breakdown (1953).

As Malvolio in *Twelfth Night* (1955).

As Malvolio in *Twelfth Night* (1955).

With Marilyn Monroe at a press conference to announce their plans to team on the film *The Prince and the Showgirl* (1956).

With Vivien Leigh in *Macbeth* (1955).

With Vivien Leigh in Venice, a lap on the tour of *Titus Andronicus* (1957).

relatively new dramatic medium of television, taking pleasure in chancing an offer of work where his distinguished peers had yet to venture. His choice of vehicle was an unfortunate one: Ibsen's dark-textured play *John Gabriel Borkman*, televised in November of 1958, proved ATV's greatest flop of that year. Undeterred, he flew to New York to play the Gauguin-like role of Charles Strickland in David Susskind's TV production of Somerset Maugham's *The Moon and Sixpence*. This time, an excellent cast and production enhanced a well-chosen vehicle, and Olivier won an Emmy Award for his performance. However, personal tragedy had already put a damper on his satisfaction with that role; during the show's rehearsal period, his brother Dickie died of leukemia at fifty-four.

The actor had attempted to arrange a legal separation from Vivien Leigh, only to find her unwilling to let him go. By then, she had attained sufficient personal stability to return to the stage in Christopher Fry's *Duel of Angels*. She also slipped into (outwardly) graceful grandmotherhood at forty-five, when her now-married daughter gave birth. Finally, though both had continued to deny their respective liaisons with others, Vivien informed him that she was now in love with her *Duel of Angels* leading man, their old friend John Merivale. Olivier could only have felt relief.

For $250,000, Olivier had agreed to a six-month Hollywood commitment to producer-star Kirk Douglas to participate with Jean Simmons, Tony Curtis, Charles Laughton, Peter Ustinov, and company in the spectacular epic *Spartacus*. During its lengthy production, Olivier—unable to afford the high cost of transatlantic calls—maintained a daily correspondence with Joan Plowright. Nevertheless, upon his return to England, the actor was met by Vivien Leigh, who would continue to disbelieve any possibility that he might leave her for good. But, since he was en route to Stratford to begin rehearsals for *Coriolanus*, there was little time for deep personal discussions, although he did bring up his interest in selling Notley Abbey.

At Stratford in 1959, Olivier found in director Peter Hall a twenty-eight-year-old disrespectful enough to challenge his distinguished star's preconceptions about a role he had played twenty-one years earlier at the Old Vic. Olivier's graceful acceptance of Hall's theatrical ideas, however, speaks eloquently both for his own artistry and actor's ego. His death scene—hanging by his ankles, held by two soldiers, after flinging himself from a twelve-foot platform—has become theatrical legend. Not unexpectedly, his *Coriolanus* was a complete triumph. While performing in the Shakespeare play by night, Olivier began filming *The Entertainer* by day, with Plowright resuming the (now-enlarged) role of his daughter,

again under Tony Richardson's direction. Late that year, with both Archie Rice and Coriolanus finally behind him, Olivier turned down an offer to play Julius Caesar opposite Elizabeth Taylor in the film *Cleopatra*, and took off with Plowright for a secret holiday in France.

Professionally, he now returned to New York to direct Charlton Heston and Rosemary Harris in *The Tumbler*, a turgid melodrama by his friend Benn Levy. It lasted a mere five performances, while earning Heston's undying gratitude: "*The Tumbler* may have been a disaster for everyone else, but I've never regreted for one moment the experience of working onstage for Olivier."

In the wake of critical conjecture as to whether the great man had lost his directorial touch, Olivier now embraced yet another unlikely acting vehicle—Eugene Ionesco's avant-garde play *Rhinoceros*. Ostensibly directed by Orson Welles, it was the scene of considerable behind-the-scenes political intrigue until, eventually, Olivier requested that Welles stay away from the final rehearsals. Again, the opening was hailed as an Olivier triumph, although Kenneth Tynan thought him wasted in an unworthy role.

By now, the Olivier-Plowright affair had become public knowledge, causing her to relinquish her role in *Rhinoceros* to Maggie Smith. Although he had discreetly written to Vivien, in care of the Broadway theatre where she was starring in *Duel of Angels*, the actor was totally unprepared for the means of her response. Via her backstage dresser, his wife had issued a statement to the press: "Lady Olivier wishes to say that Sir Laurence has asked her for a divorce in order to marry Miss Joan Plowright. She will naturally do whatever he wishes." The fact that Plowright was still Mrs. Roger Gage could hardly have made things any easier. Olivier instructed his press representative not to let the media blame either of the two women in his life; he himself would shoulder all the responsibility. A few days later, George Jessel proposed to star him and Vivien in a film to be called *Mary Todd, Kentucky Belle*. But the ridiculous idea of teaming the Oliviers as the Lincolns was quickly dismissed, and divorce proceedings commenced—to be completed before the close of 1960.

Following a relaxing ten days in France's Loire Valley, Plowright and Olivier left the Continent for North America, she for *A Taste of Honey* on the Los Angeles stage (prior to New York), and he to take on the title role in Anouilh's *Becket* in a Broadway production that would costar Anthony Quinn as Henry II, under the direction of Peter Glenville. As fate would have it, their plays opened in Manhattan on successive nights. *Becket*'s stars won high praise, but their vehicle was received less enthusiastically; ironically, it eventually won a Tony Award for the season's Best Play. As for Plowright, her performance in

With Vivien Leigh backstage in Paris, following a performance of *Titus Andronicus* (1957).

A *Taste of Honey* was a triumph, and she later copped a Best Actress Tony. With both *The Entertainer* and *Spartacus* attracting crowds to New York screens, that 1960–61 season could hardly have been more portentous for the couple. *Becket* then went off on a six-week tour, returning to Broadway without Quinn, who had to leave for a film commitment. Olivier took advantage of the situation to switch roles, playing Henry to even greater acclaim, while Arthur Kennedy stepped into the archbishop's robes. Better suited to portraying the king, Olivier took chances with a reinterpretation. As Kenneth Tynan reported, Olivier "implied what the character never suspected, namely, that his attachment to Becket was homosexual."

Only two weeks after their separate divorce decrees had become final, twenty-nine-year-old Joan Plowright became the wife of fifty-three-year-old Laurence Olivier on March 17, 1961, in Wilton, Connecticut. In Britain, the couple had bought a home in Brighton's Royal Crescent. And when a nearby Sussex benefactor named Leslie Evershed-Martin offered to make possible Olivier's own, custom-built theater in Chichester, the expectations seemed too good to be true. Tyrone Guthrie helped coordinate the project for Olivier, and the prospects of their

own neighboring theater solidified the newlyweds' plans to settle down, travel the world less in their chosen work, and raise a family of their own.

Before leaving for England, after the close of *Becket*, Olivier spent an exhausting week working again for producer David Susskind in a TV adaptation of Graham Greene's *The Power and the Glory*, whose distinguished cast included Julie Harris, George C. Scott, and Roddy McDowall. After the seven-day taping was completed, Sir Laurence and his new Lady sailed back to England on the *Queen Elizabeth*, a voyage on which it developed that she was pregnant. In Britain, they surveyed the "large mudpatch" that would eventually contain the Chichester Festival Theatre, and settled into a Brighton hotel while 4 Royal Crescent was suitably refurbished for their new home. To help with the Chichester project, Olivier committed himself, both physically and financially, and even turned down producer Sam Spiegel's offer to let him choose between two possible roles in the film *Lawrence of Arabia* that eventually went to Alec Guinness and Jack Hawkins.

With Vivien Leigh at Britain's Lydd Airport, where he met her on her return from a European holiday with her first husband, Leigh Holman (1957).

As Archie Rice in *The Entertainer* (London, 1957). (Photo by Tony Armstrong Jones)

With Dorothy Tutin in *The Entertainer* (London, 1957). (Photo by Tony Armstrong Jones)

With Joan Plowright in *The Entertainer* (New York, 1958).

On December 3, 1961, Joan gave birth to a boy whom they named Richard, after the actor's late brother. With their having finally moved into the Brighton house, and only a week after becoming a father for the second time, Olivier left for Ireland and the filming of *Term of Trial*, a drama casting him as the downtrodden schoolteacher victimized by an amorous teenage student (Sarah Miles), while married to a dominating French wife (Simone Signoret). The movie was only moderately successful, but it nevertheless brought in needed funds to a family whose hearts remained closer to the less monetarily rewarding world of the stage.

During the film's production, Olivier spent many hours mapping out plans for Chichester, whose first season would offer a trio of plays: John Ford's *The Broken Heart*, Chekhov's *Uncle Vanya*, and an obscure seventeenth-century work entitled *The Chances*. The theater opened its doors to the public on July 5, 1962, with a company that included, aside from himself and Joan, John Neville, Rosemary Harris, Keith Michell, Joan Greenwood, Andre Morell, and Fay Compton. The critics were not particularly kind to either *The Chances* or *The Broken Heart*. But *Uncle Vanya*, with Olivier directing his old colleague Michael Redgrave in the title role, was a hit that made up for its predecessors' lack. By now, Lady Olivier was already pregnant once again, and her

With Vivien Leigh, attending the London memorial service for actor Robert Donat (1958).

With Joan Plowright during the filming of *The Entertainer* (1959).

Rehearsing for a "Night of 100 Stars" charity benefit at the London Palladium (1959).

In drag for another "Night of 100 Stars" benefit at the London Palladium (1960).

Directing Charlton Heston and Rosemary Harris in the ill-fated Broadway play *The Tumbler* (1960).

With Duncan Macrae, Michael Bates, and Geoffrey Lumsden in *Rhinoceros* (1960).

With Anthony Quinn in *Becket* (1960).

husband had been named the first director of Britain's new National Theatre.

Between Chichester and the National, Olivier returned to the West End in David Turner's *Semi-De-*

tached, a contemporary work in which he played a Birmingham insurance salesman, under the direction of Tony Richardson, who had recently wed Michael Redgrave's actress-daughter, Vanessa. A hit in the provinces, *Semi-Detached* was adjudged "too suburban" for London audiences, and folded quickly.

And, as the undoubtedly formidable prospect of heading the National loomed ahead of him, Olivier expressed himself: "I don't think I'm really the right man for the job, but I can't think of anyone better." Endless red tape would have to be dealt with before promised monies could be freed for the purpose of realizing an actual theater building in London. In the meantime, the National's temporary home would be the Old Vic, while construction plans progressed for the site across Waterloo Bridge from the South Bank concert halls. Finally, it was settled that the Old Vic's final season would end in June of 1963, with the National's new-home opening set for August 5. Pausing only to observe the joyful occasion of the birth of his first daughter, Tamsin, on January 10, Olivier now drove himself steadily, dividing his activities among his National Theatre administrative duties, his performing schedule, and plans for Chichester, whose second season witnessed a revival of the hit *Uncle Vanya* production, Joan Plowright's first *Saint Joan*, and a new work by John Arden entitled *The Workhouse Donkey*. Too busy to make movies at this time, Olivier turned down both leads in Hal Wallis's film of *Becket*, and made plans to take on the difficult stage role of Othello in what would be the start of a decade's leadership of the National. And, as perhaps the most unlikely theater "lieutenant" he might have selected, the actor chose the flamboyantly opinionated Kenneth Tynan, whose criticism of Olivier's work had ranged from the ecstatic to the caustic. Surprisingly, their working partnership turned out rather well. And Chichester became a sound proving ground for productions that were later transferred to the National (*Uncle Vanya* and *Saint Joan*), while Olivier directed Peter O'Toole in *Hamlet*, and himself acted in works by Ibsen, Congreve, and, of course, Shakespeare. With William Gaskill directing, the National scored one of its earliest successes with Farquhar's Restoration comedy *The Recruiting Officer*, in which Olivier enjoyed a supporting character role. Its popularity helped establish Robert Stephens, Maggie Smith, and Colin Blakely as important additions to the company. It was only through Kenneth Tynan's persistent persuasion that Olivier finally conceded to take on *Othello*, the only major Shakespearean character he had yet to tackle. From the first read-through with the cast, Olivier offered what has been termed a "shattering" portrayal of the Moor. With Maggie Smith as Desdemona and Frank Finlay portraying the treacherous Iago, Olivier enjoyed one of his great-

est theatrical triumphs in the demanding title role. But, at fifty-seven, he found the part so taxing, both vocally and physically, that it was to mark the start of the decline of the actor's own health, which would plague and threaten the final twenty-five years of his life.

With Notley Abbey having been sold in 1959 to a Canadian businessman, Olivier now divided his private time between Brighton and the West Sussex community of Horsebridge Green, where he added a 300-year-old farmhouse to the family holdings. At the National, Olivier took over the male lead from Michael Redgrave in Ibsen's *The Master Builder*, while continuing to shoulder at least two *Othellos* a week in the company's repertory structure. And, for the first time in his career, he suffered the upsetting experience of occasionally forgetting his lines onstage. Was it the strain of working too hard? Upset over the miscarriage that Plowright had sustained on the eve of the company's October 1964 opening? Or could his continuing concern over Vivien Leigh's dwindling health and career have something to do with it? Finally, Sir Laurence Olivier was forced to come to terms with the apparent fact that, at the height of his career, he had actually encountered stage fright. Among his solutions was requesting that no fellow-actor ever look him in the eye during a performance. It was not a situation that he could easily shake off. For the next several years, the English-speaking theatre world's greatest actor would suffer . . . fear of acting!

Professionally, he directed for the National a highly respectible production of Arthur Miller's *The Crucible*, and chanced taking enough time off from his daytime duties to film a supporting role (albeit with star billing) in Otto Preminger's shot-in-London mystery melodrama *Bunny Lake Is Missing*. And now Olivier was reluctantly persuaded to film for posterity his memorable *Othello*, entrusting its direction to Stuart Burge, with whom, in 1964, he and a distinguished cast had made a "filmed record" of the Chichester *Uncle Vanya*. In September 1965, Olivier led a company of sixty-five on the National Theatre's first foreign tour when they took *Hobson's Choice*, *Love for Love*, and his powerful *Othello* to Russia.

In 1966, due to health considerations, Olivier decided to relinquish the responsibilities of Chichester, directing only one play—O'Casey's *Juno and the Paycock*—for the National, and, instead of taking on additional stage work, acting in a secondary role to Charlton Heston's in the exotic film, *Khartoum*, in which he portrayed a fanatical Arab leader.

As 1967 began, Lady Olivier was again pregnant, and her husband increased his acting schedule, beginning with Strindberg's *The Dance of Death*, opposite Geraldine McEwan, an actress heretofore best known for com-

In the title role of *Becket* (1960).

At 54, Olivier begins a second family: with Joan Plowright (now Lady Olivier) and six-day old Richard. (1961)

edy. The play moved critic Harold Hobson to rave, "Even Sir Laurence has never done anything more exciting." That summer, via emergency Caesarian birth, Julie-Kate Olivier was born just after her father's sixtieth birthday.

At the National Theatre, internal squabbles were causing Olivier undue concern over choices of plays and questions of possible experimentation with newer, less traditional works. In particular, the National's board of directors vetoed Kenneth Tynan's proposal to stage *Soldiers*, a controversial work by the German playwright Rolf Hochhuth. Halfway through 1967, Olivier's health became a major concern. Onstage, he continued to muster the theatrical strength which he had always commanded; in private life, the actor now looked poorly. In June, he was hospitalized with prostate cancer, a malignancy which, fortunately, was caught in its early stage. For a time, it seemed his career might be over.

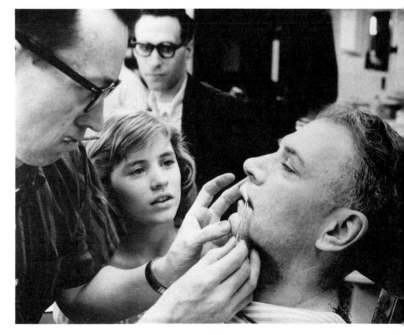

Undergoing makeup for *The Power and the Glory*, while Patty Duke looks on. (1961).

As *Othello* (1964).

As *Othello* (1964).

But it was not long thereafter that Olivier was back working at the National, rehearsing a scheduled production of Chekhov's *The Three Sisters*, with Plowright as Masha, while undergoing cancer treatments as an outpatient. He had continued to appear as Edgar in *The Dance of Death* until his work load became too much, leading to another collapse that required his replacement in the Strindberg play by his understudy, Anthony Hopkins. With his health now complicated by pneumonia, he was confined to hospital, where, on the morning of July 8, he

With director Otto Preminger on the film set of *Bunny Lake Is Missing* (1965).

With Geraldine McEwan in
Love for Love (1965).

With Peter Cellier in A *Flea
in Her Ear* (1967).

51

received an early-morning call from John Merivale to inform him that fifty-three-year-old Vivien Leigh had succumbed to tuberculosis during the night. The news motivated him to leave his hospital bed for Leigh's flat, avoiding the press by slipping in through a private entrance. In paying his respects to his late ex-wife, Olivier was surprised to note the presence in their former London home of not only his photograph beside what had once been their bed, but also numerous mementoes of their life together. That final visit to Eaton Square apparently filled the actor with a guilt that he was never able to shake off. Olivier later wrote that he stood and "prayed for forgiveness for all the evils that had sprung up between us." Then, leaving funeral arrangements to Merivale, who had been her flat-mate, Olivier quietly returned to his hospital bed.

With the cancer treatments a success, a noticeably weaker and older-looking Sir Laurence now defied his doctors' orders with plans for a six-week National Theatre tour of Canada. The company's summer hiatus he spent with his family in Switzerland, and emerged looking well and rested. Finally admitting to himself that *Othello* was now too arduous for him, he agreed to relinquish that role. Instead, for the tour, he took on the small part of the butler in *A Flea in Her Ear*, a Feydeau farce that John Mortimer had adapted for the English stage. In addition, Olivier also appeared in both of the other works performed for the Canadians—*Love for Love* and *The Dance of Death*.

Hospitalized once again, this time for an emergency appendectomy, the actor was relieved to learn that his body now contained no traces of cancer. And it was at this time that Prime Minister Harold Wilson invited him to accept a life peerage—the first ever offered to a performer. His knighthood Olivier wore proudly; it offered him prestige among others in his profession. But the idea of becoming "Lord Larry" both dismayed and intimidated him. Politely but firmly, he quietly refused the honor. And, while he recuperated from the pneumonia that followed the removal of his appendix, Olivier was heartened to receive the news that the government had finally approved an allocation of £7.4 million for the construction of Britain's new National Theatre.

His illness prevented Olivier from directing the National's production of Seneca's *Oedipus*, for which he had managed to lure John Gielgud to the National. Instead, the young and experimental Peter Brook was engaged—and eventually got into serious artistic disagreements with Olivier over such outrageous theatrical devices as staging an orgiastic dance to a disrespectful rendition of "God Save the Queen" and the unveiling onstage of a giant penis, underscored by dancers performing to "Yes, We Have No Bananas."

April 1969 marked the awarding to Olivier in New York of a special Tony Award to honor the work of the National Theatre of Great Britain. At the ceremony, playwright Arthur Miller's extravagant introduction was a profound source of embarrassment for the actor. Facing an emergency operation for piles, Olivier followed his modest acceptance words with a quick flight back to London.

With the appointment of director Frank Dunlop and actor Robert Stephens as associate directors of the National, Olivier nevertheless felt so inundated by plans and funding for the new theater that his own enthusiasm for acting and directing waned considerably. Nor did he care to take part in a new Peter Shaffer play called *The Battle of Shrivings* that had been written expressly for him and Gielgud. As he then told an interviewer, "I do get dreadfully tired at times, but I remain addicted to the idea of really getting the National launched as an actors' theater."

Olivier's return to performing in 1968 was in noticeably less demanding roles than those in which Britons were used to seeing him: the solicitor in Maugham's *Home and Beauty* and the old doctor in *The Three Sisters* (a performance that would be preserved on film the following year). He also oversaw a number of National productions that turned out far less well than had been anticipated. As a result, with the start of actual building construction beside Waterloo Bridge, the National faced a serious financial crisis.

A six-week Los Angeles engagement began 1969 for the National. At that time, Olivier startled the American theatrical community with his outlook on the profession: "It does seem sometimes that acting is hardly the occupation for an adult. False noses, lots of makeup and gum on my face. I can't stand it any more. I hope I'll never do another West End play. I don't know of any elderly actors who enjoy acting very much. One is too conscientious to enjoy it. But without it I would die, I suppose."

With the impulse to take on Shakespeare's Shylock in *The Merchant of Venice*, Olivier turned to Dr. Jonathan Miller, a brilliant young man who was combining an unusual career as a stage director with another in medicine. Joan Plowright would portray Portia in this nontraditional production, set in late nineteenth-century Italy. Most of the critics were less than kind. "Sir Laurence will not be remembered for his Shylock," said Harold Hobson of the *Sunday Times*. In *The Guardian*, Michael Billington was alone in proclaiming Olivier's Shylock "the finest of its generation." It was during this production, however, that the actor finally appeared to overcome his stage fright. After five and a half years of suffering, Olivier discovered that a popular success as Shylock (despite the critics) almost immediately restored his old self-confidence. In his own words: "Now I could feel free to retire from stage acting, if I wished and if funds allowed, without the personal trauma of knowing for the rest of my life that it was fear and not choice that had driven me from my personal metier."

Two years earlier, Olivier had declined the life-peerage offer that was now renewed. Still wary of how such an honor might alter his relationships with others in his profession, Olivier was now persuaded that he was duty-bound to accept. As a result, the Queen's Birthday Honours List of June 13, 1970, formally proclaimed the first ennoblement of an actor in his profession's history. In a letter circulated to the entire National Theatre staff, Olivier stated that the first person to address him as "Your Lordship" would be immediately dismissed.

Now known officially as Baron Olivier of Brighton, the actor made the startling announcement that he planned to take on the role of Nathan Detroit in the National Theatre's production of the hit Broadway musical *Guys and Dolls*, to be directed by the American Garson Kanin. But further illness would make that casting impossible; by August, Olivier was again hospitalized, this time with bronchial pneumonia complicated by a leg problem that had resulted from his cancer treatments. Forced to remain off the stage for some months, he was nevertheless able to accept cameo roles in films that brought in funds necessary to a family with three growing young children. And so he lent his illustrious name to the casts of *Nicholas and Alexandra*, *The Shoes of the Fisherman*, *Oh! What a Lovely War*, *Lady Caroline Lamb*, and *Battle of Britain*, while performing the unbilled narration for Franco Zeffirelli's youth-oriented *Romeo and Juliet*. For American television, he and Richard Attenborough performed what one critic called "a perfect Dickensian double-act" in a remake of *David Copperfield* that was shown in British cinemas.

One fascinating might-have-been project that fell through for want of funding was Luchino Visconti's 1971 effort to film Proust's multipart saga *Remembrance of Things Past*, in which he attempted to bring back the long-retired Greta Garbo as Queen Sofia of Naples in a cast that might also have included Marlon Brando, Alain Delon—and Laurence Olivier.

By now too long absent from his National Theatre duties, Olivier announced that he would direct Giraudoux's *Amphitryon 38* and also return to the stage as Shylock. The National had come under heavy criticism from the press, which noted a decline of artistic quality and a deficit of £100,000. With Kenneth Tynan at his side, Olivier now made some poor choices of plays. And, in employing casts of actors whose names meant nothing outside of the U.K., failed to boost the National's attraction for the tourist industry. Emergency funds were

With Anthony Quinn during the filming of *The Shoes of the Fisherman* (1968).

With director Richard Attenborough on the film set of *Oh! What a Lovely War* (1968).

Directing Joan Plowright on the film set of *Three Sisters* (1969).

With Constance Cummings onstage on *Long Day's Journey Into Night* (1971).

With producer Sam Spiegel on the film set of *Nicholas and Alexandra* (1971).

sought from the Arts Council. And, with the indisputable fact that Olivier's personal drawing power might alleviate financial problems, the actor took Tynan's advice to star in Eugene O'Neill's *Long Day's Journey Into Night.* He had not wanted to portray an actor like James Tyrone; nor, having seen Fredric March's performance in the Broadway edition, was it a role for which he had considered himself suitable. But Olivier's 1972 success in the National's production of that play proved that Tynan's casting sense was accurate. And this West End hit was quickly followed by well-received National productions of *The Front Page* and *The School for Scandal,* as well as a new Tom Stoppard play called *Jumpers.* But the strain of performing the long and demanding Tyrone role in *Long Day's Journey Into Night* took its inevitable toll on Olivier's health, along with the formal cancellation of imminent plans to stage the costly *Guys and Dolls,* for which the leading performers had already been taking song-and-dance lessons.

Dedicated to the idea that the National Theatre should be run by an actor, rather than a director, Olivier proposed the names of Richard Attenborough and Richard Burton, as well as that of a popular director who had *begun* as an actor—Michael Blakemore. It was a shock to Olivier when he was informed by the board that he was to be replaced by Peter Hall. As he later wrote: "I had expected to be consulted and had, indeed, requested to be; after ten years' hard labour one might feel it was almost an obligatory courtesy." From the reports of friends and colleagues, it was a shattering blow to Olivier, who considered the entire shift in responsibilities a "betrayal."

Though noticeably tired and drained of energy, Olivier went on to fulfill a commitment to narrate ITV's twenty-six-part television series *The World at War*, which required eighteen weeks to dub. Olivier's name was an important sales factor for the show, particularly in the U.S. With his formal resignation from the National in the spring of 1973, Olivier neared his sixty-sixth birthday with the knowledge that completion of the National's new home might still be as much as two years away . . . when Peter Hall would be its leader.

Just before stepping down at the National, Olivier returned to its stage in the supporting role of the aged grandfather in Eduardo de Filippo's *Saturday, Sunday, Monday*, an amusing Italian character comedy he had gotten Franco Zeffirelli to direct as a vehicle for Plowright. Its success was followed by a West End transfer. Later that year, Olivier took on another contemporary part—and the one which would mark the end of his stage career—as the Trotskyite politician in Trevor Griffiths's political drama *The Party*. It wasn't the leading role, but Olivier's John Tagg culminated in a marathon soliloquy that—spoken in a Glaswegian accent—took the actor some four months to master. Following a three-month

On American TV with Dick Cavett on "The Dick Cavett Show" (1973).

run, *The Party* closed on March 21, 1974, ending an era that was marked by Olivier's kneeling down to kiss the stage floor. Ironically, it was not then known, either to the actor or his colleagues, that it had been his last performance on any theater stage.

In the years that followed, much of Olivier's work in films and television involved roles, both large and small, in vehicles that many deplored as unworthy of his talents. Occasionally, there would still be rewarding parts like those in the TV-movie *Love Among the Ruins*, in which he was delightfully cast opposite Katharine Hepburn under the direction of George Cukor—and for which he would win an Emmy Award. Indeed, a TV version of *Long Day's Journey Into Night* also brought Olivier an Emmy as its year's Best Actor. And the opportunity to team with young Michael Caine, under Joseph L. Mankiewicz's direction, in a motion picture edition of the hit stage thriller *Sleuth* brought both actors Oscar nominations. Olivier also transferred his stage *Merchant of Venice* portrayal to television, opposite Joan Plowright, whom he also found time to direct in the National's stage production of *Eden End*. With a growing family to provide for (private schooling was costly), and with recurrent bouts of illness to remind him that his performing time might be running out, Olivier continued to work where the offers turned up. Much was made of an American Polaroid commercial that Olivier agreed to shoot for the fee of $1 million, with the proviso that it not be shown in the U.K.

In mid-1973, a physical encounter with an intruder in his home sent Olivier to the hospital with an injury that left his eyesight permanently impaired. The actor's physical condition was not helped when, during a vacation

With Sir Lew Grade, signing a contract to star in the TV version of *Long Day's Journey Into Night* (1972).

55

with his family at Franco Zeffirelli's Positano home, he twisted his back painfully while swimming. There followed the discovery of a rare and painful skin condition, dermato-polymyocitis, manifesting itself in a severe inflammation of his skin and musculature. Doctors predicted a six-month sojourn in the Royal Sussex Hospital. Friends who visited did not expect Olivier to survive the ordeal. And yet, from a state wherein he was unable even to ring for a nurse, he recovered sufficiently to begin physical therapy in which he had first to relearn even basic movement, before progressing to speech and voice projection. From complete and utter disability, the actor willed himself back to precarious health before returning home in February of 1975.

Olivier's eventual return to work came through the auspices of an old friend, director John Schlesinger, who sent the actor William Goldman's screen adaptation of his novel *Marathon Man*, in which a fugitive Nazi leaves the protection of South American exile with the lure of retrieving diamonds cached in New York City. The Nazi's one obstacle: a young runner, to be played by Dustin Hoffman. As a virtual warm-up, to prove that he could tackle the demands of *Marathon Man*'s New York location work, Olivier first accepted a cameo part as Sherlock Holmes's archenemy Moriarty in *The Seven-Per-Cent Solution*.

Marathon Man was not an easy film for Olivier, recuperating as he was during its production. Nor could the actor summon much sympathy for his sadistic character: "The best villains, I think, are the ones that are amusing. I really don't mind what I play, but this villain is really horrific. They tell me that's the fashion." Olivier's performance in *Marathan Man* brought him his ninth Academy Award nomination, albeit his first in the Supporting Actor category. But Jason Robards was the winner that year for *All the President's Men*.

Throughout his various and many illnesses, Olivier had thrived on work. And, although he readily admitted taking on many of the roles he accepted in commercial and less prestigious film and television projects in his later career because he needed the money for his family, the actor's very well-being depended largely on keeping in active touch with his chosen profession. Periods of respite were, of course, required between assignments for Olivier to regain the strength sapped during his bouts of filming. Yet his name continued to retain the power around which producers would assemble impressive casts—often in roles larger than Olivier's. And so there were many willing to fashion a role to Olivier's requirements—and pay him a princely fee—for the prestige of acquiring his name and talent on the cast-list of a film, in exchange for a few days' work. Thus, the actor appeared as Nicodemus in Zeffirelli's *Jesus of Nazareth* and the dedicated old Dutch doctor in Richard Attenborough's *A Bridge Too Far*.

Ill feelings over the turn of events at the National Theatre and resentment toward his successor, Peter Hall—as well as his own precarious state of health—kept Olivier from attending the formal opening in October 1976 of the new facility, one of whose three auditoriums was named the Olivier Theatre. Years thereafter, the fact that the actor had to pay, like everyone else, to get into "his own theatre" noticeably irked him.

During Olivier's 1975 hospital sojourn, his brother-in-law, David Plowright (who had charge of programming for Manchester's Granada Television), aided in the actor's recovery by suggesting an ambitious TV project in which Olivier would coproduce (with Derek Granger) and act in a series of well-known plays. Among their initial choices were Harold Pinter's *The Collection*, James Bridie's *Daphne Laureola*, Tennessee Williams's *A Streetcar Named Desire*, Paul Osborn's *Morning's at Seven*, Stanley Houghton's *Hindle Wakes*, and Eduardo de Filippo's *Saturday, Sunday, Monday*. Later on, because of a deal set up with America's NBC network, two of their selections had to be changed, with Williams's *Cat on a Hot Tin Roof* replacing *Streetcar*, and William Inge's *Come Back, Little Sheba* substituting for *Morning's at Seven*—even though Olivier had lined up a formidable cast for the latter: Jack Lemmon, Walter Matthau, Katharine Hepburn, Henry Fonda, and Myrna Loy, in addition to himself.

The fact that Granada had given him total autonomy with the project pleased Olivier immensely, and probably did more to speed his recovery from illness than any other single factor. Of the above plays, Olivier himself appeared in five out of six, while codirecting with June Howson the only one in which he did not act, *Hindle Wakes*. If the results were what might best be termed a mixed bag, there was more good than bad attached to the lot. The U.S.-saleable "names" of Joanne Woodward, Robert Wagner, and Natalie Wood were attached to *Sheba* and *Cat*, but (as is so often the case), the best productions were those with lesser international names: *The Collection*, *Daphne Laureola*, and *Saturday, Sunday, Monday*—the last two both boasting fine leading performances by Joan Plowright.

Olivier's next two films cast him in *leading* roles, for a change, although there was criticism that so distinguished an actor had "sold himself out" by signing for Harold Robbins's *The Betsy* and (to a lesser degree) Ira Levin's *The Boys From Brazil*, both popular movies derived from best-selling novels. In the actor's own words at the time: "Thank God for the movies. I can no longer be a stage actor, because I don't feel I've got the power . . . the physical attributes that are absolutely necessary

With Gawn Grainger in Olivier's last stage play, *The Party* (1973).

With Katharine Hepburn and director George Cukor on the set of *Love Among the Ruins* (1973).

With Lilli Palmer, David Hurst, and director Franklin J. Schaffner on the film set of *The Boys From Brazil* (1978).

to be a very good, powerful, meaningful actor. So we have the movies, and I get a fortune for doing it, which is absolutely what I'm after because I've always overspent in my life and now I'd better get on with it. . . . They criticize me in the papers. 'Why's he doing such muck?' I'll tell you why . . . to pay for three children in school, for a family and their future. So what should I do? Write to the critics and ask them to support us? Would that satisfy them?"

In 1977, Olivier was back in hospital, the result of his cancer treatments of a decade earlier. This time, the requisite surgery was even more serious. And again he surmounted it all and returned to his profession. *The Boys From Brazil*'s Nazi-hunter had brought him another Oscar nomination for an award that went to Jon Voight for *Coming Home*. However, Hollywood elected to give Olivier a special 1978 Academy Award for "the full body of his work, the unique achievements of his entire career and his lifetime of contribution to the art of film."

Olivier now seemed hardly to stop as he went from film to film, ignoring the continuing criticism that followed his career choices, questionable though they might seem as he appeared in roles of varying size in *A Little Romance*, *Dracula*, *The Jazz Singer*, and *Inchon*. His last contribution to the theater was directing Plowright and Frank Finlay in Eduardo de Filippo's *Filumena*, a thirty-three-performance Broadway flop in 1980. Its failure sent him back to films and television, beginning with a brief and rare appearance with his fellow knights, Sir John Gielgud and Sir Ralph Richardson, in Tony Palmer's epic TV life of *Wagner*, and far more distinguished work in the award-winning miniseries based on Evelyn Waugh's *Brideshead Revisited*, in addition to an adaptation of John Mortimer's autobiographical play, *A Voyage Round My Father*.

In 1981, the actor's position in the arts was underscored with the bestowing on him of Britain's Order of Merit, the highest of civilian honors.

The following year, Olivier's memoir, *Confessions of an Actor*, was published and sold well enough to justify

With producer Mitsuharu Ishii (in costume for a bit part) and crew, celebrating the completion of filming *Inchon* (1979).

With Jackie Gleason during a break in filming the cable television drama, *Mr. Halpern and Mr. Johnson* (1983).

the considerable sum he had been paid to write it. Initially, a ghostwriter had begun working with the actor, but the arrangements proved unsatisfactory, and Olivier decided instead to set it all down himself. Its uneven quality and his frankness, particularly with regard to Vivien Leigh, drew criticism.

The Granada TV studios in Manchester became the scene in 1983 of one of Laurence Olivier's last great triumphs—the recording at an appropriate age (seventy-five) of a role that most septuagenarians might find too difficult to perform: Shakespeare's *King Lear*. Physically frail now and vocally diminished, the actor displayed spurts of unexpected energy that illuminated this great role with power and beauty while before the cameras, but virtually collapsed when his scenes were completed. On the set, he was quoted as saying: "You know, when you get to my age, you *are* Lear, in every nerve of your body. Here I am, at the very end of myself, in both age and

In his garden during the TV production of *Laurence Olivier: A Life* (1982).

experience." For a change, his critics, both young and mature, sang Olivier's praises. And *King Lear* earned the actor his fourth Emmy Award.

In the few working years left to him, Olivier took on more questionable work in TV and films: *Mr. Halpern and Mr. Johnson, A Talent for Murder, The Last Days of Pompeii,* and *Mutiny on the Bounty* among them. As his health waxed and waned, he sometimes appeared up to his roles, while at other times, he seemed old and enfeebled. His voice now occasionally approached a high whine. With Michael Caine, he received star billing in a spy thriller, *The Jigsaw Man,* that made little impression on anyone. Olivier had suffered a collapse during London location shooting, the result of a kidney disease. His frailty seemed appropriate to his last two big-screen appearances—as the aged, Spandau-imprisoned Rudolf Hess in *Wild Geese II* and as the ancient, wheelchair-bound Old Soldier in Derek Jarman's posthumously

shown *War Requiem.* But Olivier's final outstanding performances were for television: as the expatriate English painter Henry Breasley of *The Ebony Tower* and the pathetic, elderly Archie Rice-like music hall comedian Harry Burrard in *Lost Empires.* In the words of Alan Grint, who directed him in the latter miniseries: "He's an amazing man. He acts like his age, eighty, until the cameras are about to turn. Then he's like Twiggy. He comes miraculously to life. He starts cracking jokes for the crew and telling stories, and is full of wonderful

59

energy. When it's over, nothing. He's back in the chair again. He loves to work and never wants to stop."

In May of 1987, a celebrity-studded audience turned out to fete Laurence Olivier on the occasion of his eightieth birthday, celebrated in a special performance held onstage, appropriately enough at the National's Olivier Theatre. An instant standing ovation greeted his arrival, followed by a program of skits illustrating the various aspects of theater life. Olivier is reported to have enjoyed the performance so much that he joined in singing "Happy Birthday" to himself.

Much of the essence of Olivier's art and thinking are preserved in Melvyn Bragg's remarkable 1982 television documentary, *Laurence Olivier—A Life*, a two-and-a-half-hour profile that skillfully captures the actor in the role he knew best—Laurence Olivier. In 1986, the actor followed his autobiography with another book in which he explained his craft, *On Acting*.

On July 11, 1989, this "artful lion of twentieth-century English theatre" died peacefully in his sleep, aged eighty-two, at his home in Steyning. His ashes are buried in London's Westminster Abbey.

Following are a few brief excerpts from the eulogy spoken by Sir Alec Guinness:

When Larry Olivier died, some lines of Shakespeare came to mind . . . 'The star is fallen, And time is at his period. The long day's task is done.'

Sometimes we have read in the press over the past twenty years or so of a young actor being hailed as a 'second Olivier.' That is nonsense, of course, and unfair to the actor. If he is of outstanding talent and character, then he will carve out his career in his own right and in his own name; he won't be a second anyone. In any case, there may be imitators, but there is no second Olivier. He was unique.

A shrewd man, with an acerbic wit and great charm. Ambitious, determined, brave, and daring. A full life, lived generously and shared with all of us. He has, I am sure, the nation's gratitude.

'Good night, sweet prince
And flights of angels sing
thee to thy rest.'

THE FILMS

"The theatre gives to the actor but, unfortunately, the actor gives it all back to the movies."

—Laurence Olivier

Lawrence Olivier

THE TEMPORARY WIDOW   As Peter Bille

THE TEMPORARY WIDOW

1930

A Wardour release of an UFA Production

CAST

Lilian Harvey *(Kitty Kellermann)*; Laurence Olivier *(Peter Bille)*; Athole Stewart *(President of the Court of Justice)*; Felix Aylmer *(The Public Prosecutor)*; Frederick Lloyd *(Counsel for the Defense)*; Fritz Schmuck *(Councillor Hartmann)*; Henry Caine *(Councillor Lindborg)*; Rene Hubert *(Witness Loiret)*; Frank Stanmore *(Witness Kulicke)*; Gillian Dean *(Witness Anny Sedal)*; Norman Williams *(Auctioneer Kuhnen)*; Stanley Lathbury *(Valet John)*; Johannes Roth *(Master Tailor)*; John Payne *(Old Usher)*; Erich Kestin *(Young Usher)*; Adolf Schroder *(Soldier)*; Danchell E. Hambro *(Foreman of the Jury)*; Ida Teater *(Female Juror)*; Oswald Skilbeck *(First Juror)*; Rive Job *(The Hungry Juror)*.

CREDITS

Director: Gustav Ucicky; *Producer*: Erich Pommer; *Screenwriters*: Karl Hartl, Walter Reisch, and Benn W. Levy; *Based on the play* **Hokuspokus** *by* Curt Goetz; *Cinematographer*: Carl Hoffman; *Art Direction*: Rohrig and Herith; *Running Time*: 84 minutes.

THE FILM

As was then frequently the custom, this German-made comedy-mystery was simultaneously shot in separate English and German versions, both starring the popular British expatriate Lilian Harvey. In the German cast, her costars were Willi Fritsch, Gustav Grundgens, and Oscar Homolka in roles correspondingly played in English by Laurence Olivier, Felix Aylmer, and Athole Stewart.

Harvey plays a beautiful young woman accused of killing her artist-husband in a boating accident. She pleads innocent, maintaining that her husband—whose body was never found—committed suicide. But the prosecutor (Felix Aylmer) is sure she's guilty, and establishes a reasonable case of premeditated murder that seems about to prove her the killer—until a young man (Laurence Olivier) steps forward to announce that it was *he* who was responsible. It's later revealed that the "late" artist and the self-proclaimed murderer are one and the same, minus a beard. There *was* no crime—merely an elaborate hoax to establish the painter's name and generate interest in his works.

OLIVIER:

"This was the first film I appeared in—except for one day's work as an extra for a much-needed guinea in 1925 at Cricklewood."

CRITICS CIRCLE

"Another German attempt to emulate the American comedy which fails in its object. Berlin has never yet

THE TEMPORARY WIDOW   With Felix Aylmer, unidentified actors, and Lilian Harvey

TOO MANY CROOKS   With Dorothy Boyd

managed to capture the Hollywood snap. This particular specimen is not a bad piece of work, but its fundamental story is so utterly idiotic the appeal of the finished picture is restricted. Not the least of the many hopeless drawbacks of the film is the fact the entire secret of the alleged plot is apparent from the first reel to anyone with the slightest intelligence. . . .Laurence Olivier is promising as the juvenile, and may develop into a proposition."

"Chap." in *Variety*

TOO MANY CROOKS

1930

A Fox-British Film

CAST

Laurence Olivier *(The Man)*; Dorothy Boyd *(The Girl)*; A. Bromley Davenport *(The Man Upstairs)*; Arthur Stratton *(The Burglar)*; Ellen Pollock *(Rose)*; Mina Burnett *(The Maid)*.

CREDITS

Producer-Director: George King; *Screenwriter:* Billie Bristow; *Story:* Basil Roscoe; *Running Time:* 38 minutes.

THE FILM

This "quickie" featurette—shot in four days—was one of many pictures then being turned out in haste to fulfill the British Quota Act's need for a certain proportion of English-made movies to offset the constant volume of Hollywood imports—initiating the term "Quota Quickie."

Dared by his fiancée to burgle a certain mansion one night, a young playboy (Olivier) is surprised, while opening the safe, first by a beautiful girl (Dorothy Boyd), and then by a professional crook (Arthur Stratton), who takes the valuable removed by the playboy. With the arrival of the police and the tenant (A. Bromley Davenport) of the house, it develops that the latter's actually a spy with stolen plans, the young lady's a detective, and the playboy safecracker turns out to be the owner of the mansion, which he had entered simply to get his passport.

CRITICS CIRCLE

"George King is to be congratulated on this, his first attempt at production, the result being entertainment of a pleasing order which will undoubtedly have a wide appeal. . . . Laurence Olivier's work on the screen has, up to the present time, been particularly limited, but if

TOO MANY CROOKS   With A. Bromley Davenport

his future work is up to the standard he has set here, his appearance in the leading role of a more ambitious film is assured. All, in fact, give polished performances."

Bioscope

POTIPHAR'S WIFE

(Her Strange Desire)

1931

A *First National-Pathe release of a British International Picture*

U.S. Distributor: Powers Pictures (1932)

POTIPHAR'S WIFE   With Walter Armitage, Norman McKinnell, and Nora Swinburne

CAST

Laurence Olivier (*Straker*); Nora Swinburne (*Lady Diana Branford*); Norman McKinnell (*Lord Branford*); Guy Newall (*The Hon. Maurice Worthington*); Ronald Frankau (*Maj. Tony Barlow*); Betty Schuster (*Rosita Worthington*); Marjorie Brooks (*Sylvia Barlow*); Walter Armitage (*Geoffrey Hayes*); Henry Wenman (*Stevens*); Elsa Lanchester (*Therese*); Matthew Boulton (*Rogers*); Donald Calthrop (*Counsel for the Defense*).

CREDITS

Director: Maurice Elvey; *Producer:* John Maxwell; *Screenwriter:* Edgar C. Middleton, *based on his stage play; Cinematographer:* James Wilson; *Running Time:* 78 minutes.

THE FILM

While performing on the West End stage in Noël Coward's *Private Lives*, Olivier also filmed this "sex drama" opposite Nora Swinburne, who later recalled: "He really was a very good-looking man, with thick curly hair. His teeth were uneven and he had to have them fixed. But otherwise he was quite immaculate—a very jolly personality, amusing, charming and liked by everyone."

The object of their film collaboration was less popular than its male lead. Olivier portrayed a coolly proper chauffeur named Straker, working in the employ of wealthy Lady Branford (Swinburne), whose much-older husband (Norman McKinnell) is too preoccupied with public affairs to be aware that his wife is equally involved in *private* affairs of a discreet nature. When Lady Branford becomes infatuated with her handsome chauffeur, she arranges—during a house party—for her maid Therese (Elsa Lanchester) to be absent while she plans Straker's seduction. But his cold indifference angers her,

POTIPHAR'S WIFE   With Nora Swinburne

POTIPHAR'S WIFE   Elsa Lanchester as Therese

and she rouses the household with the assertion that he has assaulted her. Straker is arrested and tried. But the case against him breaks down, and he's released.

CRITICS CIRCLE

"It should be remembered that in the stage version a moral was at least attempted. This is omitted from the film. The woman in the play, finding herself repulsed by the chauffeur, resolved to make herself worthy of his high ideals. In the picture she simply meets a punishment which arouses ribald laughter, for her husband engages a new man of abnormal ugliness. . . . Laurence Olivier is admirable in the role of the unemotional chauffeur. Nora Swinburne displays much physical witchery as the Circe."

Bioscope

"If it were not for Maurice Elvey's skillful handling of situations, the whole thing would be objectionable."

Lionel Collier in *Picturegoer*

FRIENDS AND LOVERS

1931

An RKO Radio Picture

CAST

Adolphe Menjou (*Captain Roberts*); Laurence Olivier (*Lieut. Ned Nichols*); Lily Damita (*Alva Sangrito*); Erich von Stroheim (*Victor Sangrito*); Hugh Herbert (*McNellis*); Frederick Kerr (*General Armstrong*); Blanche Friderici (*Lady Alice*); Vadim Uraneff (*Ivanoff*); Jean Del Val (*Henri*); Lal Chand Mehra (*Non Com*); Yvonne D'Arcy (*French Maid*); Kay Deslys (*French Barmaid*); Dorothy Wolbert (*English Barmaid*).

CREDITS

Director: Victor Schertzinger; *Producers:* William Le Baron and Louis Sarecky; *Screenwriter:* Wallace Smith; *Scenarists:* Jane Murfin and Wallace Smith; *Based on the story* **The Sphinx Has Spoken** *by* Maurice DeKobra; *Cinematographer:* Roy Hunt; *Sound:* Hugh Mc-Dowell; *Running Time:* 68 minutes.

THE FILM

Laurence Olivier and his wife Jill Esmond had both been signed to $700-a-week RKO movie contracts by a studio that somehow considered *her* the more valuable property. And while she was then loaned to Paramount for the Ruth Chatterton vehicle *Once a Lady*, Olivier made his Hollywood debut in this sixty-eight-minute programmer, filmed under the title of its original source material, *The Sphinx Has Spoken*.

It begins one night in London as British Army Captain Roberts (Adolphe Menjou) returns society beauty Alva

FRIENDS AND LOVERS   As Lt. Ned Nichols

66

FRIENDS AND LOVERS   With
Adolphe Menjou

FRIENDS AND LOVERS   Lily Damita and Erich von Stroheim

Sangrito (Lily Damita) to her home—to be confronted by the husband, Victor (Erich von Stroheim), Roberts never knew about! Finally admitting to their affair, Roberts expects Victor to demand "satisfaction," but instead Alva's husband agrees to a financial settlement.

Back with his regiment on the Indian frontier, Roberts is joined by his old friend and fellow officer, Lieutenant Nichols (Olivier), who he eventually is shocked to discover *also* loves Alva. After a dangerous mission, on which both men are wounded, they vow not to let any mere woman destroy their friendship.

Meanwhile, Alva is widowed when Victor angrily takes a whip to her, and is shot dead by a passing servant. And the love triangle is coincidentally united when she attends a country-house party at which Roberts and Nichols, on leave in England, are also guests. But old jealousies resurface, and Nichols makes an unsuccessful attempt to kill the other two—before urging them to run away together instead.

OLIVIER:

"The cast, apart from its eminence, was wretchedly ill-assorted. So my first Hollywood picture died the death of a dog."

CRITICS CIRCLE

"Narrative is full of discordant elements. There are probably three or four unified stories in this curious medley of romance, but they do not blend. Cast is capable, but here their personalities never get a chance to register, so swiftly are they hurried through continuity events. The exotic Miss Damita probably gets more out of her role than the others, having a number of effective theatrical scenes. The Menjou part is believable only in the polite society episodes. As a commander of soldiers he doesn't convince, and the device of making him the triumphant lover over the younger and extremely personable Maurice [sic] Olivier is an utterly false quantity."

"Rush." in *Variety*

"Victor Schertzinger, the director of this film, has not handled the situations with any marked finesse. Frederick Kerr as General Armstrong sounds a true note and curiously enough his lines are always understandable. The other players give competent performances."

Mordaunt Hall in *The New York Times*

"Laurence Olivier tends to be 'precious' as Nichols."

Picturegoer

THE YELLOW TICKET

1931

A Fox Film

CAST

Elissa Landi *(Marya Kalish)*; Lionel Barrymore *(Baron Stephan Andreev)*; Laurence Olivier *(Julian Rolfe)*; Walter Byron *(Count Nikolai)*; Arnold Korff *(Grandfather Kalish)*; Mischa Auer *(Melchior)*; Edwin Maxwell *(Alexis Balikoff)*; Rita LaRoy *(Fania Rubinstein)*; Sarah Padden *(Mother Kalish)*; Boris Karloff *(Orderly)*; Henry Kolker *(Passport Officer)*; Gilbert Emery *(Hubert)*; Ed Mortimer *(Nightclub Patron)*.

THE YELLOW TICKET With Elissa Landi

68

THE YELLOW TICKET As Julian Rolphe

CREDITS

Director: Raoul Walsh; *Screenwriters:* Jules Furthman and Guy Bolton; *Based on the play by* Michael Morton; *Cinematographer:* James Wong Howe; *Editor:* Jack Murray; *Music Director:* Carli Elinor; *Sound:* Donald Flick; *Running Time:* 83 minutes.

THE FILM

On loanout from RKO to Fox, Olivier filmed his second Hollywood picture, *The Yellow Ticket*, an old-fashioned melodrama about which he was little happier than with *Friends and Lovers*.

Ticket's cinematographer, James Wong Howe, recalls: "Raoul Walsh directed him very roughly. Olivier was a beginner, and he was very uncomfortable." The critics' applause was largely reserved for the showier performances of costars Elissa Landi and Lionel Barrymore.

Michael Morton's stage play of the same title had run for 183 performances in 1914, when it had teamed Florence Reed and John Barrymore. There followed two silent-screen adaptations: the first released in 1916, a Clara Kimball Young vehicle entitled *The Yellow Passport*; and only two years later, as *The Yellow Ticket*, with Fannie Ward, Warner Oland, and Milton Sills.

In 1931, Fox remade it handsomely, in a top-notch production directed by Walsh and beautifully photographed by Howe, as a vehicle for its contract star Elissa Landi. Lionel Barrymore took the villainous role played on stage by his brother John, and Olivier portrayed the young male lead, a British journalist who's in 1913 Russia to write about social conditions. He meets, and falls in love with, a Jewish girl (Landi) victimized by the secret police when she attempts to investigate her father's mysterious death in a St. Petersburg prison. In a complex plot that sometimes recalls *Tosca*, Landi's eventually forced to protect her honor by fatally shooting the lustful chief of Czarist secret police (Barrymore), before (*un*like the Puccini opera) escaping with her lover, who somehow manages to have a getaway plane waiting, with motor running, at the airport.

OLIVIER:

"This, to my great delight, cast me as a leading man to my sweet friend Elissa Landi, a lovely girl and a good sort of actress. Lionel Barrymore was the heavy lead, and it was really quite all right."

CRITICS CIRCLE

"Out of Michael Morton's old play . . . Raoul Walsh has produced a rugged, unrestrained but often effective pictorial drama, in which Lionel Barrymore and Elissa Landi give clever interpretations of their respective roles. Laurence Olivier portrays Rolfe quite persuasively."

Mordaunt Hall in *The New York Times*

"Its biggest asset is Lionel Barrymore, who plays with a playful relishness to be enjoyed. Olivier, as the young

WESTWARD PASSAGE   As Nick Allen

WESTWARD PASSAGE   With Ann Harding

newspaperman on assignment to write about Russia, does a decent job of it without too much credence or reliability, but likeable. The minor characters are unusually good, but Miss Landi with her English hauteur and accent looked out of focus in the role of a Russian Jewess."

"Shan." in *Variety*

"It's the moth-eaten melodrama dressed up in new clothes with Elissa Landi, who should have better stories, and Lionel Barrymore making his ridiculous role seem believable. They make a picture worth seeing."

Photoplay

WESTWARD PASSAGE

1932

An RKO Pathe Picture

CAST

Ann Harding (*Olivia Van Tyne*); Laurence Olivier (*Nick Allen*); ZaSu Pitts (*Mrs. Truesdale*); Irving Pichel (*Harry Lanman*); Juliette Compton (*Henrietta*); Irene Purcell (*Diane Van Tyne*); Emmett King (*Mr. Ottendorf*); Florence Roberts (*Mrs. Ottendorf*); Ethel Griffies (*Lady Caverly*); Bonita Granville (*Little Olivia*); Don Alvarado (*The Count*); Florence Lake (*Elmer's Wife*); Edgar Kennedy (*Elmer*); Herman Bing (*The Dutchman*); Nance O'Neil (*Mrs. Van Tyne*); Julie Haydon (*Bridesmaid*); Joyce Compton (*Girl*).

CREDITS

Director: Robert Milton; *Executive Producer:* David O. Selznick; *Associate Producer:* Harry Joe Brown; *Screenwriters:* Bradley King and Humphrey Pearson; *Based on the novel by* Margaret Ayer Barnes; *Cinematographer:* Lucien Andriot; *Editor:* Charles Craft; *Art Director:* Carroll Clark; *Music Director:* Max Steiner; *Costumes:* Margaret Pemberton; *Sound:* E.A. Wolcott; *Running Time:* 73 minutes.

THE FILM

Of his early-thirties sojourn in Hollywood, *Westward Passage* was the one film Laurence Olivier really enjoyed making, due to the professional generosity of his costar, Ann Harding, who saw to it that he had just as much benefit from good lighting and advantageous camera angles as she did. In a letter written to his family at that time, Olivier termed her "angelic" and added, "It is unbelievable for a star of her reputation to be so good."

And as Olivier wrote in *On Acting:* "RKO gave me no great acting parts. I could talk all right, but my performances were precious, lacking in vitality, charmless. I felt comparatively at ease in my last film for RKO, *Westward Passage.*"

Nine-year-old Bonita Granville, then making her movie debut as Olivier's daughter, had an unusual reason for recalling the event: "I remember that everyone on the set said he took quite a shine to me because I was the only one who pronounced his name correctly. I pronounced it 'O-live-ee-ay' because I came from a theatrical family and had been taught to learn everyone's name properly. But everyone else called him 'Mr. Oliver'!"

A superior soap opera, whose stars make us believe the less likely twists of its plot, *Westward Passage* has impoverished but temperamental would-be novelist Nick Allen (Olivier) fall in love with the serenely beautiful Olivia Van Tyne (Harding), with whom he soon elopes. Their union is anything but tranquil, as he struggles to achieve brilliance as a writer, and she gives birth to a daughter. When the child is three, Nick declares he's tired of their marriage, and Olivia obtains a divorce, subsequently marrying a well-to-do former beau, Harry Lanman (Irving Pichel).

Years later, they meet again in Lucerne. By now, Nick's become a successful writer, and Olivia's gotten used to a privileged life of servants and creature comforts. Nevertheless, their reunion is more than friendly. Nick joins her and their little Olivia (Granville) on the ship returning to America, during which he declares his ongoing love for Olivia, while they continue to enjoy one another's company. By coincidence, Lanman's prevented from meeting his family at the ship, and—sending little Olivia home with her nanny—the former marrieds impulsively drive to the little country inn where they spent their wedding night. It's thus implied that Olivia will divorce Harry for another try with Nick. Obviously, the Production Code had yet to crack down on such questionable moral transgressions!

Judging from its title, the public may justifiably have mistaken *Westward Passage* for a pioneer saga, and weren't interested. Whatever the reason, the movie failed to draw big audiences, and eventually lost $250,000.

OLIVIER:

"A truly promising picture with the pretty and highly respected Ann Harding, a woman of great charm, integrity, and beauty. My own part had splendid opportunities, and I found myself feeling the stir of optimism, but it did not last; conditions were against the fertilization of any seed."

CRITICS CIRCLE

"Another poor picture for Ann Harding. Nothing much happens within the 73 minutes the picture consumes, and those sufficiently interested will peg the finish. Tempo is lacking, and in spots the feature has been so poorly cut that there is even abrupt visual evidence of the splicing. The whereabouts of Nance O'Neil are a mystery. . . . Laurence Olivier, opposite Miss Harding, gives a fair performance behind a 'pretty' appearance, which won't endear him to male viewers. A lot of things can be blamed on this script, but Olivier's penchant to consistently appear the actor is not one of them. It will be a factor which will count against him."

"Sid." in *Variety*

"Laurence Olivier, the English actor, fails to make an attractive character out of Nick Allen, the man who marries young and without means. The role should have been an expression of love's young dream as imagined by an impetuous and volatile lover. Instead, Olivier tends to make him a bounder."

Lionel Collier in *Picturegoer Weekly*

"There are vague reminders of Noël Coward's *Private Lives*. It is a picture with bright dialogue, and the portrayals of Miss Harding, Mr. Olivier, Irving Pichel and ZaSu Pitts are emphatically clever. The story as a whole is not particularly weighty or dramatic, but notwithstanding the spats between Olivia and Nick and their divorce, there are many moments of ingratiating comedy. Robert Milton's direction is capital."

Mordaunt Hall in *The New York Times*

WESTWARD PASSAGE   With Ann Harding

PERFECT UNDERSTANDING   With Charles Cullen, Nora Swinburne, and Gloria
Swanson

Curt Courant; *Editor:* Thorold Dickinson; *Music:* Henry Sullivan; *Art Director:* Oscar Werndorff; *Sound:* A.D. Valentine; *Gowns:* Ann Morgan; *Running Time:* 80 minutes.

PERFECT UNDERSTANDING

1933

*A United Artists release of a
Gloria Swanson British Production*

CAST

Gloria Swanson *(Judy Rogers)*; Laurence Olivier *(Nicholas Randall)*; John Halliday *(Ivan Ronnson)*; Sir Nigel Playfair *(Lord Portleigh)*; Michael Farmer *(George Drayton)*; Genevieve Tobin *(Kitty Drayton)*; Nora Swinburne *(Lady Stephanie Fitzmaurice)*; Charles Cullum *(Sir John Fitzmaurice)*; O.B. Clarence *(Dr. Graham)*; Mary Jerrold *(Mrs. Graham)*; Peter Gawthorne *(Jackson, the Butler)*; Rosalinde Fuller *(Cook)*; Evelyn Bostock *(Maid)*.

CREDITS

Director: Cyril Gardner; *Producer:* Gloria Swanson; *Screenwriter:* Michael Powell; *Based on a story by* Miles Malleson; *Cinematographer:*

THE FILM

Having married an Englishman, Michael Farmer, and with little in the way of any further Hollywood prospects, producer-star Gloria Swanson now decided to make her next project a British-based film that would reach American cinemas via United Artists, which had been releasing all of her recent movies and of which she was a stockholder. However, before this "easy and straightforward film" had reached completion, so many problems had arisen to complicate production that *Perfect Understanding* required Swanson to seek the aid of a group of South African investors, putting up her U.A. stock as collateral. Swanson reasoned that her fans would enjoy a look at her attractive new husband, and thus gave him a supporting role that would not be ruined by his inexperience as an actor. With a sophisticated but verbose script by future director Michael Powell *(The 49th Parallel, The Red Shoes)*, Swanson now anticipated bringing 1930s audiences the talkie equivalent of the sort of society dramas her largely-female fans had flocked to in the silent 1920s. But *Perfect Understanding*—a comedy about marital independence—was such frothy nonsense, released amid the Depression problems of 1933, that few could identify with the trivialities of its pseudo-Coward characters. In the thin plotting, Swanson and

Olivier marry, only to hit a snag when, following a whirl-about-Europe honeymoon, she returns to oversee the decoration of their London flat, while he joins his wealthy circle of friends holidaying on the French Riviera. There, he becomes the romantic target of a married friend, Nora Swinburne, with whom he spends an ill-advised night—which drives Swanson to act romantic with an older admirer, John Halliday. But despite their disagreements, Swanson and Olivier are reconciled for the fadeout.

As the star recalled her leading man in her autobiography, *Swanson on Swanson*: "I had told Noël Coward I wanted a Ronald Colman type. Laurence Olivier was much better than that. His good looks were positively blinding. He was 25 but looked 21, and that worried me until he grew the mustache I suggested for him; it aged him to where we became a perfectly believable couple." (Swanson was then thirty-three, and looked it.) Upon its British release, *Perfect Understanding* did respectable business; but in the U.S., it was a disaster.

PERFECT UNDERSTANDING   With Gloria Swanson

OLIVIER:

"My film with Gloria Swanson, *Perfect Understanding*, [was] a misnomer if ever there was one. It was, I'm afraid, no great sadness to me to learn later that it had been seen only by very few people indeed."

CRITICS CIRCLE

"An all-around disappointment, on story, on entertainment and on most other counts. Gist of the situation is that it is ultra-British in idea and in execution and will prove dull to American fans to the extent that their loyalty to a former film idol will not make up. . . . Laurence

Olivier looks like a romantic lead and plays a stilted part with all the grace and aplomb that seems to be the special gift of young English actors. But when they bring him into the sunlight of Cannes in a bathing suit minus the shirt, he shrinks sadly in romantic suggestion and never quite recovers his glamor."

"Rush." in *Variety*

"The story is drawn out, the dialogue is frequently childish and Miss Swanson is by no means at her best. Michael Farmer, Miss Swanson's husband, is entrusted with a minor role, and it cannot be said that he reveals any marked promise as an actor. Laurence Olivier gives a sterling performance in a none too fortunate role."

Mordaunt Hall in *The New York Times*

NO FUNNY BUSINESS

(Professional Co-Respondents)

1933

A United Artists-British Picture
U.S. Distributor: Principal Films (1934)

CAST

Gertrude Lawrence *(Yvonne Kane)*; Laurence Olivier *(Clive Dering)*; Jill Esmond *(Ann Moore)*; Edmond Breon *(Edward Kane)*; Gibb McLaughlin *(Monsieur Florey)*; Muriel Aked *(Mrs. Fothergill)*.

CREDITS

Directors: John Stafford and Victor Hanbury; *Producer*: John Stafford; *Screenwriters*: Victor Hanbury and Frank Vosper; *Based on a story*

NO FUNNY BUSINESS   With Jill Esmond

NO FUNNY BUSINESS With Gibb
McLaughlin and Jill Esmond

by Dorothy Hope; *Cinematographers:* W. Blakeley and D. Langley; *Editor:* Elmer McGovern; *Music:* Noël Gay; *Running Time:* 75 minutes.

THE FILM

This stagy farce not only had the ring of inferior imitation-Coward about it, but also reunited two members of the original *Private Lives* cast, Gertrude Lawrence and Laurence Olivier. And there were other reminders of that 1931 comedy classic, as well. But Olivier had nothing to say about the movie in either his autobiography *Confessions of an Actor* or the subsequent *On Acting.* It was his only film with then-wife Jill Esmond.

Esmond and Olivier are employees of an agency that services professional co-respondents for couples seeking divorces. As such, each is sent, unknown to the other, to the French Riviera as a co-respondent for Yvonne and Edward Kane (Gertrude Lawrence and Edmond Breon), also unknown to one another. Mistaking one another for the client, Esmond and Olivier fall in love, quarrel, and get back together again. Also reunited by all the confusion, Lawrence and Breon realize they don't really want a divorce either. The story concludes as they're all heading back to London on the same train.

CRITICS CIRCLE

"It is surprising that an artist of Gertrude Lawrence's standing should accept so frivolous a scenario for a starring vehicle in pictures. There are a couple of musical numbers and a lot of smart, clean comedy. The entire

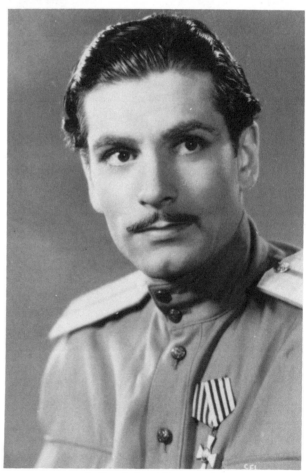

MOSCOW NIGHTS As Captain Ignatoff

74

production breathes class, but the whole thing cries out for plot."

Jolo." in *Variety*

"*No Funny Business* deserves some sort of booby prize for its success in reaching such a devastating level of mediocrity with a cast that includes Gertrude Lawrence, Edmond Breon, Jill Esmond, Laurence Olivier and Gibb McLaughlin. One of the less distinguished products of the recently rejuvenated British film studios. The pace is laboriously slow, the camera static, the recording bad and the direction gifted with a supreme talent for telegraphing its intentions several scenes ahead. It is all excessively silly and makes almost no sense at any point."

Andre Sennwald in *The New York Times*

"Gertrude Lawrence conveys a good deal of vitality and assurance, although playing in a manner long outmoded. Laurence Olivier, however, looks somewhat unhappy as the conventional juvenile lead of the period."

Monthly Film Bulletin
(1951 Reissue)

MOSCOW NIGHTS

(I Stand Condemned)

1935

A General Film Distributors release of a Denham-London Films-Capitol Production

U.S. Distributor: United Artists (1936)

CAST

Harry Baur (*Brioukow*); Laurence Olivier (*Captain Ignatoff*); Penelope Dudley Ward (*Natasha*); Robert Cochran (*Polonsky*); Morton Selten (*Kovrin*); Athene Seyler (*Mme. Sabline*); Walter Hudd (*Doctor*); Kate Cutler (*Mme. Kovrin*); C.M. Hallard (*President of Court-Martial*); Edmund Willard (*Officer for the Prosecution*); Charles Carson (*Officer for the Defence*); Morland Graham (*Brioukow's Servant*); Hay Petrie (*The Spy*); Richard Webster (*Confederate Spy*); Anthony Quayle (*Soldier in Hospital*).

CREDITS

Director: Anthony Asquith; *Executive Producer:* Alexander Korda; *Producers:* Alexis Granowsky and Max Schach; *Assistant Director:* Teddy Baird; *Screenwriters:* Anthony Asquith and Eric Siepmann; *Based on the novel by* Pierre Benoit; *Cinematographer:* Philip Tannura; *Editors:* William Hornbeck and Francis Lyon; *Art Director:* Vincent

MOSCOW NIGHTS   With Charles Carson and extras

Korda; *Music Director:* Muir Mathieson; *Costumes:* John Armstrong; *Sound:* A.W. Watkins; *Running Time:* 74 minutes.

THE FILM

Like its 1934 French-made original, this English adaptation by Eric Siepmann and Anthony Asquith (who also directed) had French character actor Harry Baur repeating his part of Brioukow, albeit this time with his lines expertly dubbed by an uncredited British actor.

In Russia, amid World War I, it's arranged that the well-born but impoverished Natasha (Penelope Dudley Ward) becomes engaged to Brioukow (Baur), an unattractive but prosperous, middle-aged contractor. However, while nursing in a hospital, she falls in love with a wounded officer named Ignatoff (Olivier), while explaining that she's promised to another, to whom she remains faithful. Later, both men quarrel over Natasha and, after accusing Brioukow of war-profiteering, Ignatoff gambles beyond his means. He's left owing Brioukow far more than he can hope to repay—until he's promised financial help by Mme. Sabline (Athene Seyler), an elderly eccentric who comes to his aid. But it turns out that she's actually a German spy, and Ignatoff's arrested as her accomplice. Forced to admit that the faithful Natasha will never love him as she loves Ignatoff, Brioukow finally clears him, in a moment of noble self-sacrifice.

Following on the heels of his cameo appearance in the ill-starred *Conquest of the Air*, this picture marked Olivier's second screen performance under his contract with the British-based Hungarian producer, Alexander Korda.

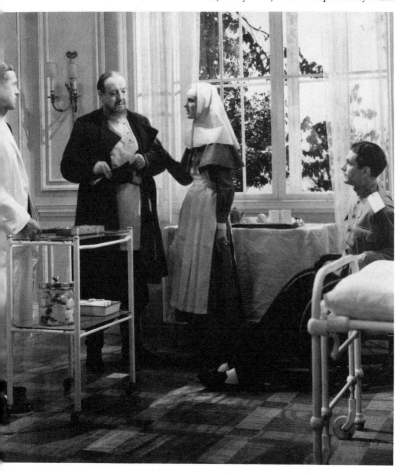

MOSCOW NIGHTS   With Harry Baur

hospitals, and Mr. Laurence Olivier as an embittered front-line officer who loves a young society nurse engaged to the profiteer. The acting of Miss Penelope Dudley Ward belongs to another class altogether, to country-house charades."

Graham Greene in *The Spectator*

"Laurence Olivier's portrayal of Ignatoff is rather too clipped and flippant, and his voice cracked a couple of times just when folks were expecting great things in the way of diction to complete his resemblance to Ronald Colman."

John T. McManus in *The New York Times*

AS YOU LIKE IT

1936

*A 20th Century-Fox release of an
Inter-Allied Pictures Production*

CAST

Elisabeth Bergner (*Rosalind*); Laurence Olivier (*Orlando*); Henry Ainley (*Banished Duke*); Sophie Stewart (*Celia*); Mackenzie Ward (*Touchstone*); Leon Quartermaine (*Jaques*); Richard Ainley (*Sylvius*); Felix Aylmer (*Duke Frederick*); Aubrey Mather (*Corin*); J. Fisher White (*Adam*); George Moore Marriott (*Dennis*); John Laurie (*Oliver*); Lionel Braham (*Charles*); Austin Trevor (*Le Beau*); Stuart Robertson (*Amiens*); Cyril Horrocks (*First Lord*); Ellis Irving (*Second Lord*);

OLIVIER:

"*Moscow Nights* was an almost simultaneous remake of a film which looked really rather good when it was in French (even the title *Les Nuits Muscovites* was already better). It contained an imaginatively advanced series of lap-dissolves, all of which were pushed straight into the English picture, which must have been why Korda bought the original."

CRITICS CIRCLE

"*Moscow Nights*, Anthony Asquith's new film, is completely bogus. This absurd romantic spy-drama of war-time Russia opens with Volga boatmen and carries on with every worn-out property of a Hollywood Russia, even to the gypsy orchestra. The direction is puerile; no one can drop a tray or a glass without Mr. Asquith cutting to a shell-burst. But he is well served by his players, by Harry Baur as an awkward, pathetic war-profiteer, by Miss Athene Seyler as an old, genteel spy who haunts the

Lawrence Hanray (*Third Lord*); Joan White (*Phebe*); Dorice Fordred (*Audrey*); Peter Bull (*William*); Muriel Johnson (*Hisperia*); W.H. Clark, A.H. Scott, G. Hall, and G. Lawrence (*Pages*).

CREDITS

Producer-Director: Paul Czinner; *Assistant Directors:* Teddy Baird and Dallas Bower; *Screenwriters:* Robert J. Cullen, James M. Barrie and Carl Meyer; *Based on the play by* William Shakespeare; *Cinematographers:* Hal Rosson and Jack Cardiff; *Editor:* David Lean; *Art Director:* Lazare Meerson; *Music Director:* William Walton; *Choreographer:* Ninette De Valois; *Costumes:* John Armstrong and Joe Strassner; *Running Time:* 97 minutes.

THE FILM

During his Hollywood sojourn, Olivier had been approached to play Romeo opposite Norma Shearer in MGM's second bout with Shakespeare, *Romeo and Juliet*. He had declined on the theory that the Bard wasn't suitable material for the screen. Subsequently Olivier played Romeo—and Mercutio, alternating in these roles with John Gielgud—on the British stage, and Elisabeth Bergner, suitably impressed with what she saw, told her producer-director husband Paul Czinner, who was planning a Shakespearean film vehicle for her: "This is the

AS YOU LIKE IT   As Orlando

man I want as my partner." The result was *As You Like It*, Olivier's first motion picture experience with Shakespeare. The actor had some reservations about the project, but *money* was the ultimate decision maker: for thirteen weeks of filming, he received what was then considered a fantastic sum. Added to which, the opportunity of performing opposite Bergner, then an important star, was a major consideration. As Olivier said in an interview at the time: "I hope I can do something with Orlando, something reasonably intelligent. No one can play with Bergner without learning something from her."

Ironically, their professional relationship was not ideal; Bergner later reported of Olivier: "He was *not* charming or friendly to work with. He could be inspirational, but he treated us both—me and my husband—as foreigners."

The end result was a heavily edited version—albeit by no less a personage than J. M. Barrie—of Shakespeare that frequently substituted livestock for actors in an approach that adhered more to cinematic movement than to the intelligent verbiage that is the essence of Shakespeare. As Anthony Holden points out in his voluminous biography, *Olivier*, "If Olivier was proving nothing else, he was displaying early signs of the versatility which he would make the hallmark of his career." It might be noted in passing that, although Olivier left out any mention of either Bergner or *As You Like It* in his autobiography, he made up for the omission in his 1986 volume, *On Acting*.

OLIVIER:

"My performance in *As You Like It* looked eccentric, playing to a Rosalind with a Geman accent, whose impersonation of a boy hardly attempted to deceive the audience; but they loved her whatever she did. I made my humble most of Orlando, but the circumstances were too much charged against me. The director's flocks of sheep ran away with the film."

CRITICS CIRCLE

"This is the most Shakespearean Shakespeare screenplay yet. It is as true to the original as is possible in films. Elisabeth Bergner, who is starred, is another problem; she is cute, she is good, but she does not speak English clearly. In her earlier British films, her Teutonic accent didn't matter. Here it most decidedly does; it is a nuisance and it jars. There is a fine supporting cast. Olivier as Orlando is well cast, intelligent and a fine reader of lines."

"Kauf." in *Variety*

"Mr. Laurence Olivier, who plays Orlando, has not been on the scene two minutes before he shows how

AS YOU LIKE IT   With Elisabeth Bergner

AS YOU LIKE IT   With Leon Quartermaine

much progress he has made in the art not only of poetic diction but of poetic feeling. Orlando is generally regarded as a part for a stick; Mr. Olivier plays the lover with great feeling."

James Agate in *Around Cinemas*

"The production is praiseworthy and sincere but is not wholly satisfactory, and this in some measure is due to the miscasting of Elisabeth Bergner as Rosalind. Laurence Olivier delivers his lines as Orlando, although he lacks robustness as a lover and is apt to overdo an air of worried bewilderment."

Picturegoer

"I have said before that Laurence Olivier seems to me to be one of the most brilliant actors in the world. In *As You Like It*, his triumph as Orlando is all the more striking for its contrast to his glamorous Romeo and his fiery Mercutio in John Gielgud's recent [stage] production of *Romeo and Juliet*."

Campbell Dixon in *The Daily Telegraph*

FIRE OVER ENGLAND

1937

A London Films release of a Mayflower-Pendennis Production

U.S. Distributor: United Artists

CAST

Flora Robson (*Queen Elizabeth*); Laurence Olivier (*Michael Ingolby*); Leslie Banks (*Earl of Leicester*); Vivien Leigh (*Cynthia*); Raymond Massey (*King Philip of Spain*); Tamara Desni (*Elena*); Morton Selten (*Burleigh*); James Mason (*Hillary Vane*); Herbert Lomas (*Richard Ingolby*); Robert Newton (*Don Pedro*); Robert Rendell (*Don Miguel*); Charles Carson (*Admiral Veldes*); Henry Oscar (*Spanish Ambassador*); Lawrence Hanray (*French Ambassador*); Roy Russell (*Cooper*); Howard Douglas (*Lord Amberley*); Cecil Mainwaring (*Illingworth*); Frances de Wolf (*Tarleton*); Graham Cheswright (*Maddison*); George Thirlwell (*Gregory*); A. Corney Grain (*Hatton*); Donald Calthrop (*Don Escobal*); Lyn Harding (*Sir Richard*).

CREDITS

Director: William K. Howard; *Executive Producer:* Alexander Korda; *Producer:* Erich Pommer; *Assistant Director:* W. O'Kelly; *Screen-*

FIRE OVER ENGLAND   With Vivien Leigh

writers: Clemence Dane and Sergei Nolbandov; *Based on the novel by* A.E.W. Mason; *Cinematographer:* James Wong Howe; *Editor:* John Dennis; *Music:* Richard Addinsell; *Running Time:* 92 minutes.

THE FILM

Fire Over England marked the first professional association of Olivier with his future wife, Vivien Leigh, with whom he'd later team in two other films, as well as various stage productions. At that time, he was still married to Jill Esmond and Leigh to her first husband, Leigh Holman. But, as Vivien later stated: "It was during the making of *Fire Over England* that Larry and I . . . fell in love. Alex Korda was like a father to us; we went to him with every little problem we had. Well, one day we went to him and said, 'Alex, we must tell you our great secret—we're in love and we're going to be married.' " He smiled and said: 'Don't be silly—everybody knows that. I've known that for weeks and weeks.' " And so the Leigh-Olivier affair that began here did not culminate in wedlock until four years later, when each was, finally, legally free.

After the success of his 1933 *Private Life of Henry VIII*, producer Alexander Korda planned a follow-up concentrating on the monarch's willful daughter Elizabeth I, and designed as a vehicle for the talented, young British character actress Flora Robson, who played Elizabeth in Korda's 1934 *Catherine the Great*.

The resultant movie offered a romanticized patriotic drama of England's Virgin Queen versus Philip of Spain (Raymond Massey) and the formidable Spanish Armada.

FIRE OVER ENGLAND   With Vivien Leigh and Flora Robson

And although history was liberally rearranged for the occasion, the result was a colorful entertainment in which an athletic Laurence Olivier impersonated Michael Ingolby, the impetuous naval lieutenant who arouses his Queen's envy by courting her lady-in-waiting Cynthia (Vivien Leigh). Otherwise, he's engaged in spy missions to Spain on behalf of Elizabeth. By the finale, this fictitious hero has saved England from Spain in some swashbuckling Armada scenes, is knighted by his monarch, and wins Lady Cynthia's hand.

OLIVIER:

"Korda provided me with a very good costume part in *Fire Over England* with Vivien, but I emoted too much and, in the American version, they had to cut one of my scenes because the New York preview audience got the giggles."

CRITICS CIRCLE

"The sets are magnificent, the direction (until the closing scenes, which are spoilt by the absurdity of the story) spirited, and the acting is far better than we are accustomed to in English films. Mr. Laurence Olivier can do the hysterical type of young romantic hero with ease, Mr. Leslie Banks is a Leicester who might have been on the board of governors of any school, and Mr. Raymond Massey presents a fine and plausible portrait of King

FIRE OVER ENGLAND   With Vivien Leigh

Philip. Mr. Massey is the only memorable thing about the film."

Graham Greene in *The Spectator*

"This picture stands head and shoulders above any historical drama yet made in this country and it has few rivals from other countries. As the young lovers, Vivien Leigh and Laurence Olivier are exceedingly good. Their love scenes have a naturalness and tenderness that is particularly attractive."

Lionel Collier in *Picturegoer*

"Erich Pommer's rich production has all the solid virtues of the better British pictures. It is dignified, sound, carefully filmed, extremely well played, and reasonably faithful to the events it sought to reenact. It has, too, a curious lack of vitality for all its wealth of vibrant material. . . . Mr. Olivier is properly impetuous, and Vivien Leigh and Tamara Desni are lovely as the fortunate chap's two leading ladies. The materials, in brief, were there; only the vital spark to fuse them into a stirring historical drama was missing."

Frank S. Nugent in *The New York Times*

"The film is exciting and colorful on the lines of Henry VIII when content to remain a piece of derring-do. At other times it appears too self-conscious a piece of special pleading in a significant period of contemporary dismay.

FIRE OVER ENGLAND   With Tamara Desni

81

FIRE OVER ENGLAND   As Michael Ingolby

FIRE OVER ENGLAND   With Leslie Banks

Laurence Olivier is magnificently acrobatic. He is not called on to be much more."

Ivan Butler in *Cinema in Britain*

Counsel's Opinion by Gilbert Wakefield; *Technicolor Cinematographers:* Harry Stradling and Jack Hildyard; *Special Effects:* Ned Mann; *Art Directors:* Lazare Meerson, P. Sherriff and A. Waugh; *Editors:* William Hornbeck and L.J.W. Stockviss; *Music:* Miklos Rozsa; *Sound:* A.W. Watkins and Charles Tasto; *Costumes:* Rene Hubert; *Running Time:* 92 minutes.

THE DIVORCE OF LADY X

1938

A United Artists release of a London Films Production

CAST

Merle Oberon (*Leslie Steele*); Laurence Olivier (*Logan*); Binnie Barnes (*Lady Mere*); Ralph Richardson (*Lord Mere*); Morton Selten (*Lord Steele*); J.H. Roberts (*Slade*); Gertrude Musgrove (*Saunders*); Gus McNaughton (*Waiter*); Eileen Peel (*Mrs. Johnson*); H.B. Hallam (*Jeffries*).

CREDITS

Director: Tim Whelan; *Producer:* Alexander Korda; *Assistant Director:* Philip Brandon; *Screenwriters:* Robert E. Sherwood, Ian Dalrymple and Arthur Wimperis; *Based on* Lajos Biro's *adaptation of the play*

THE FILM

The Divorce of Lady X, still another of Olivier's 1930s movies overlooked in both his *Confessions of an Actor* and *On Acting*, teamed him with Merle Oberon and stage colleague Ralph Richardson at the same time his close friend Vivien Leigh was filming *A Yank at Oxford* with Robert Taylor and Maureen O'Sullivan.

The story had been used earlier—and some critics thought better—in a 1932 Korda "Quota Quickie" called *Counsel's Opinion*, (after the Gilbert Wakefield stage play of that title). In the 1938 remake, Olivier's a young barrister inadvertently caught up in a romantic web of mistaken identity, beginning with a night in a hotel suite in which he's innocently forced to share his sleeping quarters—and pajamas—with an attractive young lady (Merle Oberon). He later mistakes her for the wife of a lord (Ralph Richardson), who's actually wed to Binnie Barnes, a much-married woman from whom he wants a divorce. It's all very trivial and fluffy, with Richardson reconciling with Barnes, and Olivier winding up with the one he's fallen in love with—Oberon.

Olivier's first bout with the Technicolor cameras comes off well—indeed, at times his close-ups are almost more beautiful than Oberon's—and his comedy technique is smooth. Only Miklos Rozsa's persistent background score occasionally becomes intrusive.

CRITICS CIRCLE

"A gay and urbane comedy, jauntily played by a British cast. Merle Oberon enjoys comedy, and vice versa. And Laurence Olivier has an engaging inability to defend masculine integrity against the feminine foe."

> Frank S. Nugent in *The New York Times*

"It's never exceptionally complicated—just the story of Merle Oberon twisting Olivier prettily around her little finger—but the excellent acting and Tim Whelan's smooth, resourceful direction give it wit, distinction and body. Laurence Olivier is in unusually good form and gives what is his best screen performance yet."

> "N.D." in *Film Weekly*

"Alexander Korda's Technicolored comedy is rich, smart entertainment. Miss Oberon impresses more than she has in recent efforts. Olivier does his role pretty well,

THE DIVORCE OF LADY X   With Merle Oberon

THE DIVORCE OF LADY X   With Gertrude Musgrove and Ralph Richardson

THE DIVORCE OF LADY X   With Merle Oberon

THE DIVORCE OF LADY X   With Merle Oberon

retarded somewhat by an annoysome bit of pouting business. Richardson will win much attention with his work."

"Bert." in *Variety*

Q PLANES

(Clouds Over Europe)

1939

A Columbia Pictures release of a Harefield Production

CAST

Laurence Olivier *(Tony McVane)*; Ralph Richardson *(Major Hammond)*; Valerie Hobson *(Kay Hammond)*; George Curzon *(Jenkins)*; George Merritt *(Barrett)*; Gus McNaughton *(Blenkinsop)*; David Tree *(Mackenzie)*; Sandra Storme *(Daphne)*; Hay Petrie *(Stage Door Keeper)*; Frank Fox *(Karl)*; George Butler *(Air Marshall Gosport)*; Gordon McLeod *(The Baron)*; John Longden *(Peters)*; Reginald Purdell *(Pilot)*; John Laurie *(Editor)*; Pat Aherne *(Officer)*.

CREDITS

Director: Tim Whelan; *Executive Producer:* Alexander Korda; *Producer:* Irving Asher; *Screenwriter:* Ian Dalrymple; *Based on a story by*

Q PLANES   With Reginald Purdell

Brook Williams, Jack Whitlingham, and Arthur Wimperis; *Cinematographer:* Harry Stradling; *Art Directors:* Vincent Korda and Frederick Pusey; *Editors:* William Hornbeck and Hugh Stewart; *Music Director:* Muir Mathieson; *Sound:* A.W. Watkins; *Running Time:* 82 minutes.

THE FILM

Producer Alexander Korda got the idea for this far-fetched comedy-adventure yarn from a news item concerning an aircraft which took off but allegedly was never seen again. Ian Dalrymple's resultant screenplay unfolds like a 1930s preview of the James Bond series, dealing as it does lightheartedly with an improbable plot, leavened with sly British humor. Olivier plays a young test pilot, who becomes romantically involved with an airport lunch counter attendant (Valerie Hobson), ignorant of the fact that she's not only an undercover reporter—hot on the story of plans that have disappeared—but also the sister of an eccentric Scotland Yard man (Ralph Richardson) on the case of a German spy ship employing radio waves to disable British bombers and force them down for detailed study.

CRITICS CIRCLE

"Despite its subject, *Q Planes* is mainly a comedy—a sort of *Thin Man* in an espionage setting. Much of its success is due to Ralph Richardson, who cleverly holds together the comedy and dramatic ingredients as Major Hammond. Olivier is good, as always, as one of the test pilots, and Valerie Hobson provides the necessary romance interest as a girl reporter with whom he falls in love."

Lionel Collier in *Picturegoer*

"One of the wittiest and pleasantest comedies that have come a capering to the American screen this season. It doesn't lose its sense of humor once, not even when the melodrama is at its most melodramatic. Ian Dalrymple and his writing aides have written chuckles into every fourth line of the script and grins into every second; and what the script has not provided, Ralph Richardson has as the Scotland Yard man. The others in the cast are not quite so good—how could they be?—but Laurence Olivier, Valerie Hobson, George Curzon and the rest are most acceptable."

Frank S. Nugent in *The New York Times*

"Laurence Olivier has comparatively little to do beyond look virile and masculine as the nominal hero of the piece, and Valerie Hobson lends her compensating charm to one of those phoney girl-reporter roles."

Film Weekly

Q PLANES   With Ralph Richardson and Valerie Hobson

Q PLANES   With Valerie Hobson

WUTHERING HEIGHTS

1939

*A United Artists release of a
Samuel Goldwyn Production*

CAST

Merle Oberon *(Catherine Earnshaw)*; Laurence Olivier *(Heathcliff)*; David Niven *(Edgar Linton)*; Flora Robson *(Ellen Dean)*; Donald Crisp *(Dr. Kenneth)*; Hugh Williams *(Hindley Earnshaw)*; Geraldine Fitzgerald *(Isabella Linton)*; Leo G. Carroll *(Joseph)*; Cecil Humphreys *(Judge Linton)*; Miles Mander *(Mr. Lockwood)*; Romaine Callender *(Robert)*; Cecil Kellaway *(Mr. Earnshaw)*; Rex Downing *(Heathcliff as a child)*; Sarita Wooton *(Cathy as a child)*; Douglas Scott *(Hindley as a child)*; Mme. Alice Ehlers *(Harpsichordist)*.

CREDITS

Director: William Wyler; *Producer:* Samuel Goldwyn; *Screenwriters:* Ben Hecht and Charles MacArthur; *Based on the novel by* Emily Brontë; *Cinematographer:* Gregg Toland; *Editor:* Daniel Mandell; *Art Director:* James Basevi; *Set Decorator:* Julie Heron; *Costumes:* Omar Kiam; *Musical Director:* Alfred Newman; *Special Character Makeup:* Blagoe Stephanoff; *Running Time:* 104 minutes.

THE FILM

When, back on the London stage, Olivier received Samuel Goldwyn's offer to play Heathcliff in *Wuthering Heights*, he consulted his acting colleague Ralph Richardson, who replied cryptically: "Yes, dear boy. Bit of fame. Good."

Goldwyn's earlier plan was to team Olivier romantically with his *Divorce of Lady X* costar Merle Oberon as Cathy—and the actor's offscreen inamorata Vivien Leigh in the secondary part of Isabella. Olivier knew Vivien would have made a perfect Cathy, while doubting Merle's emotional qualifications for the role. Leigh refused to accept a supporting part in *Wuthering Heights*, reportedly scoffing at William Wyler's protestation that she'd never get as good a first role in America!

Emily Brontë's melodramatic tale of tragic love, jealousy and revenge was first published in 1847 under the *nom de plume* of Ellis Bell, to hide the fact that the author was a woman. It was her only novel, this wildly imaginative story of conflicting passions on the wild and stormy moors of her native Yorkshire. Its focus is on the moody and unrefined gypsy youth known only as "Heathcliff" who, through his unfulfilled love for the well-born and self-centered Cathy Earnshaw, is driven to extremes of vindictiveness, ending in either death or tragedy for everyone involved.

A number of other versions of Brontë's book have reached the screen—a 1920 silent British adaptation with Milton Rosmer and Colette Brettel; Luis Buñuel's 1953 Mexican translation, *Abismos de Pasion*, with Jorge Mistral and Irasema Dilian; a 1970 British remake, realistically filmed in Yorkshire with Timothy Dalton and Anna Calder-Marshall; a French adaptation in 1985, and a Japanese one three years later. (At this writing, a new British remake is in production for 1992 release.) But the only lasting classic has proved to be Goldwyn's haunting, California-made, 1939 production, sensitively directed by the demanding William Wyler and artfully photographed in black-and-white by Gregg Toland. Ben Hecht and Charles MacArthur confined their simplified adaptation of Brontë's complex plot to only the novel's initial half, while retaining much of its original dialogue.

In a vintage year for Hollywood movies, *Wuthering Heights* held its own among intense competition, even surpassing *Gone With the Wind* to win the New York Film Critics' Award as 1939's Best Picture. And though it only took home one Academy Award—for Toland's atmospheric photography—there were Oscar nominations for Best Picture, Screenplay, Director Wyler, Supporting Actress Geraldine Fitzgerald (in the role Vivien Leigh rejected), Alfred Newman's score—and, in the first of his Best Actor nominations—Laurence Olivier (who had been cast only after fellow British actor Robert Newton had tested unsuccessfully).

Although generally popular with both critics and audiences, *Wuthering Heights* was not a financial success until after its eventual reissue. Nevertheless, it remained Goldwyn's favorite among all of his own productions.

OLIVIER:

"If any film actor is having trouble with his career, can't master the medium and, anyway, wonders whether it's worth it, let him pray to meet a man like William Wyler. Wyler was a marvelous sneerer, debunker; and he brought me down. I knew nothing of film acting or that I had to learn its technique; it took a long time and several unhandsome degrees of the torture of his sarcasm before I realized it."

CRITICS CIRCLE

"It is Goldwyn at his best and, better still, Emily Brontë at hers. Out of her strange tale of a tortured romance, Mr. Goldwyn and his troupe have fashioned a strong and somber film, poetically written as the novel not always was, sinister and wild as it was meant to be, far more compact dramatically than Miss Brontë had made it. And it has been brilliantly played. Laurence Olivier's Heathcliff is the man. He has Heathcliff's broad lowering brow, his scowl, the churlishness, the wild tenderness, the bearing, speech and manner of the demon-possessed.

WUTHERING HEIGHTS   As Heathcliff

WUTHERING HEIGHTS   Heathcliff hears Cathy's voice in the night

WUTHERING HEIGHTS   With Merle Oberon and Donald Crisp

Merle Oberon has matched the brilliance of his characterization with hers. William Wyler has directed it magnificently. It is, unquestionably, one of the most distinguished pictures of the year."

Frank S. Nugent in *The New York Times*

"Sam Goldwyn's version of the novel turns out to be among the best pictures made anywhere. Laurence Olivier makes a fine, cryptic and dominant job of Heathcliff, and Merle Oberon opposite him gets over the difficulties of being beautiful, wild and sweet all at once very well. David Niven triumphs over a weak and unhappy part as he always does. For the rest, the cast was as near perfection as you could ask."

Otis Ferguson in *The New Republic*

"*Wuthering Heights* will have to depend on class audiences. Its general sombreness and psychological tragedy is too heavy for general appeal. Samuel Goldwyn's film retains all of the grim drama of the book. Stark tragedy is vividly etched throughout. . . . Olivier provides a fine portrayal as the moody, revengeful lover. Oberon is excellent throughout, nicely tempering her changing

WUTHERING HEIGHTS   With Merle Oberon and David Niven

WUTHERING HEIGHTS   With Merle Oberon

WUTHERING HEIGHTS With Geraldine Fitzgerald

moods. Niven handles his role satisfactorily, while Miss Fitzgerald is impressive as Niven's sister, who comes under the spell of Olivier and finds nothing but unhappiness in her marriage to him. Direction by William Wyler is slow and deliberate, accenting the tragic features of the piece."

Variety

"Laurence Olivier puts over a magnificent performance as Heathcliff. The character seldom deserves sympathy, while the transformation from clod to man of wealth and vengeance is, to say the least, fantastic, but he not only brings conviction to his portrayal but translates intelligently its mystical quality."

Kinematograph Weekly

"This Heathcliff would never have married for revenge. Mr. Olivier's nervous, breaking voice belongs to balconies and Verona and romantic love."

Graham Greene in *The New Statesman*

CONQUEST OF THE AIR   As Vincent Lunardi with bit players

CONQUEST OF THE AIR

1940

A United Artists release of a London Films Production

CAST

Laurence Olivier (*Vincent Lunardi*); Franklin Dyall (*Jerome de Ascoli*); Henry Victor (*Otto Lilienthal*); Hay Petrie (*Tiberius Cavallo*); John Turnbull (*Von Zeppelin*); Charles Lefaux (*Louis Bleriot*); Bryan Powley (*Sir George Cayley*); Frederick Culley (*Roger Bacon*); Alan Wheatley (*Borelli*); John Abbott (*De Rozier*); Ben Webster (*Leonardo da Vinci*); Percy Marmont (*Wilbur Wright*); Dick Vernon (*Simon the Magician*); Denville Bond (*Oliver the Monk*); Charles Hickman (*Orville Wright*); Margaretta Scott (*Isobella d'Este*); Charles Frend (*Narrator*).

CREDITS

Directors (all uncredited): Zoltan Korda, Alexander Esway, Donald Taylor, Alexander Shaw, John Monk Saunders, and William Cameron Menzies; *Producer:* Alexander Korda; *Associate Producer/Technical Advisor:* Nigel Tangye; *Screenwriters:* Hugh Gray and Peter Bezencenet; *Based on stories by* John Monk Saunders and Antoine de St. Exupery; *Cinematographers:* Wilkie Cooper, Hans Schneeberger, and George Noble; *Editors:* Charles Frend, Peter Bezencenet, and Adam Dawson; *Art Directors:* Vincent Korda and John Bryan; *Music:* Arthur Bliss; *Sound:* A.W. Watkins; *Production Supervisor:* John J. Croyden; *Running Time:* 71 minutes.

THE FILM

Understandably, Olivier had nothing to say about this odd little film in either of his books; it was a partially-dramatized documentary tracing man's efforts to fly, from 57 A.D. into the 1930s, and Olivier's cameo—as eighteenth-century balloonist Vincent Lunardi—was brief. Produced chiefly during 1935, the movie was shelved due to various problems with which producer Alexander Korda could not immediately come to terms. *Conquest of the Air* was tradeshown in 1938 in a sixty-minute version, but did not reach British cinemas until 1940, when it ran seventy-one minutes. A 1944 reissue, cut to a mere forty-six minutes, appealed to some critics as preferable to the "original."

CRITICS CIRCLE

"It is certainly scrappy, but the camera work is good and the commentary quite well put over."

Kinematograph Weekly

"As is well known, this picture was planned long ago, and its conception frequently changed as it spasmodically progressed. This has inevitably resulted in its being a bit scrappy. It is perhaps overlong, and in spite of the absorbing interest of the subject, is rather heavy and lacking in inspiration."

Monthly Film Bulletin

"*Conquest*'s erratic production history is at once apparent in the final result, a scrappy mixture of newsreel footage and reconstructed dramatic scenes which star most of Korda's contract players in the key roles of aviation pioneers. With the exception of one stunning visual sequence—D'Annunzio's leaflet 'bombing' of Vienna—the film lacks imagination and inspiration, and pales in comparison with the contemporary work done by British documentary filmmakers and with present-day television documentaries. Its main virtue is the musical score which Arthur Bliss was persuaded to compose during the early stage of production and which, as a concert piece on its own, has since become dissociated from the film."

Karol Kulik in *Alexander Korda* (1975)

21 DAYS

(21 Days Together)

1940

A Columbia Pictures release of a London Films/ Denham Production

CAST

Vivien Leigh (*Wanda Walenn*); Laurence Olivier (*Larry Durrant*); Leslie Banks (*Keith Durrant*); Francis L. Sullivan (*Mander*); Hay Petrie (*John Aloysius Evans*); Esme Percy (*Henry Walenn*); Robert Newton (*Tolly*); Victor Rietti (*Antonio*); Morris Harvey (*Alexander Macpherson*); Meinhart Maur (*Carl Grunlich*); Lawrence Hanray (*Solicitor*); David Horne (*Beavis*); Wallace Lupino (*Father*); Muriel George (*Mother*); William Dewhurst (*Lord Chief Justice*); Frederick Lloyd (*Swinton*); Elliot Mason (*Frau Grunlich*); Arthur Young (*Asher*); Fred Groves (*Barnes*); Aubrey Mallalieu (*Magistrate*).

CREDITS

Director/Associate Producer: Basil Dean; *Producer:* Alexander Korda; *Screenwriters:* Graham Greene and Basil Dean; *Based on the play* **The First and the Last** *by* John Galsworthy; *Cinematographer:* Jan Stallich; *Editors:* William Hornbeck, Charles Crichton, and John Guthrie; *Art Directors:* Vincent Korda and Frederick Pusey; *Music:* John Greenwood; *Sound:* A.W. Watkins; *Running Time:* 75 minutes.

THE FILM

Olivier's autobiography omits any mention of this John Galsworthy drama, and although the movie's not highly respected today, neither is it anything of which those involved should be ashamed. Basil Dean, the martinet stage director with whom Olivier had earlier had to contend in the theatre, directed this second teaming of the actor with Vivien Leigh in 1937. But it was considered a poor box-office prospect, and was shelved—so it didn't reach the cinemas until 1940, by which time *Wuthering Heights* and *Gone With The Wind* had made them major film stars. Both do earnest jobs of acting roles which tend to make the viewer suspend belief, but they eventually manage to make us accept the unlikely—and there are enough striking close-ups of those beautiful faces to satisfy the staunchest followers.

The slight plot offers slow and heavy going; Olivier plays the ne'er-do-well younger brother of distinguished London barrister Leslie Banks. The former's in love with a Russian refugee, Vivien Leigh, who has a secret, older husband (Esme Percy) she hasn't seen in two years. When the latter shows up, demanding money and threatening the lovers, Olivier struggles with him, and Percy is killed. Olivier drags the body out into the foggy night, leaving him in an alley where authorities puzzle over who's culpable. Concerned about the eventual scandal, Banks prevents Olivier from going to the authorities, instead allowing an alcoholic vagrant to take the blame. When the latter is put on trial, he's remanded for twenty-one days, during which Olivier weds Leigh and battles with his conscience. Just as he's about to turn himself in, it's revealed that the suspect has succumbed to a heart attack without repudiating his false confession, and Olivier is free to enjoy a new lease on life with Leigh.

Despite its stars, *21 Days* was a failure, both in Britain and the U.S., where—cut by some ten minutes—it was retitled *21 Days Together*.

21 DAYS   With Vivien Leigh

21 DAYS   With Vivien Leigh and Esme Percy

CRITICS CIRCLE

"My first script was a terrible affair and typical in one way of the cinema-world. I had to adapt a story of John Galsworthy—a sensational tale of a murderer who killed himself and an innocent man who was hanged for the suicide's crime. If the story had any force, it lay in its extreme sensationalism; but as the sensationalism was impossible under the rules of the British Board of Film Censors, who forbade suicide and forbade a failure of British justice, there was little left of Galsworthy's plot when I had finished. This unfortunate first effort was suffered with good-humored nonchalance by Laurence Olivier and Vivien Leigh."

Graham Greene in *International Film Annual* (1958)

"There is a lack of balance both in the direction and acting, which prevents the underlying theme from being clearly defined. Leslie Banks makes Keith's conduct, fantastic that it is, understandable. But Laurence Olivier is lacking in restraint as Larry, and Vivien Leigh is not much better as Wanda. These two, unfortunately, do not help to render the drama thematically plausible."

Kinematograph Weekly

"Considering their recent film successes, Mr. Olivier and Miss Leigh are on a spot, and it is gratifying to report that *21 Days Together* does not let them down, nor they it, which is not generally the case with such intentionally delayed products. Mr. Olivier, who is a great one for tension, never lets you feel for a moment that he isn't a tortured soul—and well it might be, with Miss Leigh and all her tantalizing graces slipping momentarily away from him."

Bosley Crowther in *The New York Times*

REBECCA

1940

*A United Artists release of a
Selznick International Picture*

CAST

Laurence Olivier *(Maxim de Winter)*; Joan Fontaine *(Mrs. de Winter)*; George Sanders *(Jack Favell)*; Judith Anderson *(Mrs. Danvers)*; Nigel Bruce *(Major Giles Lacy)*; C. Aubrey Smith *(Colonel Julyan)*; Reginald Denny *(Frank Crawley)*; Gladys Cooper *(Beatrice Lacy)*; Florence Bates *(Mrs. Van Hopper)*; Melville Cooper *(The Coroner)*; Leo G. Carroll *(Dr. Baker)*; Leonard Carey *(Ben)*; Lumsden Hare *(Tabb)*; Edward Fielding *(Frith)*; Philip Winter *(Robert)*; Forrester Harvey *(Chalcroft)*.

CREDITS

Director: Alfred Hitchcock; *Producer:* David O. Selznick; *Screenwriters:* Robert E. Sherwood and Joan Harrison; *Adapted by* Phillip MacDonald and Michael Hogan *from the novel by* Daphne du Maurier; *Cinematographer:* George Barnes; *Editors:* Hal C. Kern and James E. Newcomb; *Art Directors:* Lyle Wheeler and James B. Platt; *Music:* Franz Waxman; *Special Effects:* Jack Cosgrove; *Running Time:* 130 minutes.

THE FILM

After some fifteen years as a respected British filmmaker, specializing in movies of mystery and suspense, director Alfred Hitchcock was lured to the U.S. by master producer David O. Selznick. Selznick's first picture following his enduring Civil War epic *Gone With the Wind* was Daphne du Maurier's best-selling novel *Rebecca*. For Hollywood, it was the perfect "pre-sold" package of romance and mystery—in short, the ideal "woman's picture" (to employ a long-outmoded term from yesteryear's cinema). The producer, celebrated for his worldwide search for a Scarlett O'Hara for his 1939 classic, launched a minor-league *Rebecca* search for his female lead that considered Loretta Young, Anita Louise, Margaret Sullavan, Olivia de Havilland, Anne Baxter—and even his Scarlett, Vivien Leigh—before taking a chance on Joan Fontaine, a mostly-"B"-picture leading lady who was then on the verge of abandoning her unpromising career for marriage to Brian Aherne—and retirement. Her eventual selection for the role cast her romantically opposite a visibly dismayed Laurence Olivier, who had hoped to team again with Vivien Leigh.

Fortunately for *Rebecca*, much of the action required Olivier to maintain a moody and slightly remote distance from his leading lady, while she had to project a certain shy and naïve charm as the young bride swept into surroundings of old-world wealth and sophistication, for which she's ill-prepared. With the paternally patient Hitchcock (who nonetheless suffered minor worries with Olivier's tendencies toward mannered speech habits) in *Rebecca*'s director's chair, a certain behind-the-scenes chill proved no hindrance to creating the on-film atmosphere appropriate to the du Maurier book. Fontaine's character—mysteriously nameless in both film and novel (told in the first person) is introduced as the demure Riviera companion-secretary to a wealthy and vulgar American (Florence Bates). While out sketching by a cliff, she encounters an attractive, moody Englishman (Olivier), and they begin to meet (unknown to the girl's employer) for meals, walks, and tennis dates. On the eve of the women's departure for America, Olivier proposes marriage and Fontaine accepts, entering an intimidating new world as the unprepared mistress of his rambling Cornish manor house, Manderley. Most formidable of all is his sinister housekeeper (Judith Anderson), whose sustained devotion to Olivier's late first wife (the "Rebecca" of the title) leads her to attempt driving Fontaine to contemplate a departure from Manderley—or suicide in the crashing surf below. The conflicts aroused by these clashing personalities, augmented by numerous of Olivier's friends, servants, and hangers-on, blends with the ever-burgeoning mystery surrounding Rebecca's drowning death to create a fascinating romantic melodrama that drew audiences as much to the movie as to its literary predecessor. Very much an "English" film in both atmosphere and cast (save for Florence Bates), *Rebecca* garnered no less than eleven Academy Award nominations—and was named 1940's Best Picture. Olivier and Fontaine were among the Oscar losers, he to James Stewart of *The Philadelphia Story*, and she to Ginger Rogers for *Kitty Foyle*.

OLIVIER:

"Selznick was shrewd enough to choose an English cast and to advise me to grey up my temples because, at thirty-two, I looked too young. I admired and liked

REBECCA   As Maxim de Winter

REBECCA   With Joan Fontaine

REBECCA   With Joan Fontaine and Judith Anderson

Hitchcock tremendously, and we had a jolly time; all English pros together. He didn't treat us like cattle—although he boasted that that was what he thought about all actors, and although my leading lady to my mind implacably qualified as a female of that species.

"I could manage the smooth, impervious Englishman; but the haunted quality, the mystery element, was thinly written. I was used to tragedy; this was melodrama. I couldn't find the reality of the part. Joan Fontaine played the girl beautifully, but I was never sure how much she was to be deceived; nor indeed how much the audience were to be deceived."

98

REBECCA   With Joan Fontaine, Gladys Cooper, and Reginald Denny

CRITICS CIRCLE

"*Rebecca* is an altogether brilliant film, haunting, suspenseful, handsome and handsomely played. Laurence Olivier's brooding Maxim de Winter is a performance that almost needs not to be commented upon, for Mr. Olivier last year played Heathcliff, who also was a study in dark melancholy, broken fitfully by gleams of sunny laughter. The real surprise, and the greatest delight of them all, is Joan Fontaine's second Mrs. de Winter, who deserves her own paragraph."

Frank S. Nugent in *The New York Times*

"Laurence Olivier is excellent as the sardonic Maxim and makes him credible and not unsympathetic."

Monthly Film Bulletin

"Rarely has any writer had a book translated to the medium of the screen with the care and attention obviously lavished on Daphne du Maurier's *Rebecca*. Laurence Olivier is admirably suited to the role of Maxim de Winter, playing it with a moody intensity that is exactly right, but it is Joan Fontaine's portrait of the second wife that is outstanding."

The Cinema

"Laurence Olivier may be too perfect, and surely he must know how, when he clasps that fine anguished forehead with those fine despairing hands, ladies weep and moan; but he has grace and self-command and the most offhand of elegance, and I like him at it."

Otis Ferguson in *The New Republic*

REBECCA With Joan Fontaine

"Magnificent romantic-gothic corn, full of Alfred Hitchcock's humor and inventiveness. It features one of Laurence Olivier's rare poor performances; he seems pinched and too calculated—but even when he's uncomfortable in his role he's more fascinating than most actors. Joan Fontaine gives one of her rare really fine performances—she makes her character's shyness deeply charming. And with Judith Anderson, George Sanders and Florence Bates—all three showing their flair for playing rotten people."

Pauline Kael in *5001 Nights at the Movies* (1982)

PRIDE AND PREJUDICE

1940

A Metro-Goldwyn-Mayer Picture

CAST

Greer Garson *(Elizabeth Bennet)*; Laurence Olivier *(Fitzwilliam Darcy)*; Mary Boland *(Mrs. Bennet)*; Edna May Oliver *(Lady Catherine de Bourgh)*; Maureen O'Sullivan *(Jane Bennet)*; Ann Rutherford *(Lydia Bennet)*; Heather Angel *(Kitty Bennet)*; Marsha Hunt *(Mary Bennet)*; Edmund Gwenn *(Mr. Bennet)*; Frieda Inescort *(Miss Caroline Bingley)*; Karen Morley *(Charlotte Lucas)*; Bruce Lester *(Charles Bingley)*; Edward Ashley *(Mr. Wickham)*; Melville Cooper *(Mr. Collins)*; Marten Lamont *(Mr. Denny)*; E. E. Clive *(Sir William Lucas)*; May Beatty *(Mrs. Phillips)*; Marjorie Wood *(Lady Lucas)*; Gia Kent *(Miss de Bourgh)*; Gerald Oliver-Smith *(Fitz William)*; Vernon Downing *(Captain Carter)*; Buster Slaven *(Beck's Assistant)*; Wyndham Standing and Lowden Adams *(Committeemen)*; Clara Reid *(Maid in Parsonage)*; Claud Allister *(Yardgoods Clerk)*.

CREDITS

Director: Robert Z. Leonard; *Producer:* Hunt Stromberg; *Screenwriters:* Aldous Huxley and Jane Murfin; *Based on the dramatization by* Helen Jerome *of the novel by* Jane Austen; *Cinematographer:* Karl Freund; *Editor:* Robert J. Kern; *Art Directors:* Cedric Gibbons and Paul Groesse; *Set Decorator:* Edwin B. Willis; *Music:* Herbert Stothart; *Gowns:* Adrian; *Dance Director:* Ernst Matray; *Running Time:* 117 minutes.

THE FILM

Jane Austen's witty classic of late-eighteenth-century manners and mores in Britain was published in 1813—sixteen years after its completion. It was not an era in which female novelists could readily find a publisher. Indeed, the Brontë sisters found it easier—in the 1840s—to get their initial works published by using male pseudonyms.

MGM's 1940 version of *Pride and Prejudice*—its only

English-language theatrical film adaptation thus far—updates the original setting to early-nineteenth-century England, where the well-born Mr. Bennet (Edmund Gwenn) and his vulgar, working-class wife (Mary Boland) are preoccupied with the formidable prospect of finding suitable uppercrust husbands for their five daughters (Greer Garson, Maureen O'Sullivan, Ann Rutherford, Marsha Hunt, and Heather Angel). The two most eligible, Elizabeth (Garson) and Jane (O'Sullivan), manage to attract a pair of wealthy bachelor prospects, Messrs. Darcy and Bingley (Laurence Olivier and Bruce Lester), but pride of their noble birthrights initially prevent the men from considering marriage into a family with such "common" roots—until a lengthy battle of wills and wiles between Elizabeth and the arrogant Darcy eventually leads him to amend his snobbery and accept her, as well as her family.

Initially, *Pride and Prejudice* had been planned as a George Cukor project, to star Norma Shearer and Clark Gable in an Irving Thalberg production. But the latter's untimely 1936 death changed all that. Both Melvyn Douglas and Robert Donat were earlier candidates for Darcy, before Metro settled on Olivier, who vainly attempted to get his offscreen love Vivien Leigh for Elizabeth. Instead, MGM preferred to promote its newest British contract star Greer Garson, who had ironically been given her first big break by director-star Olivier in his unsuccessful 1936 London stage production, *Golden Arrow*.

OLIVIER:

"Then came Darcy in *Pride and Prejudice* for MGM, which I accepted because Vivien was to be my costar and George Cukor the director. But no. Greer Garson became Elizabeth Bennet and Robert Z. Leonard the director, and I was very unhappy with the picture. It was difficult to make Darcy into anything more than an unattractive-looking prig, and darling Greer seemed all wrong as Elizabeth. To me, Jane Austen had made Elizabeth different from her affected, idiotic sisters; she was the only down-to-earth one. But Greer played her as the most affected and silly of the lot."

CRITICS CIRCLE

"Metro reaches into the remote corners of the library bookshelf for this old-time novel about English society and the vicissitudes of a British mother faced with the task of marrying off five daughters in a limited market. As a film, it possesses little of general interest, except as a costarring vehicle for Greer Garson and Laurence Olivier. Their new joint venture is in a boxoffice category somewhat below the high mark of their recent pictures. Olivier appears very unhappy in the role of Darcy, rich

PRIDE AND PREJUDICE As Fitzwilliam Darcy

PRIDE AND PREJUDICE   With Greer Garson, Maureen O'Sullivan, and Bruce Lester

young bachelor, who is first spurned and then forgiven for his boorishness, conceit and bad manners."

"Flin." in *Variety*

"The most deliciously pert comedy of old manners, the most crisp and crackling satire in costume that we in this corner can remember ever having seen on the screen. It isn't often that a cast of such uniform perfection is assembled. Greer Garson is Elizabeth stepped right out of the book, or rather out of one's fondest imagination: poised, graceful, self-contained, witty, spasmodically stubborn, and as lovely as a woman can be. Laurence Olivier is Darcy, that's all there is to it—the arrogant, sardonic Darcy whose pride went before a most felicitous fall."

Bosley Crowther in *The New York Times*

"Animated and bouncing, the movie is more Dickens than Austen; once one adjusts to this, it's a happy and carefree viewing experience. The movie belongs to Lau-

PRIDE AND PREJUDICE   With Greer Garson

rence Olivier, who plays Darcy, and to that great old dragon Edna May Oliver, as Lady Catherine. In the role of Elizabeth Bennet, Greer Garson is not as intolerably noble as she became later. She's effective and has nice diction, though she's arch and incapable of subtlety, and a viewer can get weary of watching that eyebrow that goes up like the gold curtain at the old Met."

Pauline Kael in *5001 Nights at the Movies*

THAT HAMILTON WOMAN

(Lady Hamilton)

1941

A United Artists release of an Alexander Korda Production

CAST

Vivien Leigh *(Emma Hart, Lady Hamilton)*; Laurence Olivier *(Lord Horatio Nelson)*; Alan Mowbray *(Sir William Hamilton)*; Sara Allgood *(Mrs. Cadogan-Lyon)*; Gladys Cooper *(Lady Nelson)*; Henry Wilcoxon *(Captain Hardy)*; Heather Angel *(Street Girl)*; Miles Mander *(Reverend Lord Keith)*; Ronald Sinclair *(Josiah)*; Luis Alberni

(*King of Naples*); Norma Drury (*Queen of Naples*); Olaf Hytten (*Gavin*); Georges Renavent (*Hotel Manager*); Leonard Carey (*Orderly*); Alec Craig (*Gendarme*); Juliette Compton (*Lady Spencer*); Guy Kingsford (*Captain Troubridge*).

CREDITS

Producer-Director: Alexander Korda; *Screenwriters:* Walter Reisch and R.C. Sherriff; *Cinematographer:* Rudolph Maté; *Special sequences photographed by* Edward Linden; *Editor:* William Hornbeck; *Art Directors:* Vincent Korda and Lyle Reynolds Wheeler; *Set Decorator:* Julia Heron; *Music:* Miklos Rozsa; *Costumes:* Rene Hubert; *Makeup Artist:* Blagoe Stephanoff; *Special Effects:* Laurence Butler; *Assistant Director:* Walter Mayo; *Sound:* William A. Wilmarth; *Running Time:* 128 minutes.

THE FILM

Widely celebrated as the favorite movie of Winston Churchill (he reputedly saw it some eleven-odd times), *That Hamilton Woman* (or *Lady Hamilton*, as it was called in the U.K.) was an American production—albeit turned out by the Hungarian-born British producer Alexander Korda—that had all the earmarks of an English film due to its almost-all-British cast.

The story is told in flashback form, as a middle-aged slattern (Vivien Leigh) recounts the story of her life to a younger streetwalker (Heather Angel). The older woman it seems had been a sexually inexperienced English girl named Emma Hart, who had journeyed to the Court of Naples in 1786 to marry her lover, the British ambassador's nephew. Instead, she finds that she's been deceived by the young rascal, rebounding to become the mistress—and eventual wife—of the ambassador, Sir William Hamilton (Alan Mowbray). Seven years pass, and Emma meets the British naval hero Lord Horatio Nelson (Laurence Olivier), whom she befriends, interceding with the Neapolitan Queen (Norma Drury) to get aid for the English fleet anchored there. During Nelson's sojourn in Naples, he and Emma realize a romantic attraction that deepens when he returns, having lost an arm and an eye, to recuperate there following his victory over Napoleon in the Battle of the Nile. Hamilton stoically puts up with Emma's infidelity for patriotic reasons, while the lovers' illicit affair becomes common knowledge back in Britain, where they're forced to return when revolution overthrows the Neapolitan throne. Emma's now expecting Nelson's child, but when he asks his wife (Gladys Cooper) for a divorce, she adamantly refuses him. The lovers settle into unmarried, rural domesticity. But, with the war going badly for England, Emma persuades Nelson to serve his country again by returning to command the fleet. Battling Napoleon's forces at Trafalgar, he's mortally wounded, leaving his mistress to descend to the streets, where, in an epilogue, Emma ends her incredible story.

Because of the difficulties attendant on filmmaking in wartime Britain, Alexander Korda had moved his operations to Hollywood, where he continued to turn out films like *The Thief of Bagdad, Lydia* and *The Jungle Book.* Despite its handsome production values, *That Hamilton Woman* had to be made with a maximum of technical ingenuity, since Korda's financial resources were then at a low ebb, requiring economical sets (his brother Vincent took charge of the film's art direction) and model shots to represent the naval-battle scenes. The film was completed in a record (for Korda) six weeks in a small Hollywood studio. Korda was thought to have scored a coup by engaging Olivier and Leigh, but both stars were then in dire financial need, having just lost all of their considerable savings on an ambitious 1940 stage production of *Romeo and Juliet.* That, with the newly popular stars of *Gone With the Wind* and *Wuthering Heights*, appeared a certain success, but proved an overwhelming disaster.

Just prior to *That Hamilton Woman*'s production, in August of 1940, the celebrated illicit lovers, Leigh and

THAT HAMILTON WOMAN   As Lord Horatio Nelson

all professionals, mutually respectful and efficient. The years of happy association that Vivien, Alex and I had shared were evident in the final result. I played the English hero, Lord Nelson, not as the neurotic I discovered in my researches, but as the gallant yet gentle sailor in the patriotic convention of the times. Nelson had the most extraordinary girlish mouth, so I wore rose lips because I was now becoming relatively at ease in the medium, didn't have a star's face that couldn't be changed from one film to the next, and wanted to practice my craft of acting."

CRITICS CIRCLE

"Miss Leigh hits the peaks with her delineation of Lady Hamilton, a vivacious girl who is pictured as a victim of men, but whose ingenuity in statecraft saves the Empire. She dominates the picture throughout with her reserved love for Nelson and her determination to aid his success from the background. Olivier's characterization of Nelson, the British naval hero, carries the full dignity and reserve of the historical figure."

"Walt." in *Variety*

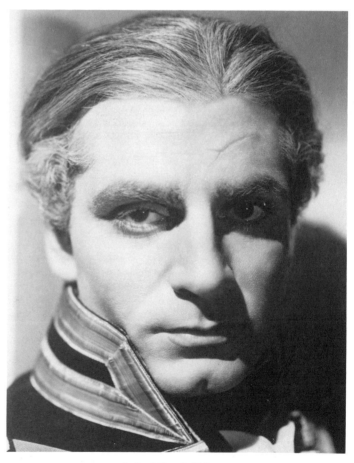

THAT HAMILTON WOMAN   As Lord Horatio Nelson

Olivier, finally and legally free of their respective former mates, were married in Santa Barbara. But their on-screen roles as *That Hamilton Woman*'s scandalous lovers could hardly have failed to attract moviegoers, both at home and abroad.

Subsequent movies dealing with the subject included the 1969 *Lady Hamilton*, an international coproduction with Richard Johnson and Michele Mercier as the lovers, and the 1973 *Bequest to the Nation* (aka *The Nelson Affair*), with Peter Finch and Glenda Jackson.

OLIVIER:

"The picture was shot in a small, little-known studio right in the middle of Hollywood, then called General Services. The work was harmonious throughout; we were

106

THAT HAMILTON WOMAN
With Vivien Leigh

THAT HAMILTON WOMAN   With Vivien Leigh and
bit players

THAT HAMILTON WOMAN   With Vivien Leigh

THE 49TH PARALLEL   As Johnnie the Trapper

"Vivien Leigh and Laurence Olivier are dressed like Nelson and Lady Hamilton, they go through all the joys which beset that not so ill-fated couple; but they are seldom other than two modern film stars led in and out of the scenes by the accepted clichés."

Richard Winnington in *The News Chronicle*

"The death scene is finely done, a moving piece of acting. Laurence Olivier's performance as Nelson, indeed, is within its conventions good throughout."

Dilys Powell in *The Sunday Times*

"In short, the whole film is just a running account of a famous love affair, told with deep sympathy for the participants against a broad historic outline of the times. Vivien Leigh's entire performance as Lady Hamilton is delightful to behold. All of the charm and grace and spirit which Miss Leigh contains is beautifully put to use to capture the subtle spell which Emma most assuredly must have weaved. Laurence Olivier's Nelson is more studied and obviously contrived, and his appearance is very impressive, with the famous dead eye and empty sleeve. But our impression of Nelson, at least, has been one of less forbidding austere, of a man who gave off more heat in his tender or impassioned moments."

Bosley Crowther in *The New York Times*

49TH PARALLEL

(The Invaders)

1941

A General Film Distributors release of an Ortus Films production

U.S. Distributor: Columbia Pictures (1942)

CAST

Laurence Olivier *(Johnnie the Trapper)*; Finlay Currie *(The Factor)*; Anton Walbrook *(Peter)*; Glynis Johns *(Anna)*; Leslie Howard *(Philip Armstrong Scott)*; Raymond Massey *(Andy Brock)*; Charles Victor *(Andreas)*; Eric Portman *(Lieutenant Hirth)*; Frederick Piper *(David)*; Tawera Moana *(George the Indian)*; Eric Clavering *(Art)*; Charles Rolfe *(Bob)*; Richard George *(Kommandant Bernsdorff)*; Raymond Lovell *(Lieutenant Kuhnecke)*; Niall MacGinnis *(Vogel)*; Peter Moore *(Kranz)*; John Chandos *(Lohrmann)*; Basil Appleby *(Jahner)*; Ley On *(Nick the Eskimo)*; Theodore Salt and O.W. Fonger *(U.S. Customs Officers)*.

THE 49TH PARALLEL   With Raymond Lovell, Finlay Currie, and Eric Portman

108

CREDITS

Director: Michael Powell; *Producers:* Michael Powell and John Sutro; *Associate Producers:* Roland Gillett and George Brown; *Screenwriters:* Emeric Pressburger and Rodney Ackland; *Cinematographer:* Frederick A. Young; *Editors:* David Lean and Hugh Stewart; *Art Director:* David Rawnsley; *Music:* Ralph Vaughan Williams; *Sound:* A.W. Watkins; *Canadian Adviser:* Nugent M. Cloucher; *Running Time:* 123 minutes. (U.S. length: 105 minutes.)

THE FILM

Britain's Ministry of Information was persuaded to finance this episodic, propagandistic adventure drama (for a mere $100,000), because producer-director Michael Powell assured them he had commitments from such notable performers—working at half their usual fee—as Laurence Olivier, Elisabeth Bergner (Glynis Johns later replaced her), Leslie Howard, and Anton Walbrook. Filmed on location in Montreal, as well as at Britain's Denham Studios, *49th Parallel* follows the six-member crew of a U-37 German submarine, which surfaces in Canada's Gulf of St. Lawrence, only to be attacked and sunk by RCAF bombers. Stranded in a strange land, the crew members, commanded by the brutal Lieutenant Hirth (Eric Portman), find their way to a Hudson's Bay trading post, where they encounter an agent (Finlay Currie) and his spirited friend, a French-Canadian trapper (Olivier) whom they kill when he tries to radio a message about them to the authorities. The Germans move on to a Hutterite settlement, ruthlessly heading for the then-neutral U.S.; but they're either captured or killed as they go, eventually leaving only Hirth to the mercy of an AWOL Canadian soldier (Raymond Massey), who stops him with a bullet aboard a train near the border.

The first motion picture to commission a score from the noted British composer Ralph Vaughan Williams, *49th Parallel* became a huge financial success in Britain, as well as the U.S., where it was more commercially retitled *The Invaders*.

OLIVIER:

"They'd bring us actors down from time to time to make Ministry of Information films, and I was released for *49th Parallel*, a film with a patriotic theme directed by the imaginative Michael Powell, who allowed actors to act. I was happy with my simple and gentle French-Canadian trapper, which I established in only ten minutes' screentime. Had I learnt something about the economy and directness of film acting from my days in Hollywood?"

CRITICS CIRCLE

"Among the best of the anti-Nazi pictures—it was made in Canada and England by a group of selfless stars,

THE 49TH PARALLEL   With Eric Portman

playing in small but vital roles for the sake of the main idea. The picture is made immeasurably effective by the realistic manner in which it has been put together by Michael Powell. *The Invaders* is an absorbing and exciting film."

Bosley Crowther in *The New York Times*

"A famous cast interprets the leading roles with a perfection of light and shade that keeps the theme in perspective and gives an irresistible force to speech and action. To our mind, the most appealing of the roles is that of the French-Canadian trapper played by Laurence Olivier, for he breaks away from the convention and gives a plain study of a simple soul aghast at the vicious cruelty of the Nazi doctrines and their adherents, in comprehending the politics of the war but ready to die for his faith."

Today's Cinema

"This is an important and effective propaganda film. Started in April 1940, it took 18 months to complete and included two expeditions to Canada. The main criticism is its title. Even this reviewer, an American, did not know until he saw the film that 49th parallel means the dividing line between the U.S. and Canada. . . . Every part, to the smallest bits, is magnificently played in a vast canvas that contributes to the dignity of the undertaking. The stars are Leslie Howard, with his comedy gifts at high tide; Laurence Olivier (a bit, but best thing he has ever done); Raymond Massey (also a bit, but outstanding), and Anton Walbrook as a dignified Hitlerite [sic!] leader. Despite heartbreaking difficulties encountered, such as the defection of Elisabeth Bergner after the picture was well under way, Michael Powell, the director, has managed to maintain his stature among the top directors."

"Jolo." in Variety

THE DEMI-PARADISE

(Adventure for Two)

1943

*A General Film Distributors release of a
Two Cities Films production*

U.S. Distributor: Universal Pictures (1945)

THE DEMI-PARADISE   With Leslie Henson

CAST

Laurence Olivier *(Ivan Dimitrievich Kouznetsoff)*; Penelope Ward *(Ann Tisdall)*; Marjorie Fielding *(Mrs. Tisdall)*; Margaret Rutherford *(Rowena Ventnor)*; Felix Aylmer *(Mr. Runalow)*; George Thorpe *(Herbert Tisdall)*; Guy Middleton *(Richard Christie)*; Michael Shepley *(Mr. Walford)*; Edie Martin *(Aunt Winnie)*; Muriel Aked *(Mrs. Tisdall-Stanton)*; Jack Watling *(Tom Sellars)*; Everley Gregg *(Mrs. Flannel)*; Joyce Grenfell *(Mrs. Pawson)*; Wilfrid Hyde-White *(Waiter)*; Miles Malleson *(Box-Office Manager)*; Marion Spencer *(Mrs. Teddy Beckett)*; John Laurie and John Boxer *(Sailors)*; David Keir *(Mr. Jordan)*; Brian Nissen *(George Tisdall)*; Josephine Middleton *(Mrs. Tremlow)*; Aubrey Mallalieu *(Toomes)*; Charles Paton *(Mr. Bishop)*; Leslie Henson *(Himself)*; John Schofield *(Ernie)*; Margaret Withers *(Mrs. Elliston)*; Beatrice Harrison *(Herself)*; Inge Perten *(Russian Doctor)*; Alexis Chesnakoff *(Russian Delegate)*; Mavis Clair *(Barmaid)*; George Street and Ben Williams *(Hecklers)*.

CREDITS

Director: Anthony Asquith; *Producer/Screenwriter:* Anatole de Grunwald; *Cinematographer:* Bernard Knowles; *Editors:* Reginald Beck and Jack Harris; *Art Directors:* Paul Sheriff and Carmen Dillon; *Music:* Nicholas Brodsky; *Sound:* J.C. Cook; *Assistant Director:* George Pollock; *Running Time:* 115 minutes.

THE FILM

Olivier portrayed a young Soviet marine engineer named Kouznetsoff who's the inventor of a new style propellor. When, in 1939, he's sent to England to oversee its manufacture there, Kouznetsoff becomes the weekend houseguest of eccentric shipowner Mr. Runalow (Felix Aylmer) and his granddaughter Ann (Penelope Ward). The difference in manners and customs initially bewilders and repels the Russian visitor, who returns home without seeing his propellor as a feasible proposition. Two years later, Kouznetsoff comes back to Britain, and is once again the country guest of the Runalows under much-altered circumstances, for now the country's at war—a situation which serves to break down differences of class and cultural attitudes. In time, his propellor becomes a success, and the Russian leaves for the Soviet Union, promising Ann to see her—and Britain—again when the war ends.

OLIVIER:

"I was summoned to the Ministry of Information to see Jack Beddington, who was sidekick for the Minister on any question which concerned show-business propaganda. He asked me to undertake two pictures intended to enhance the British cause. One was *The Demi-Paradise*, whose object was to win the British public over to the idea of liking the Russians—hardly an insurmountable task, you would have thought, since Russia had by then come into the war heavily on our side.

"*Demi-Paradise* was amusing to do, Russian accent and all. I had, at first, a Russian lady to teach me the accent until I began to find my consonants becoming alarmingly, not to say suspiciously, effeminate. I turned to a Russian male, who immediately declared, 'Avreesink see huss tolld yu iss alll wrongg,' at which point I decided I might do worse than invent my own Russian accent. I knew the basic principles of it anyway.

"The work was pleasant. Anthony (Puffin) Asquith was

THE DEMI-PARADISE With Wilfrid Hyde-White and Penelope Ward

the excellent, experienced and very charming director, and Tolly de Grunwald was the fine, delightfully friendly [Russian] producer, always helpful and encouraging about my accent."

CRITICS CIRCLE

"The film is made by a dazzling performance from Laurence Olivier and the skillful direction of Asquith. The section describing the 1939 visit of the Russian to this country is the best part, the nearest thing yet to English René Clair, the Russian providing an ironic commentary on Asquith's previous presentations of this stratum of our life."

William Whitebait in *The New Statesman and Nation*

"*Demi-Paradise*'s script consists of a wealth of character drawings with a thin web of a story about a young Russian engineer. Outstanding is a performance by Laurence Olivier. It is an accumulation of matured acting greatly exceeding the normal development that comes to an artist with increased experience. Replete with Russian accent, he gives a dignified and serious performance full of sincerity and repose that puts him in the top rank of British actors. For years an ace artist, he reaches a height in this film that will court comparison with the greatest of his contemporaries."

"Jolo." in *Variety*

THE DEMI-PARADISE Margaret Rutherford and extras

"Except for one mousey little character (played by Edie Martin) who looks on the Russians as wild barbarians, the people in this picture seem pompous, artificial and unmercifully dull. Mr. Olivier's melancholy Russian is a

111

THE DEMI-PARADISE   With Felix Aylmer

ponderous caricature, and Penelope Ward's English maiden is a skinny reed responsive to light whims. . . . Blame the writer-producer and the director—Anatole de Grunwald and Anthony Asquith, respectively—for the general incompetence of the picture. It's a limp and dampish hand across the sea."

Bosley Crowther in *The New York Times*

"The picture drew a picture, ironic and yet at the same time affectionate, of British foibles. *The Demi-Paradise* has innumerable touches of pictorial satire. It is remarkable too for the beautiful performance of Laurence Olivier as the bewildered Russian, a performance which puts him for the first time in the top flight of British film actors."

Dilys Powell in *Film Since 1939*

HENRY V

1944

*An Eagle-Lion release of a
Two Cities Films production*

U.S. Distributor: United Artists (1946)

CAST

Laurence Olivier *(King Henry V)*; Robert Newton *(Ancient Pistol)*; Leslie Banks *(Chorus)*; Renée Asherson *(Princess Katherine)*; Esmond

Knight *(Fluellen)*; Leo Genn *(Constable of France)*; Ralph Truman *(Mountjoy)*; Harcourt Williams *(King Charles VI)*; Ivy St. Helier *(Alice)*; Ernest Thesiger *(Duke of Berri)*; Max Adrian *(The Dauphin)*; Francis Lister *(Duke of Orleans)*; Valentine Dyall *(Duke of Burgundy)*; Russell Thorndike *(Duke of Bourbon)*; Morland Graham *(Sir Thomas Erpingham)*; George Cole *(Boy)*; Felix Aylmer *(Archbishop of Canterbury)*; Nicholas Hannen *(Duke of Exeter)*; Robert Helpmann *(Bishop of Ely)*; Freda Jackson *(Mistress Quickly)*; Jimmy Hanley *(Williams)*; John Laurie *(Jamy)*; Niall MacGinnis *(McMorris)*; George Robey *(Sir John Falstaff)*; Roy Emerton *(Bardolph)*; Griffith Jones *(Earl of Salisbury)*; Frederick Cooper *(Corporal Nym)*; Michael Shepley *(Gower)*; Arthur Hambling *(Bates)*; Brian Nissen *(Court)*; Gerald Case *(Earl of Westmoreland)*; Michael Warre *(Duke of Gloucester)*; Janet Burnell *(Queen Isabel of France)*; Frank Tickle *(Governor of Harfleur)*; Jonathan Field *(French Messenger)*; Vernon Greeves *(English Herald)*; Ernest Hare *(A Priest)*.

CREDITS

Directors: Laurence Olivier and Reginald Beck; *Producers:* Laurence Olivier and Filippo Del Giudice; *Associate Producer:* Dallas Bower; *Based on the play* **The Chronicle Historie of King Henry the Fifth** *by* William Shakespeare; *Text Editors:* Laurence Olivier and Alan Dent; *Technicolor Cinematographers:* Robert Krasker and Jack Hildyard; *Editor:* Reginald Beck; *Art Directors:* Paul Sheriff and Carmen Dillon; *Music:* William Walton; *Costumes:* Roger Furse and Margaret Furse; *Sound:* John Dennis and Desmond Dew; *Running Time:* 137 minutes.

THE FILM

Laurence Olivier's only previous motion picture bout with Shakespeare was with the rather indifferent 1936 *As You Like It*—an experience that left the actor convinced that the Bard's works were best left to the stage. In the theater, of course, Olivier was a well-seasoned Shakespearean, but it took the influence of an enterprising Italian immigrant named Filippo Del Giudice to change his way of thinking about filming the classics. In 1937, Del Giudice had established Two Cities Films, and had later been the guiding force behind Noël Coward's much-praised *In Which We Serve*, as well as the Olivier vehicle *The Demi-Paradise*. During the latter movie's production, the actor had starred in a full-length radio adaptation of *Henry V*, a broadcast that so impressed Del Giudice that he set about producing a film version of that play, in which Olivier would have complete artistic freedom.

Olivier had not originally planned to *direct* this movie; to do that, he unsuccessfully sought the services first of his *Wuthering Heights* director William Wyler, and then Carol Reed and Terence Young—none of whom were available. With no other appropriate choice at hand, Olivier decided to assume the direction himself, at the same time engaging film cutter Reginald Beck, not only to edit, but also to take the director's chair in the many scenes when Olivier himself was before the cameras. Theatre critic Alan Dent was signed to assist with preparing the Shakespearean text and, to assure the finest tech-

HENRY V As King Henry V

HENRY V   As King Henry V

nical qualities of sight and sound, the Technicolor cameras were in the expert hands of Robert Krasker and Jack Hildyard, and William Walton would compose the score. To fulfill *Henry* V's unusual and daring production concept, Paul Sheriff collaborated with Carmen Dillon, while the team of Roger and Margaret Furse was made responsible for the lavish costumes.

The majority of the movie's large cast was recruited from the British theater community, concentrating on colleagues with whose work Olivier was familiar. However, the one casting idea he couldn't realize was to have his wife, Vivien Leigh, play Katherine, the French princess. David O. Selznick, the independent Hollywood producer who had Leigh under personal contract, considered the role too small for his illustrious Scarlett O'Hara, and he refused to let her take it. And so Olivier settled for the lesser-known English stage actress Renée Asherson, who went on to play Katherine to such perfection that many assumed she was a new French discovery.

The "framing" device with which *Henry* V opens and closes was suggested to Olivier by director Anthony Asquith: the movie begins by focusing in on an ingeniously detailed miniature set of Shakespeare's London, before descending to focus on the stage of his famed Globe Theatre, where the play itself commences—and eventually concludes. In between, the film's audience is treated to a blend of painted stage sets and sweepingly natural outdoor scenery—for the naturalistic Battle of

HENRY V   As King Henry V

HENRY V   Henry meets the French delegation at Agincourt

115

HENRY V   With Felix Aylmer,
Robert Helpmann, Griffith
Jones, and bit players

Agincourt sequence, which was shot in Enniskerry, Ireland. If this odd amalgam of styles confused some viewers, it was wholly attributable to Olivier himself, who reasoned that mixing the real with the theatrical would help sustain the attention of filmgoers, many of whom would be unfamiliar with the antique cadences of Shakespearean speech.

Filmed in the midst of World War II, *Henry V* not unexpectedly became Britain's most costly picture to that date, forcing Filippo Del Giudice to relinquish control of Two Cities Films to J. Arthur Rank, in order to save the movie.

Shakespeare intended his *Chronicle Historie of King Henry the Fifth* as a straightforward account of men and war, and of an embryo king's coming of age. At twenty-eight, Henry is an endearingly exuberant youth who proves himself by leading his army into battle. Invading Britain's longtime enemy, France, he takes Harfleur, before attempting to withdraw his weary, outnumbered ranks to Calais. At Agincourt, confronted by the French forces, Henry's men are driven to an incredible victory by their valorous leader. And, following the truce at Rouen, King Henry successfully courts Katherine, the French princess.

Henry V was released in Great Britain in the autumn of 1944, where it enjoyed a huge success.

Nearly two years would pass before its eventual U.S. release—to even greater acclaim. First, however, the censors saw fit to cut a few offending "damns" and "bastards," and United Artists warily devised a clever plan of raised-price, reserved-seat "road show" distribution. In New York alone, it played continuously for a record

116

HENRY V With
Renée Asherson

eleven months, and won Olivier the New York Film Critics Award as Best Actor of 1946. In Hollywood, the motion picture Academy gave him a special Oscar for producing, directing, and starring in a film which had gone far to raise the British film industry's prestige abroad.

In 1989, the young British actor-director Kenneth Branagh turned out an equally impressive remake of *Henry V* that won new converts to the Bard.

OLIVIER:

"After *Demi-Paradise*, I would be required to make a picture of Shakespeare's *Henry V*. The pull of this play as popular propaganda, I could see, might be far more potent than the first project, and the pull on my artistic ambitions was intoxicating.

"I have been luckier than most because I was ultimately given the opportunity to take Shakespeare from the wooden O and place him on the silver screen. 'Not possible,' I was told. Initial attempts to do this had been absolutely appalling. The audiences had stayed away in the multitudes. But I had the good fortune to be something of a movie star; I already had a following, so whatever I did was looked upon with curiosity. Somehow, it worked, and I think it had much to do with the way I adapted the sound of the lines to the modern ear. The film-going public, many of whom had never been in a theatre in their lives, understood, enjoyed and were entertained. Once the public had been wooed and won by *Henry V*, the critics and the studios came round to the idea that it was possible to put Shakespeare on the screen. *Henry* was a box-office success. Shakespeare had been

117

given to the people. He was no longer for a small band of the select."

CRITICS CIRCLE

"A fine group of British film craftsmen and actors, headed by Laurence Olivier, have concocted a stunningly brilliant and intriguing screen spectacle, rich in theatrical invention, in heroic imagery and also gracefully regardful of the conventions of the Elizabethan stage. Mr. Olivier and his editor, Reginald Beck, have simply cut large chunks out of the play . . . to get at the action and the meat. Thus reduced of excessive conversations (though it might have been trimmed even more), they have mounted the play with faithful service to the spirit and the word. That service is as truly magnificent as any ever given to a Shakespearean script, both in visual conception and in the acting of an excellent cast. Mr. Olivier's own performance of Henry sets a standard for excellence. His majestic and heroic bearing, his full and vibrant use of his voice, create a kingly figure around which the other characters spin. Thanks to him and to all those who helped him, we have a glowing 'touch of Harry in the night.' "

Bosley Crowther in *The New York Times*

"It is not, I repeat, the most exciting or inspiring or original film that I have seen. But I cannot think of any that seems to be more beautiful, more skillfully and charmingly achieved within its wisely ordered limits, or more thoroughly satisfying."

James Agee in *The Nation*

"Laurence Olivier produces, directs and stars in *Henry V*. He deserves credit for undertaking the most ambitious film of our time. But it is also the most difficult, annoying, beautiful, boring, exciting, wordy, baffling picture yet made. It has a sort of damnable excellence."

Ernest Betts in *The People*

"Mr. Olivier and his colleagues have produced a film that is probably the highest compliment this generation can pay to an age of less conscious culture. They have worked from a clean Shakespearean text, cut to about two-thirds of its original length. There are two interpolations—an inserted speech from *Henry IV* to explain the reference to Falstaff, and a couple of resounding lines from Marlowe's *Tamburlaine* to send Pistol off to the wars with a flourish. They have collected a cast of some of the finest Shakespearean actors on the English stage, so that every speech gets its due, every slightest word its weight."

C. A. Lejeune in *The Observer*

118

"Olivier's *Henry V* burst like a rising sun on the cinema screen at the end of 1944: seldom can a film's timing have been more apt. The word of the day was 'breakthrough'—for the war, for the Britain of the future—and for Shakespeare on the screen. Justified though some criticisms may be, the film remains a landmark in the presentation of Shakespeare and in the history of British cinema. The battle charge of Agincourt, to Walton's most stirring music, and culminating in the whirring flight of a thousand arrows, is unlikely ever to be surpassed."

Ivan Butler in *Cinema in Britain*

HAMLET

1948

A General Film Distributors/J. Arthur Rank release of a Two Cities Films production

U.S. Distributor: Universal Pictures

CAST

Laurence Olivier (*Hamlet*); Eileen Herlie (*Gertrude*); Basil Sydney (*Claudius*); Jean Simmons (*Ophelia*); Felix Aylmer (*Polonius*); Norman Wooland (*Horatio*); Terence Morgan (*Laertes*); Harcourt Williams (*First Player*); Patrick Troughton (*Player King*); Tony Tarver (*Player Queen*); Peter Cushing (*Osric*); Stanley Holloway (*Gravedigger*); Russell Thorndike (*Priest*); John Laurie (*Francisco*); Esmond Knight (*Bernardo*); Anthony Quayle (*Marcellus*); Niall MacGinnis (*Sea Captain*); John Gielgud (*Voice of Hamlet's Ghost*); Christopher Lee (*Guard*).

CREDITS

Producer-Director: Laurence Olivier; *Associate Producer*: Reginald Beck; *Assistant Producer*: Anthony Bushell; *Assistant Director*: Peter Bolton; *Based on the play by* William Shakespeare; *Text Editor*: Alan Dent; *Cinematographer*: Desmond Dickinson; *Editor*: Helga Cranston; *Production Designer*: Roger Furse; *Art Director*: Carmen Dillon; *Set Dresser*: Roger Ramsdell; *Music*: William Walton; *Sound*: John Mitchell, L.E. Overton and Harry Miller; *Special Effects*: Paul Sheriff, Henry Harris, and Jack Whitehead; *Running Time*: 155 minutes.

THE FILM

Shakespeare's poetic revenge drama is quite possibly the best known—and most variously interpreted—classic in the English language. Olivier had originally portrayed the enigmatic, introspective Prince of Denmark onstage at the Old Vic in 1937. At forty-one, he followed his triumphant *Henry V* film with this fascinating Freudian interpretation of the Bard's masterpiece, in which the

HAMLET   As Hamlet

HAMLET   Hamlet's death scene

bleached, cornsilk hair, Olivier brings a brutal Oedipal poignancy to the scenes with his mother the Queen (Eileen Herlie, a mature-looking actress actually thirteen years Olivier's junior!) and a sadomasochistic torment to those with Ophelia (eighteen-year-old Jean Simmons in her only experience with Shakespeare). In the film's deadly climactic duel scene, Olivier's athletic panache and demonic energy are ingeniously captured and enhanced by the joint artistry of cinematographer Dickinson and editor Helga Cranston.

Hamlet cost backer J. Arthur Rank nearly £580,000—more than twice what he had initially anticipated. Understandably, he was anxious at that high an expenditure on a black-and-white picture of "specialized" appeal—especially considering that Olivier maintained an adamant "closed-set" policy toward anyone not actively involved in the filming. Eventually, when an executive revealed that the star had let him view half an hour's

four-and-one-half-hour play was condensed into a 155-minute motion picture. Again, the actor produced and directed, as well as starred in what turned out to be a brilliant rendition of the play, tightened to eliminate such excess baggage as Rosencrantz and Guildenstern. Helping Olivier realize his concept of the work, Desmond Dickinson's restless, constantly exploring cameras roam the massive Elsinore Castle sets, brought period flavor by the court fanfares and incidental background music of the incomparable William Walton. Olivier's *Hamlet* is a perfect visualization of Shakespeare, craftily devised in terms of the motion picture screen. The action never stops long for speeches; instead the visual images keep changing and moving as the cameras rove the halls, parapets, and private castle chambers with a relentless purpose appropriate to the fateful tragedy that Olivier so uncannily realizes in this all-encompassing production. Nor does he confine his action to those bloodthirsty towered corridors; visualized exteriors represent a chilling graveyard scene, an abbreviated sea skirmish, and the watery death of young Ophelia in a reedy stream.

Olivier's own reading of the Prince of Denmark is as silver-tongued as anyone might anticipate, an intelligent blend of violent emotion and intellectual calm. His delivery of the "To be or not to be" speech is, for its day, quite unusual—presented in the form of an interior, soundtrack monologue. As pale of feature as his

122

HAMLET   With Basil Sydney, Eileen Herlie, Jean Simmons, and bit players

"rushes," J. Arthur eagerly inquired, "And what's it like?" "Mr. Rank," ventured the informant, "it's wonderful. You wouldn't know it was Shakespeare."

Shown in the U.S. as a reserved-seat "road show" attraction, *Hamlet* won immediate critical acclaim and audience interest, as well. At home, it copped the British Film Academy's Best Picture Award for 1948, but less expected was its precedent-breaking Academy Award for Best Picture, coupled with Oscars for Best Actor Olivier, as well as the art direction and costume design of Roger Furse and Carmen Dillon's set decoration. Sir Laurence (for such he became during *Hamlet*'s production) also won the New York Film Critics citation for 1948's best male acting.

As this volume was being compiled, *Hamlet* returned to the screen in the person of Mel Gibson in a 1990 production devised by Franco Zeffirelli. Bridging the gap: a 1969 British film, directed by Tony Richardson and starring the eccentric Nicol Williamson in an uneven movie considerably overshadowed by its 1948 predecessor.

OLIVIER:

"In 1947, I made a film of *Hamlet*. It could well be left at that, but there are credits; others contributed vitally to it. It was designed entirely by [Roger] Furse. I chose black-and-white for it rather than color, to achieve through depth of focus a more majestic, more poetic image, in keeping with the statute of the verse. In one shot Ophelia, in close foreground, sees Hamlet down a long corridor through a mirror, seated 120 feet away; her every hair is in focus and so are his features.

"Of course, I had to be ruthless in the cutting. Half of *Henry V* went, so did half of *Hamlet*. I approached the job with terror and the utmost respect, not terror of the purists, but fear that my concept and its execution would

be unfaithful to Shakespeare or to the medium; it must be utterly respectful to the spirit of Shakespeare or to the medium; it must be utterly respectful to the spirit of Shakespeare and to the audience's consciousness of Hamlet."

CRITICS CIRCLE

"It may come as something of a rude shock to the theatre's traditionalists to discover that the tragedies of Shakespeare can be eloquently presented on the screen. So bound have these poetic dramas long been to the culture of our stage that the very thought of their transference may have staggered a few profound diehards. But now the matter is settled; the filmed *Hamlet* of Laurence Olivier gives absolute proof that these classics are magnificently suited to the screen. Actually, a lot of material which is in the conventional *Hamlet* text is missing from the picture—a lot of lines and some minor characters, notably those two fickle windbags, Rosencrantz and Guildenstern. And it is natural that some fond Shakespeareans are going to be distressed at the suddenly discovered omission of this or that speech. But some highly judicious editing has not done damage to the fullness of the drama nor to any of its most familiar scenes."

Bosley Crowther in *The New York Times*

HAMLET   With Jean Simmons

HAMLET   With Felix Aylmer

124

"A man who can do what Laurence Olivier does for Shakespeare is certainly among the more valuable men in his time. [*Hamlet*] in every piece of casting, in every performance, is about as nearly solid as gold can be. The most moving and gratifying thing in this film is to watch this talented artist [Olivier], in the height of his accomplishment, work at one of the most wonderful roles ever written."

James Agee in *Time* Magazine

"To some it will be one of the greatest films ever made, to others a deep disappointment. Laurence Olivier leaves no doubt that he is one of our greatest living actors. His rich, moving voice, his expressive face, make of the tortured Dane a figure of deep and sincere tragedy. Arguments about his age and his blond hair cannot detract from the personal triumph of his performance. His liberties with the text, however, are sure to disturb many."

Milton Shulman in *The Evening Standard*

"The bravura of performance so clear to Laurence Olivier reveals him to be a theatrical showman as well as

HAMLET   With Terence Morgan, Basil Sydney, Norman Wooland, Eileen Herlie, Peter Cushing, and extras

HAMLET   With Peter Cushing, Terence Morgan, Norman Wooland, and extras

a great artist. The duel scene, lasting ten minutes and taking fourteen days to shoot, is magnificently intense, with the growing rage of the contestants. The melodramatic flying leap down from a height onto Claudius, when Hamlet plunges his sword into his uncle's body at the end of the play . . . was sufficiently dangerous to be made the final shot in the production. . . . Of the three Shakespearean films directed by Olivier, *Hamlet* is possibly the one which most repays detailed examination. The film, though over-long, suffers from certain important losses through the drastic cutting of the text. But this *Hamlet* remains nevertheless arguably the most imaginative of the three films in treatment and realization, as it is, obviously, by far the most demanding of the three as a play."

Roger Manvell in *Shakespeare and the Film* (1971)

THE MAGIC BOX

1951

A British Lion release of a Festival Film production
U.S. Distributor: Mayer-Kingsley (1952)

CAST

Robert Donat *(William Friese-Greene)*; Margaret Johnston *(Edith Harrison)*; Maria Schell *(Helena Friese-Greene)*; John Howard Davies *(Maurice Friese-Greene)*; David Oake *(Claude Friese-Greene)*; Renée Asherson *(Miss Tagg)*; Richard Attenborough *(Jack Carter)*; Robert Beatty *(Lord Beaverbrook)*; Michael Denison *(Connaught Rooms Reporter)*; Henry Edwards *(Butler)*; Leo Genn *(Maida Vale Doctor)*; Marius Goring *(House Agent)*; Joyce Grenfell *(Mrs. Clare)*; Robertson Hare *(Sitter)*; Kathleen Harrison *(Mother)*; William Hartnell *(Recruiting Sergeant)*; Stanley Holloway *(Broker's Man)*; Jack Hulbert *(First Holborn Policeman)*; Glynis Johns *(May Jones)*; Mervyn Johns *(Pawnbroker)*; Barry Jones *(Bath Doctor)*; Miles Malleson *(Orchestra Conductor)*; Muir Matheson *(Sir Arthur Sullivan)*; A.E. Matthews *(Old Gentleman)*; John McCallum *(Sitter)*; Bernard Miles *(Cousin Alfred)*; Laurence Olivier *(Second Holborn Policeman)*; Cecil Parker *(First Platform Man)*; Eric Portman *(Arthur Collings)*; Dennis Price *(Bond Street Assistant)*; Michael Redgrave *(Mr. Lege)*; Margaret Rutherford *(Lady Pond)*; Ronald Shiner *(Fairground Barker)*; Sheila Sim *(Nursemaid)*; Basil Sydney *(William Fox-Talbot)*; Sybil Thorndike *(Sitter)*; David Tomlinson *(Bob)*; Cecil Trouncer *(John Rudge)*; Peter Ustinov *(Industry Man)*; Frederick Valk *(Maurice Guttenberg)*; Kay Walsh *(Hotel Receptionist)*; Emlyn Williams *(Bank Manager)*; Harcourt Williams *(Tom)*; Googie Withers *(Sitter)*; Edward Chapman *(Father)*; Roland Culver *(First Company Promoter)*; Joan Dowling *(Friese-Greene Maid)*; Mary Ellis *(Mrs. Collings)*; Marjorie Fielding *(Elderly Viscountess)*; Robert Flemyng *(Doctor in Surgery)*; Everley Gregg *(Bridegroom's Mother)*; Joan Hickson *(Mrs. Stukely)*; Thora Hird *(Doctor's Housekeeper)*; Patrick Holt *(Sitter)*; Michael Hordern *(Official Receiver)*; Sidney James *(Sergeant)*; James Kenney *(Kenneth Friese-*

Greene); Herbert Lomas *(Warehouse Manager)*; John Longden *(Speaker)*; Bessie Love *(Bride's Mother)*; Peter Reynolds *(Bridegroom)*; Janette Scott *(Ethel Friese-Greene)*; John Stuart *(Second Platform Man)*; Marianne Stone *(Bride)*; Ernest Thesiger *(Earl)*; Joan Young *(Glove Shop "Dragon")*.

CREDITS

Director: John Boulting; *Producer:* Ronald Neame; *Screenwriter:* Eric Ambler; *Based on the book* **Friese-Greene** *by* Ray Allister; *Technicolor Cinematographer:* Jack Cardiff; *Editor:* Richard Best; *Production Designer:* John Bryan; *Assistant Art Director:* T. Hopewell-Ash; *Set Dresser:* Dario Simoni; *Music:* William Alwyn; *Costumes:* Julia Squire; *Running Time:* 118 minutes.

THE FILM

Laurence Olivier was among the all-star supporting cast of this belated tribute to the English cinematograph pioneer William Friese-Greene (portrayed by Robert Donat) in a film designed as that industry's contribution to the 1951 Festival of Britain.

THE MAGIC BOX   As the Second Holborn Policeman

THE MAGIC BOX   With Robert Donat

CARRIE   As the derelict George Hurstwood

CRITICS CIRCLE

"Without material of high drama to build on, director and writer have been content to create a number of episodes in the cinema pioneer's private and personal life, often amusing, sometimes moving and only occasionally dull. Robert Donat is quietly charming, and Laurence Olivier stands out in his two-minute scene as a stolidly sceptical policeman."

Ivan Butler in *Cinema in Britain*

"It is a picture of great sincerity and integrity, superbly acted and intelligently directed. This story of the British motion-picture pioneer is charged with real-life drama, with the major incidents in his often-tragic life handled with a delicate degree of emotion and poignancy. The selection of Robert Donat as Friese-Greene is an excellent one. His two wives are portrayed with infinite charm by Maria Schell and Margaret Johnston. For the remainder of the cast, all the top names of British films have been recruited. Many front-ranking stars have little more than walk-on bits, and quite a few just make a brief appearance without even a line of dialogue. The names are too numerous to list, but mention must be made of a fine cameo from Sir Laurence Olivier as a policeman who is the first to see the inventor's moving picture."

"Myro." in *Variety*

"Sir Laurence Olivier appears as a bewildered city policeman, dragged off his beat by the inventor in the middle of the night to form an audience for one of his first public performances of moving pictures. This scene is brilliant in its economy and incisiveness, and in the subdued eloquence of its pantomime. It is also unselfish, with one of the greatest actors of our time deliberately serving as a 'feed' in the interests of the story."

Britain Today

"The policeman is played by a be-whiskered Laurence Olivier, and he and Donat milk the big moment of more tenseness and eye-moistening emotion than you would have thought possible."

The London Daily Express

CARRIE

1952

A Paramount Picture

CAST

Laurence Olivier *(George Hurstwood)*; Jennifer Jones *(Carrie Meeber)*; Miriam Hopkins *(Julia Hurstwood)*; Eddie Albert *(Charles*

127

CARRIE   With Jennifer Jones and Eddie Albert

Drouet); Basil Ruysdael (Mr. Fitzgerald); Ray Teal (Allan); Barry Kelley (Slawson); Sara Berner (Mrs. Oransky); William Reynolds (George Hurstwood, Jr.); Mary Murphy (Jessica Hurstwood); Harry Hayden (O'Brien); Charles Halton (Factory Foreman); Walter Baldwin (Carrie's Father); Jacqueline de Wit (Minnie); Dorothy Adams (Carrie's Mother); Harlan Briggs (Joe Brant); Melinda Plowman (Little Girl); Donald Kerr (Slawson's Bartender); Lester Sharpe (Mr. Blum); Don Beddoe (Mr. Goodman); John Alvin (Stage Manager); Royal Dano (Captain); James Flavin (Mike, the Bartender); Margaret Field (Servant Girl); Lois Hall (Lola); Irene Winston (Anna); Albert Astar (Louis the Headwaiter).

CREDITS

Producer-Director: William Wyler; *Associate Producer:* Walter Koenig; *Screenwriters:* Ruth and Augustus Goetz; *Based on the novel* **Sister Carrie** *by* Theodore Dreiser; *Cinematographer:* Victor Milner; *Editor:* Robert Swink; *Art Directors:* Hal Pereira and Roland Anderson; *Music:* David Raksin; *Costumes:* Edith Head; *Runnng Time:* 118 minutes.

THE FILM

Although Olivier barely mentions it in his autobiography, *Carrie* (reuniting him professionally with director William Wyler) contains what many consider one of his finest performances on film. But it wasn't a very popular movie, and its downbeat, old-fashioned story undoubtedly worked against its being fully appreciated by the critics *or* the award-givers, despite the excellence of its cast and production.

Based on Theodore Dreiser's tear-jerking novel *Sister Carrie*, this followed on the heels of an earlier Paramount

CARRIE   With Miriam Hopkins

CARRIE   With Jennifer Jones

picture derived from the same author, 1951's more popular *A Place in the Sun*, adapted from *An American Tragedy*. Actually, *Carrie* was produced in 1950, and Olivier accepted the role (already turned down by Cary Grant) as a means of keeping busy in Hollywood while his wife Vivien Leigh filmed *A Streetcar Named Desire* there. That it took Paramount until 1952 to release *Carrie* may have had as much to do with that studio's sales strategy as with editing the final cut (it seems that some of Olivier's later footage was eliminated, both to relieve the gloom and to bring the finished product in under two hours in length).

Carrie's predictable plot follows the turn-of-the-century misfortunes of an impressionable small-town girl (Jones) who intends to make her living in Chicago, at first staying with her married sister, while working in a sweatshop. But a sewing-machine accident loses Carrie her job, and she's driven to look up Charlie Drouet (Eddie Albert), the cheerful traveling salesman she met on her train journey to the big city. Cleverly, he worms his way into her good graces, and soon she's living with him,

although more suitably impressed with George Hurstwood (Olivier), the married manager of a swank restaurant where Charlie wines and dines her. Trapped in a socially comfortable but loveless marriage with a wife (Miriam Hopkins) and grown children, the middle-aged Hurstwood becomes rejuvenated through his feelings for Carrie. His subsequent liaison with her, after she leaves Drouet, leads to Hurstwood's losing his livelihood and his dignity. And, when his wife refuses him a divorce, he embezzles $10,000, moving to New York with Carrie. After they're found and he returns the money, the impoverished couple hits financial bottom, with Carrie leaving him to pursue a stage career, while her lover drifts to the streets. Later, when she's found theatrical success, they're reunited in her dressing room, and she tries to help him. A somewhat ambiguous ending suggests suicide as the solution for Hurstwood's ongoing despair.

CRITICS CIRCLE

"When the word first came that Mr. Olivier had been cast in the difficult role of this reckless Chicago gentle-

129

CARRIE   With Jennifer Jones

man out of America's raw Gilded Age, there were those who regarded his selection as a perilously chancy choice, likely to lead to a distortion that would throw the whole story askew. The eminent British actor was thought too elegant and alien for the role of Mr. Dreiser's middle-aged hero who went to ruin out of love for a pretty girl. Mr. Olivier gives the film its closest contact with the book, while Miss Jones' soft, seraphic portrait of Carrie take it furthest away."

Bosley Crowther in *The New York Times*

"Wyler has delicately caught the tragedy of a man's downfall and decay; and Sir Laurence Olivier's acting is a triumph of autumnal sensibility."

Dilys Powell in *The Sunday Times*

"It is a somber, low-key entertainment almost totally unrelieved during its nearly two-hour unfolding. Yet it's conceivably a tearjerker with some box-office lure for the distaff side. . . . Jennifer Jones, playing Carrie, gives one of the bright performances of her career. For Laurence Olivier, it is mostly a thankless performance, through no fault of his own, since it is a role that gives him little opportunity for shading or the dramatic intensity that has established him as one of the great actors of the generation. As the cultured restaurant manager, he never quite

130

fits the role, nor looks the part, of a man reduced to begging when all else has failed him."

"Kahn" in *Variety*

"William Wyler's version of Theodore Dreiser's *Sister Carrie* is graced by one of Laurence Olivier's finest screen performances. Olivier has always given credit to Wyler for teaching him to act in the movies when they did *Wuthering Heights* together, but it's in *Carrie* that he showed how much he had learned. As George Hurstwood, the manager of an elegant Chicago grog-and-steak house, who ruins himself for a pretty face (Jennifer Jones), Olivier is so impassioned and so painfully touching that everyone else in the movie, including the girl whose story it's meant to be, fades into insignificance."

Pauline Kael in *5001 Nights at the Movies*

A QUEEN IS CROWNED

1953

*A General Film Distributors release of a
J. Arthur Rank production*

U.S. Distributor: Universal-International

CREDITS

Producer: Castleton Knight: *Commentary written by:* Christopher Fry; *Narrator:* Sir Laurence Olivier; *Original Music:* Guy Warrack; *Musical Adviser:* Sir Malcolm Sargent; *Photographed in* Technicolor; *Running Time:* 89 minutes.

THE FILM

This was the longest and most widely distributed of the various documentaries covering the June 2, 1953 Coronation of Queen Elizabeth II, which culminated in the ceremony at Westminster Abbey. Among its competitors were two British twenty-minute shorts, *Coronation Day* and *The Coronation Ceremony*, and a fifty-six-minute feature entitled *Elizabeth Is Queen*. While nominated for an Oscar, *A Queen Is Crowned* was named 1953's best documentary by the International Press.

CRITICS CIRCLE

". . . with an eloquent commentary by Christopher Fry finely spoken by Sir Laurence Olivier, *A Queen Is Crowned* is the richest and most stirring film I have ever seen."

Campbell Dixon in *The Daily Telegraph*

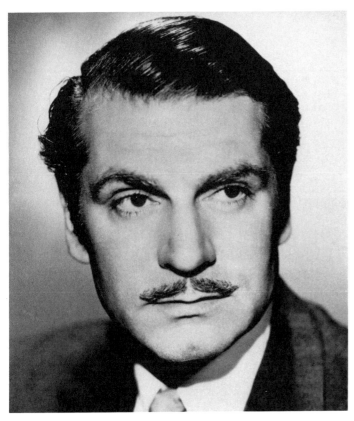

A QUEEN IS CROWNED

"The memory of the brilliant B.B.C. television version of the Coronation ceremony . . . overshadows both *Elizabeth Is Queen* and *A Queen Is Crowned*. The probability of the overwhelming richness of colour and movement patterning this unique ceremony should have warned the producers of these colour films against the dangers of over-production—a pitfall into which both have fallen with the use of pretentious but uninformative commentaries, and superfluous introductory sequences. The results are disappointing, except for the colour, which has been most effectively caught in both films."

Monthly Film Bulletin

"In their documentation of the coronation of their Sovereign, the British film makers have made history themselves. A masterful, dignified and cohesive tribute to Queen Elizabeth II and an unsurpassed illustration of this historic event. From the moment that Sir Laurence Olivier, speaking dramatist Christopher Fry's poetic lines, reverently says, "this royal throne of kings—this England," the camera, capturing scenes of the rolling hills of Wales, the mountains of Scotland, and the drowsy hamlets and bustling towns, sets a picturesque and reverential tone for the events to follow. Credit must be given to Mr. Fry and Sir Laurence for not intruding

THE BEGGAR'S OPERA   As Captain Macheath

on the camera's precincts. They speak and are heard only as a necessary footnote to the majestic proceedings. With *A Queen Is Crowned* the British have fashioned a historic, beautiful and living document."

A. H. Weiler in *The New York Times*

"Christopher Fry's commentary, intensely spoken by Sir Laurence Olivier, struck me as being too overawed for the occasion. It never descended to the natural."

Milton Shulman in *The Evening Standard*

THE BEGGAR'S OPERA

1953

A British Lion release of an Imperadio Pictures production

U.S. Distributor: Warner Bros.

CAST

Laurence Olivier *(Captain Macheath)*; Stanley Holloway *(Lockit)*; George Devine *(Peachum)*; Mary Clare *(Mrs. Peachum)*; Athene Seyler *(Mrs. Trapes)*; Dorothy Tutin *(Polly Peachum)*; Daphne Anderson *(Lucy Lockit)*; Hugh Griffith *(The Beggar)*; Margot Grahame *(The Actress)*; Denis Cannan *(The Footman)*; Yvonne Furneaux *(Jenny*

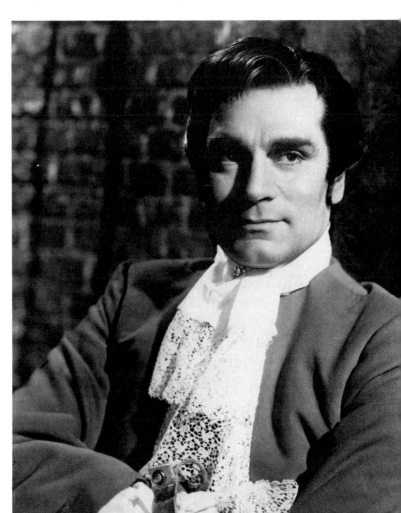

THE BEGGAR'S OPERA Macheath imprisoned

Diver); Kenneth Williams (*Jack, The Pot Boy*); Eric Pohlmann (*Innkeeper*); Laurence Naismith (*Matt of the Mint*); George Rose (*First Turnkey*); Sandra Dorne (*Sukey Tawdrey*); Jocelyn James (*Molly Brazen*); Isabel George (*Mrs. Vixen*); Helen Christie (*Betty Doxey*); Stuart Burge (*First Prisoner*); Cyril Conway (*Second Prisoner*); Gerald Lawson (*Third Prisoner*); Eileen Harvey (*Female Traveler*); Edward Pryor (*Filch*); Edith Coates (*Mrs. Coaxer*); Max Brent (*Drunkard*); Mercy Haystead (*Dolly Trall*); Patricia Raine (*Mrs. Slammekin*); John Kidd (*Second Turnkey*); H.C. Walton (*Third Turnkey*); Eugene Leahy (*Fourth Turnkey*); Edgar Norfolk (*Fifth Turnkey*); Oliver Hunter (*First Chairman*); John Baker (*Second Chairman*); Madge Brindley (*Gin Seller*); Felix Felton (*The Governor*); Tamba Alleney (*Negro Page*); Terence Greenidge (*Chaplain*); Billy Wells (*Hangman*).

CREDITS

Director: Peter Brook; *Producers*: Herbert Wilcox and Laurence Olivier; *Associate Producer*: Eric Goodhead; *Screenwriter*: Denis Cannan, *adapted by* Christopher Fry *from the operetta by* John Gay; *Technicolor Cinematographer*: Guy Green; *Editor*: Reginald Beck; *Art Director*: William C. Andrews; *Music*: Sir Arthur Bliss; *Opera Sets and Costumes*: George Wakhevitch; *Sound*: Peter Handford and Red Law; *Special Effects*: Wally Veevers and George Samuels; *Running Time*: 94 minutes.

THE FILM

This adaptation of John Gay's 1728 musical marked the movie debut of noted stage director Peter Brook, whose theatrical expertise failed to make a cinematic success of this distinctly "art-house" project, despite the box-office name of Laurence Olivier.

For twentieth-century audiences, this work is better known in its more popular Bertolt Brecht-Kurt Weill variation, *The Threepenny Opera*, of which there have been several film versions of varying success.

In brief, the work is set in 1741 London, where the highwayman Macheath (Olivier) awaits execution in Newgate Prison. From his cell, he overhears from outside an "opera" composed by a beggar that tells of Macheath's previous escapades and of the countless women in his life—one of whom caused his incarceration. As the opera ends, the highwayman gets a reprieve and returns to his freedom.

OLIVIER:

"Stanley [Holloway] and I were the only two who did our own singing; the rest were all dubbed by first-class British singers, both Peter Brook and Arthur Bliss insisting that the sound be critically unassailable. This seemed reasonable, but it had the effect of making me sound inferior to the rest of the cast. The main point of the enterprise was supposed to be that I was now a singing actor. The fact that I was not known to be a singer would cast doubts, while possibly promoting some curiosity. But the unhappy result was that the sounds that I made were not up to the general standard of the music. I had

THE BEGGAR'S OPERA With Daphne Anderson, Dorothy Tutin, and George Devine

begged my two partners to think again about using professional singers. The voices of almost all in the acting cast were good enough to pass muster; it might not be a musical event, but it would be all of a pattern and the unpretentious can sometimes have its own special charm. I maintained that, in the final analysis, this would be better for the film itself, but failed wretchedly to carry the day. There is little satisfaction in being right in prognosticating a failure when it happens to be one's own. I just hope and pray that my personal flop in *The Beggar's Opera* will be the worst that I shall ever disenjoy."

CRITICS CIRCLE

"A bold experiment which does not come off. *The Beggar's Opera* is another example of the uneasy partnership between screen and opera. Olivier's light baritone, pleasant enough in its own way, is no match for the other voices. This apart, his performance is as robust and as lively as could be expected. He makes the highwayman Macheath a bold and lovable adventurer and the amo-

THE BEGGAR'S OPERA With Dorothy Tutin

THE BEGGAR'S OPERA   With Daphne Anderson

rous intrigues, particularly during his sojourn in jail, are staged with the right measure of frivolity."

"Myro." in *Variety*

"Much—perhaps too much—was to be expected of *The Beggar's Opera*, the first film of Peter Brook, the most gifted stage director of his generation. Unfortunately, the failure is equalled only by the ambition. One has the feeling that much went wrong with this film almost from the start. The ragged construction, the scrappy, often unfinished-looking succession of episodes, the variable colour, the discordant mixture of styles, the whole potted 90 minutes of a work more than twice that length—all this suggests an initial lack of grasp. Sir Laurence Olivier proves a pleasant light baritone, but it is hardly fair to surround him with professionals like Bruce Boyce or Joan Cross. For the rest, his performance seems curiously muted, lacking the swagger, the roistering, that Macheath requires."

"G.L." in *Monthly Film Bulletin*

"Olivier's Macheath, to my mind, is the most comfortable piece of work he has given us yet in pictures. He romps through the part, whether acting, singing, dancing

or riding, without any touch of self-consciousness, and as though all these exercises were a joy, and the player's impression of ease, of relaxation, is irresistibly communicated to the audience."

C. A. Lejeune in *The Observer*

"Since he is a man who has taken bold liberties with the movie medium before, Sir Laurence is not surprising a moviegoer too greatly by raising his voice in song for the first time. The surprise is that Sir Laurence's baritone is light, audible but not especially distinguished. Perhaps it is adequate, but it strikes a layman's ear as a faint obbligato to his portrayal of the athletic and amorous brigand. Abetted by the racy dialogue supplied by both Gay and Fry, Sir Laurence is, alternately, a reckless daredevil, a wily but manly lover and a fearless, brooding adventurer. It is a characterization that he endows with genuine abandon, stature and feeling."

A. H. Weiler in *The New York Times*

RICHARD III

1955

An Independent Film Distributors/British Lion release of a London Films production

U.S. Distributor: Lopert Films (1956)

CAST

Laurence Olivier *(Richard III)*; John Gielgud *(Clarence)*; Claire Bloom *(Lady Anne)*; Ralph Richardson *(Buckingham)*; Cedric Hardwicke *(Edward IV)*; Stanley Baker *(Henry Tudor)*; Laurence Naismith *(Stanley)*; Norman Wooland *(Catesby)*; Alec Clunes *(Hastings)*; Mary Kerridge *(Queen Elizabeth)*; Pamela Brown *(Jane Shore)*; Helen Haye *(Duchess of York)*; John Laurie *(Lovel)*; Esmond Knight *(Ratcliffe)*; Michael Gough *(Dighton)*; Andrew Cruickshank *(Brakenbury)*; Clive Morton *(Rivers)*; Nicholas Hannen *(Archbishop)*; Russell Thorndyke *(Priest)*; Paul Huson *(Prince of Wales)*; Stewart Allen *(Page)*; Wally Bascoe and Norman Fisher *(Monks)*; Terence Greenidge *(Scrivener)*; Dan Cunningham *(Grey)*; Douglas Wilmer *(Dorset)*; Michael Ripper *(Second Murderer)*; Andy Shine *(Young Duke of York)*; Roy Russell *(Abbot)*; George Woodbridge *(Lord Mayor of London)*; Peter Williams *(Messenger to Hastings)*; Timothy Bateson *(Ostler)*; Willoughby Gray *(Second Priest)*; Anne Wilton *(Scrubwoman)*; Bill Shine *(Beadle)*; Derek Prentice and Deering Wells *(Clergymen)*; Richard Bennett *(George Stanley)*; Patrick Troughton *(Tyrell)*; John Philipps *(Norfolk)*; Brian Nissen, Alexander Davion, Lane Meddick, and Robert Bishop *(Messengers to Richard)*.

CREDITS

Director: Laurence Olivier; *Associate Director*: Anthony Bushell; *Producers*: Laurence Olivier and Alexander Korda; *Screenwriters*: Alan

Dent and Laurence Olivier; *Based on the play by* William Shakespeare; *VistaVision-Technicolor Cinematographer:* Otto Heller; *Editor:* Helga Cranston; *Production Designer:* Roger Furse; *Art Director:* Carmen Dillon; *Music:* William Walton; *Sound:* John Cox; *Special Effects:* Wally Veevers; *Swordplay:* Bernard Hepton and John Greenwood; *Assistant Director:* Gerry O'Hara; *Running Time:* 161 minutes.

THE FILM

Of Olivier's first three bouts with filmed Shakespeare in the joint capacity of actor-director-producer, *Richard III* is largely considered to be the most vivid, straightforward, and satisfying. And once again his unflagging vitality and penchant for self-criticism inspired an excellent cast of Bard-seasoned actors to give of their talents unstintingly. Thus lies the secret of Olivier's successes with Shakespeare—the energetic example he set for all of his colleagues. *Richard III* reportedly took half the time he needed to complete filming his Academy Award-winning *Hamlet* and a third of that lavished on his wartime production of *Henry V.* Alan Dent, the critic and Shakespearean scholar who helped edit *Richard's* text for the film, has said of his friend and collaborator, "In his acting and direction, Olivier combines the strength of Hercules with the ubiquity of Mercury." Together, the pair made some shrewd alterations, opening their movie with the final scene from *Henry VI, Part 3*—the coronation of Edward IV (Cedric Hardwicke)—thereby establishing some of the existent court intrigues and tensions which reinforce Richard's subsequent soliloquy, "Now is the winter of our discontent . . ."

In *Richard III*, Olivier frequently seizes the opportunity of sharing his monologues, confidentially, with the film's audiences—at first with sly humor, but with increasing sobriety as his ruthless machinations advance his court career. And here this boldly theatrical device succeeds somewhat better than his deployment of closemouthed, voice-over soliloquies in *Hamlet.*

Visually, the entire production is as colorful as are the historical details of its source material surrounding that treacherous, humpbacked Duke of Gloucester, who inveigled and murdered his way to the throne of fifteenth-century England. Roger Furse's striking production design, again beautifully complemented by the art direction of Carmen Dillon, emphasizes the spaciousness of setting and imaginatively colorful costuming, appropriately centering on the blacks and reds favored by the flamboyant Richard. Had it been a silent film, this *Richard* would remain a masterpiece of spectacular and im-

RICHARD III   With Paul Huson and Ralph Richardson

peccable period detail, magnificently photographed in depth-affirming VistaVision and vivid Technicolor by the Czech-born British-films veteran Otto Heller.

But even the most wonderful showcase would be of little use without a show, and Olivier and company give *Richard III* so full-bodied a performance that it would be difficult to justify another screen version in the foreseeable future. The actor's direction is courageously bold and striking. But this is, after all, an *actor's* picture, and Olivier's performance dominates the film with his rich, classical portrayal of this subtly deformed monster, making him a figure of clever calculation and frightening evil. With his black pageboy wig and elongated false nose (affording him at time a Sid Caesar look)—full of nuance and unpredictable movement—that it becomes difficult to recognize this handsome actor, despite his mellifluous tones and brilliant vocal interpretation. This is truly a great Shakespearean performance, right through to the climactic (if modestly reproduced) Battle of Bosworth Field and the dying Richard's desperate final outcry, "My kingdom for a horse!"

Despite the Master's earlier comments about his casting, one must also cite Ralph Richardson's scheming Buckingham, John Gielgud's brief but distinguished Clarence (whose murder in a large keg of wine provides one of the film's few lurid moments) and Cedric Hardwicke's forceful characterization of elderly Edward IV, whose throne Richard both covets and gets. In *Richard III*, distaff players defer to the men, though Claire Bloom makes a beautiful, well-spoken Anne, who's at once stirred and repelled by Richard's crude courting. Mary Kerridge is a colorful Queen Elizabeth, and Pamela Brown, as court mistress Jane Shore, proves anew the eloquence of silence and an expressive face.

In the U.S., *Richard III* was initially seen in March of 1956 on NBC television, as the result of an agreement between the network and producer Alexander Korda. However, because of NBC "standards and practices," three brief murder scenes deemed too shocking for home viewing, were deleted from that version.

Although the Academy of Motion Picture Arts and Sciences voted Olivier a Best Actor Oscar nomination, it took the British Film Academy to reward his work more tangibly, naming *Richard III* 1955's Best Film from Any Source, as well as the Best British Film. And it justly gave Sir Laurence Olivier its Best Actor prize.

OLIVIER:

"I'd played Richard III so often on stage, I'd let ham fat grow on my performance. I had to rid myself of this before the cameras got me. So for two weeks I hid myself away and studied the text and my inflections anew, hacked off the extra flesh and the broad gestures I needed

137

RICHARD III   As King Richard III

RICHARD III   With Claire Bloom

ish and sardonic wit. Heavily made-up with one dead eyelid, a hatchet nose, a withered hand, a humped back, a drooping shoulder and a twisted, limping leg, he is a freakish-looking figure that Sir Laurence so articulates that he has an electric vitality and a fascinatingly grotesque grace. A grating voice, too, is a feature of his physical oddity. More important to the character, however, is the studiousness and subtlety with which Sir Laurence builds up tension within him as his mischiefs and crimes accumulate. . . . Since he presents us a Richard who is vivid, exciting and sound in his psychological complication, Sir Laurence may be readily forgiven some slight liberties with Shakespeare's text. And he has seen to it that none of the other characters has

RICHARD III   With Laurence Naismith, Claire Bloom, Ralph Richardson, and bit players

on stage to reach the back row of the upper circle some fifty yards away, made myself clean and austere in my expressions, and changed the phrasing, because Richard would be flirting with the camera—sometimes only inches from his eyes—and would lay his head on the camera's bosom if he could. He is the classical actor's favorite bravura part, but he must be kept credible, and the bravura must be carefully marshalled.

"I made a mistake casting Ralph [Richardson] as Buckingham. He wasn't oily enough. There was always a twinkle in his eye. I should have got Orson Welles."

CRITICS CIRCLE

"A more exciting *Richard III* than anything that the stage has ever done or is ever likely to do."

Milton Shulman in *The Sunday Express*

"The measure of Sir Laurence Olivier's genius for putting Shakespeare's plays on the screen is beautifully and brilliantly exhibited in his production and performance of *Richard III*. Sir Laurence's Richard is tremendous—a weird, poisonous portrait of a super-rogue whose dark designs are candidly acknowledged with lip-lick rel-

RICHARD III   With Andrew Cruickshank and
Norman Wooland

RICHARD III   With Norman
Wooland

quite the air of importance—or vitality and definition—
that Richard has."

Bosley Crowther in *The New York Times*

"In bringing Shakespeare's historical melodrama to the
screen, Laurence Olivier has chosen a style more forth-
right and direct, less 'cinematic,' than in *Hamlet* or even
Henry V, and the result is perhaps the most exciting
Shakespearean film yet made. Olivier's performance was
brilliant on the stage; here it is even more impressive, the
irony sharpened, the arrogance made even more breath-
taking by the camera's intimacy. Rightly, it dominates
the film, and although the other parts are excellently
played, the lasting impression is of this richly drawn
portrait, surely one of the classic Shakespearean interpretations."

"G.L." in *Monthly Film Bulletin*

"It embalms in celluloid one of the greatest
Shakespearean performances of our day. Olivier plays his
Richard for laughs. And he raises the grisly humour of
the horror comic to the level of genius."

Alan Brien in *The Evening Standard*

"It is notably a performer's picture, with the major credit going to Olivier for his classic playing of the deformed Richard. This is a portrayal full of subtlety and understanding. *Richard III* is more than just a prestige picture. It is a screen achievement of the highest order."

"Myro." in *Variety*

THE PRINCE AND THE SHOWGIRL

1957

A Warner Bros. release of a Marilyn Monroe-Laurence Olivier coproduction

CAST

Laurence Olivier *(The Regent)*; Marilyn Monroe *(Elsie Marina)*; Sybil Thorndike *(Queen Dowager)*; Richard Wattis *(Northbrooke)*; Jeremy Spenser *(King Nicholas)*; Esmond Knight *(Colonel Hoffman)*; Jean Kent *(Maisie Springfield)*; Daphne Anderson *(Fanny)*; Vera Day *(Betty)*; Paul Hardwick *(Major Domo)*; Rosamund Greenwood *(Maud)*; Aubrey Dexter *(The Ambassador)*; Maxine Audley *(Lady Sunningdale)*; Harold Goodwin *(Call Boy)*; Andreas Malandrinos *(Valet with Violin)*; Gillian Owen *(Maggie)*; Margot Lister *(Lottie)*; Charles Victor *(Theatre Manager)*; David Horne *(The Foreign Officer)*; Dennis Edwards *(Head Valet)*; Gladys Henson *(Dresser)*.

CREDITS

Producer-Director: Laurence Olivier; *Executive Producer:* Milton H. Greene; *Screenwriter:* Terence Rattigan, *based on his play* **The Sleeping Prince**; *Technicolor Cinematographer:* Jack Cardiff; *Editors:* Jack Harris and (uncredited) Laurence Olivier; *Production Designer:* Roger Furse; *Art Director:* Carmen Dillon; *Music:* Richard Addinsell; *Choreographer:* William Chappell; *Running Time:* 117 minutes.

THE FILM

Having set up her own company, in association with portrait photographer Milton H. Greene, Marilyn Monroe surprised almost everyone by making her first independent production an alliance with Britain's most celebrated actor. It was agreed that, in a joint collaboration with his L.O.P. Ltd., she and Laurence Olivier would also costar in a London-made screen version of Terence Rattigan's romantic comedy *The Sleeping Prince*, as adapted for the screen by the playwright.

The production had its problems, largely attributable to the insecurities of its leading lady, whose behavior frequently exasperated Olivier. He preferred its original title, *The Sleeping Prince*, which had enjoyed a London

THE PRINCE AND THE SHOWGIRL   With Marilyn Monroe

success with Vivien Leigh playing opposite her then-husband. Later, as *The Girl Who Came to Supper*, the work would turn up again as a short-lived 1963 Broadway musical starring José Ferrer and Florence Henderson.

Warned accordingly by Monroe's *Bus Stop* director Joshua Logan, Olivier handled his costar with such care that his own performance took a back seat to his direction. Especially disconcerting was the constant on-set presence of Marilyn's meddlesome drama coach, Paula Strasberg—who even gave Olivier some acting tips, until he requested her departure. Although he later reflected more generously about it, the three months spent filming *The Prince and the Showgirl* with the ever-tardy Monroe proved a hellish experience for Olivier. Nor was its eventual public reception as favorable as anticipated. The recipient of generally favorable reviews, this gentle Ruritanian love story about an American musical-comedy star who becomes the romantic object of a Carpathian prince visiting London during the Coronation of 1911, was not, however, a box-office success.

OLIVIER:

"I had been amused by Terence Rattigan's original script for *The Sleeping Prince* on the stage, but found it hard to love the character in the film version, which the

THE PRINCE AND THE SHOWGIRL   With Jeremy Spenser and Marilyn Monroe

money men had christened *The Prince and the Showgirl*, making it sound like an Edwardian musical.

"My feathers were considerably ruffled by Marilyn's erratic behavior on and around the set; her spikiness and spite were frightening, split from her sweetness and vulnerability. Half the time her head was so full of the rigamarole of 'method,' her natural talent was suppressed. She'd take ages over a shot, keep people waiting for hours. However, she could be a dream, listening and understanding my idea of a scene, taking off-camera directions beautifully, and proving her physical beauty and comic timing to be historical facts.

"In the editing room I had a happier time than I expected. I loved cutting away to Marilyn's reaction shots; no one had such a look of hurt innocence or of unconscious wisdom, and her personality was strong on the screen. She gave a star performance."

CRITICS CIRCLE

"What is perhaps the most diverting piece of casting in many a year—Britain's Sir Laurence Olivier with Hollywood's Marilyn Monroe—turns out to be the most diverting thing about their film, *The Prince and the Showgirl*. And the mere sight of them together is equally rewarding—for a while. Sir Laurence is kept pretty much

THE PRINCE AND THE SHOWGIRL   With Sybil Thorndike and Marilyn Monroe

141

THE PRINCE AND THE SHOWGIRL   With Marilyn Monroe

a stuffed shirt, wearing a monocle and speaking in Teutonic accents that are unpleasant and hard to understand. And Miss Monroe mainly has to giggle, wiggle, breathe deeply and flirt. The main trouble with *The Prince and the Showgirl*, when you come right down to it, is that both characters are essentially dull."

Bosley Crowther in *The New York Times*

"Terence Rattigan is just playing a game, amusing us for two hours, and the actors enjoy the charade immensely. They try to look earnest, but a twinkle in the eye betrays them. In the case of Olivier, the twinkle must fight its way through a thick monocle to reach the outside world, and it does. This is a performance of rich, subtle humor."

William K. Zinsser in *New York Herald Tribune*

"Terence Rattigan's play was a rather thin piece of Ruritanian love whose success was largely due to its star casting. It might still have been successful as a film, given a Lubitsch delicacy or an Ophuls elegance; but with handling which is admirably efficient, but as heavy as the same director's *Hamlet*, the piece drags on rather slowly. One can only look for pleasure in the performances. Olivier's humorless, Teutonic politician is as complete a creation as one would expect; and a perfect and unselfish foil to Marilyn Monroe's Elsie. She is, of course, splendid as the sophisticated innocent."

"D.R." in *Monthly Film Bulletin*

142

"The Ruritanian romance, directed by Laurence Olivier, is slanted to show off the talents of Marilyn Monroe as an innocent abroad. Olivier, perhaps with excess gallantry, makes his prince something of a cold cod, but even in this uningratiating role he has a high gloss—an irony that shines. Monroe's breathy little-girl voice and polymorphous-perverse non-acting have a special mock-innocent charm that none of her imitators seem able to capture."

Pauline Kael in *5001 Nights at the Movies*

THE DEVIL'S DISCIPLE

1959

A United Artists release of a Brynaprod and Hecht-Hill-Lancaster coproduction

CAST

Burt Lancaster *(Anthony Anderson)*; Kirk Douglas *(Richard Dudgeon)*; Laurence Olivier *(General Burgoyne)*; Janette Scott *(Judith Anderson)*; Eva Le Gallienne *(Mrs. Dudgeon)*; Harry Andrews *(Major Swindon)*; Basil Sydney *(Lawyer Hawkins)*; George Rose *(British Sergeant)*; Neil McCallum *(Christopher Dudgeon)*; Mervyn Johns *(Rev. Maindeck Parshotter)*; David Horne *(William)*; Jenny Jones *(Essie)*; Erik Chitty *(Titus)*.

CREDITS

Director: Guy Hamilton; *Producer:* Harold Hecht; *Screenwriters:* John Dighton and Roland Kibbee; *Based on the play by* George Bernard Shaw; *Cinematographer:* Jack Hildyard; *Editor:* Alan Osbiston; *Art Directors:* Terence Verity and Edward Carrere; *Set Decorator:* Scott Slimon; *Music:* Richard Rodney Bennett; *Costumes:* Mary Grant; *Running Time:* 82 minutes.

THE FILM

Coproduced by the movie companies earlier established by its stars, Burt Lancaster and Kirk Douglas, this adaptation of Shaw's 1897 comedy was filmed in England. Whereas previous motion pictures derived from the plays of Shaw were generally either directed by—or overseen by—the late producer Gabriel Pascal, Burt, Kirk, and writers John Dighton and Roland Kibbee held no such reverence. Cuts were made in the text, and considerable alterations followed, with only the celebrated court-martial scene (the play's best asset) treated with the respect justifiably due it. Onstage, this relatively minor Shaw comedy, set in 1777 New Hampshire during America's War for Independence, centers largely on the irresponsible Dick Dudgeon (Douglas), whose father was

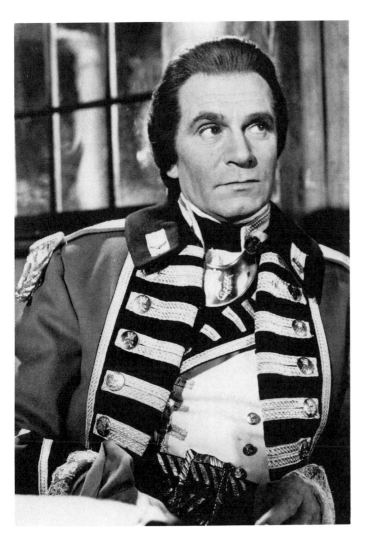

THE DEVIL'S DISCIPLE   As General Burgoyne

"I was particularly amused by the dry irony of Shaw's Burgoyne in *The Devil's Disciple*; there's no harm in an audience seeing an actor's enjoying himself. I was awful in the part, as dull as dishwater; you wouldn't think anyone could be with that pearl among parts. After three or four weeks, [Producer Harold] Hecht sent for me; he really was a thoroughly nice little man, and gave me an instruction which sent me off into uncontrollably hysterical giggles. "Larry," he said, "we want you to put more Mr. Puff into your General Burgoyne." I can't recall having such a miserable time in a job ever. I never heard one word about how the film was eventually received around the world. Somehow I never inquired."

hanged by the British—under General "Gentleman Johnny" Burgoyne (Olivier)—as an example to the colonists. Dudgeon is subsequently mistaken for the Rev. Anthony Anderson (Lancaster), the Redcoats' next target, and displays his contempt for authority as he's led off to prison. At the court-martial that follows, Dudgeon enjoys a lively battle of wits with Burgoyne, before being sentenced to the gallows. It's revealed that Dudgeon isn't really the Rev. Anderson, followed by a battle royal in which the latter intercepts an important dispatch meant for Burgoyne. With this as leverage, Anderson gets Dudgeon pardoned. Burgoyne, correctly anticipating that England is about to lose her colonies, invites Dudgeon for tea.

Alexander Mackendrick *(The Man in the White Suit)*, the film's original British director, left the project after two weeks of "differences of opinion" with the actor/producers, who replaced him with a fellow Brit, Guy Hamilton.

THE DEVIL'S DISCIPLE   As General Burgoyne

143

THE DEVIL'S DISCIPLE   With
Burt Lancaster, Harry Andrews,
and players

THE DEVIL'S DISCIPLE   With Kirk Douglas, Janette Scott, and Harry Andrews

144

CRITICS CIRCLE

"Although his role is relatively minor, once he gets onscreen for good, Olivier takes over. His character, that of 'Gentleman Johnny' Burgoyne, is a witty, mocking figure and mouthpiece for Shaw's wicked shafts into convention and history, in this case the American Revolution. Olivier certainly gets most of the good lines. But few players could equal his bland under-playing, his sunny urbanity in the face of British Military atrocities."

"Powe." in *Variety*

"Olivier is in enormous good humor, delivers his speeches with a rare bite, and is exactly what Shaw might have asked for, if he had been able to advise on casting and playing. I rather think that, in the process, he has given an acting lesson to Messrs. Lancaster and Douglas, for he represents style and finish (along with an impeccable diction), while they represent something closer to industriousness and good will, rather than the Shavian method. Douglas and Lancaster can't be said to be bad; they just aren't terribly good."

Hollis Alpert in *Saturday Review*

"And though, as the English General Burgoyne, Olivier loses the American War of Independence, he wins the fight for screen supremacy (over Douglas and Lancaster) while barely stretching his talents to a tenth of their capacity."

Margaret Hinxman in *The Daily Herald*

"Olivier gives the performance of his life, making Lancaster and Douglas look like stupid oafs who wandered back from a western."

The Evening Standard

"Guy Hamilton's direction is brisk enough, but insufficiently stylized to make the production consistently and acceptably artificial—the only way, surely, of successfully presenting such basically uncinematic material. With the exception of Laurence Olivier, who romps away with the film in the expanded and inevitably scene-stealing part of General Burgoyne, Hamilton has not been lucky in his players."

"D.H." in *Monthly Film Bulletin*

SPARTACUS   As Crassus

SPARTACUS

1960

*A Universal-International release of a
Bryna production*

CAST

Kirk Douglas *(Spartacus)*; Laurence Olivier *(Crassus)*; Jean Simmons *(Varinia)*; Tony Curtis *(Antoninus)*; Charles Laughton *(Gracchus)*; Peter Ustinov *(Batiatus)*; John Gavin *(Julius Caesar)*; Nina Foch *(Helena)*; Herbert Lom *(Tigranes)*; John Ireland *(Crixus)*; John Dall *(Glabrus)*; Charles McGraw *(Marcellus)*; Joanna Barnes *(Claudia)*; Harold J. Stone *(David)*; Woody Strode *(Draba)*; Peter Brocco *(Ramon)*; Paul Lambert *(Gannicus)*; Nicholas Dennis *(Dionysius)*; Robert J. Wilke *(Guard Captain)*; John Hoyt *(Roman Officer)*; Frederic Worlock *(Laelius)*; Dayton Lummis *(Symmachus)*.

CREDITS

Director: Stanley Kubrick; *Executive Producer:* Kirk Douglas; *Producer:* Edward Lewis; *Screenwriter:* Dalton Trumbo; *Based on the novel by* Howard Fast; *Supertechnirama-70/Technicolor Cinematographer:* Russell Metty; *Additional-scenes Photographer:* Clifford Stine; *Editors:* Robert Lawrence, Robert Schulte and Fred Chulak; *Production De-*signer: Alexander Golitzen; *Art Director:* Eric Orbom; *Set Decorators:* Russell A. Gausman and Julia Heron; *Music:* Alex North; *Costumes:* Roger Furse and Peruzzi; *Miss Simmons's Costumes:* Bill Thomas; *Sound:* Waldon O. Watson, Joe Lapis, Murray Spivack, and Ronald Pierce; *Historical/Technical Advisor:* Vittorio Nino Novarese; *Running Time:* 196 minutes.

THE FILM

Coming from Stanley Kubrick, director of such small-scale black-and-white cinematic gems as 1956's *The Killing* and 1957's *Paths of Glory*, this lengthy $12-million "thinking man's" spectacle about a slave revolt against Rome a century before the birth of Christ, was produced by Kirk Douglas's Bryna Productions, which scored both an artistic and popular success with such a costly gamble. Douglas also became the first Hollywood producer to run the risk of hiring—and according screen credit to—the blacklisted screenwriter Dalton Trumbo (one of the "Hollywood Ten"), who based his *Spartacus* adaptation on the novel by another "enemy" of the House Committee on Un-American Activities, Howard Fast.

Casting himself in the film's title role, producer Douglas hired a distinguished supporting cast, topped by Laurence Olivier and (replacing a German import named Sabina Bethmann, who hadn't worked out) Jean Sim-

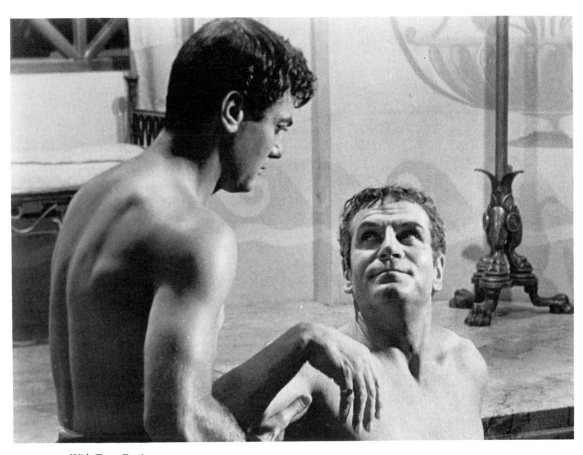

SPARTACUS   With Tony Curtis

147

SPARTACUS With Jean Simmons

mons—the British star's teenage leading lady twelve years earlier in *Hamlet*—as well as Charles Laughton and Peter Ustinov, to team with Hollywood lightweights John Gavin and Tony Curtis. All gave of their best to the ambitious enterprise. (Initially, Anthony Mann was engaged by Douglas to direct, but "creative differences" brought about a parting of the ways, along with the departure of Miss Bethmann, Mann's Varinia.)

Although minor cuts were made in the film, prior to release in order to satisfy the then-powerful Legion of Decency, there has recently been shown a "restored" version of *Spartacus*. This includes two brief moments of violence—where Olivier is spattered with blood during his killing of gladiator Woody Strode, and a battle scene detailing the severing of a Roman soldier's arm—as well as a deleted scene in which Roman officer Olivier makes no secret of his sexual interest in the good-looking male slave impersonated by Curtis. With the consent of Olivier's widow, Joan Plowright, the voice of Anthony Hopkins was used to dub her husband's dialogue in the restored footage.

The movie's four Oscars included Peter Ustinov's as 1960's Best Supporting Actor.

OLIVIER:

"For Crassus in *Spartacus*, I was passing through a patrician phase, but I gave him a touch of that flirting femininity of Richard III, the cool eyes, suddenly a

SPARTACUS With Woody Strode, Nina Foch, John Dall, and Joanna Barnes

flame—second cousin to Coriolanus, several times removed.

"It was pleasant to be with Peter Ustinov, Charles Laughton and my darling Jeannie Simmons again, and, considering the weighty subject, the work on *Spartacus* went by pleasantly enough under the direction of Stanley Kubrick, hitherto little known."

CRITICS CIRCLE

"A far-above-average spectacle. It is an opulent story that the movie tells, and it is further enriched by another rarity in the genre: good acting. Laurence Olivier has the meaty role of Marcus Crassus. Peter Ustinov has fine, often humorous, moments as Batiatus. Charles Laughton, in full toga as a Roman politician, is wondrous to behold. When these people get together, you can be sure that some old-fashioned eloquence will result. It does. . . . A help, too, is the sharp direction of Stanley Kubrick, who evidently doesn't believe in relaxing his vigilant camera, even when he has more than three hours in which to dawdle. All in all, Mr. Douglas and company have managed to breathe new life into ancient Rome."

Hollis Alpert in *Saturday Review*

"*Spartacus* is a very unequal work, a knitting of sophistication with the commonplace, the extraordinary with the ordinary, dramatic or intellectual excitement with mere trivia of spectacle. The actors are at one point severely in character, but at another fall into obvious posturing. Douglas is as manly a Spartacus as he was a Viking, though not as savage. Olivier's Crassus is sly and stand-offish, but stubbornly patrician. . . . But the very unevenness forces one to recommend that, in spite of the laborious or dreary passages, moviegoers see the picture for the delight of its many exciting or comic or linguistically delightful highlights. When it is routine it is humdrum, but when it is moving it is supple, vigorous and exciting."

Paul V. Beckley in *New York Herald-Tribune*

SPARTACUS   With Peter Ustinov, Nina Foch, Jean Simmons, and Joanna Barnes

150

"*Spartacus* is a trap for snobs. They assume that because it is a costume drama three and a half hours long and has seven stars and a cast of many thousands, it must ipso facto be bad. In proof, it is an entertaining show. Olivier, as the rich Crassus, gives an impeccably patrician performance that fits a certain aloof element in his personality. A lot of first-rate professionals have pooled their abilities to put on a first-rate circus."

Stanley Kauffmann in *The New Republic*

"It is Sir Laurence Olivier whom you'll remember—as a cold-lipped Crassus whose pettish pulling at his necklace hints at effeminacy while ruthlessness looks out of those foxy eyes."

Alexander Walker in *The Evening Standard*

THE ENTERTAINER

1960

A British Lion Films release of a Bryanston Films/Woodfall production

U.S. Distributor: Continental Film Distributing

CAST

Laurence Olivier (*Archie Rice*); Brenda de Banzie (*Phoebe Rice*); Joan Plowright (*Jean Rice*); Roger Livesey (*Billy Rice*); Alan Bates (*Frank Rice*); Daniel Massey (*Graham*); Albert Finney (*Mick Rice*); Shirley Ann Field (*Tina Lapford*); Thora Hird (*Mrs. Lapford*); Miriam Karlin (*Soubrette*); Geoffrey Toone (*Hubbard*); James Culliford (*Cobber Carson*); Gilbert Davis (*Brother Bill*); Tony Longridge (*Mr. Lapford*); McDonald Hobley (*Film Star*); Charles Gray (*Columnist*); Antony Oliver (*Interviewer*); Jo Linden (*Gloria*); Mercia Turner (*Britannia*); Vicky Travers (*Other Nude*); Beryl & Bobo (*Trampoline Act*); Herman & Constance Welles (*Scots Singers*); The Clippers (*Rock 'n' Roll Trio*).

CREDITS

Director: Tony Richardson; *Producer:* Harry Saltzman; *Associate Producer:* John Croyden; *Screenwriters:* John Osborne and Nigel Kneale; *Based on the play by* John Osborne; *Cinematographer:* Oswald Morris; *Editor:* Alan Osbiston; *Art Director:* Ralph Brinton; *Music:* John Addison; *Choreographer:* Honor Blair; *Sound:* Peter Handford and Bob Jones; *Assistant Director:* Peter Yates; *Running Time:* 96 minutes.

THE FILM

In a 1975 *Time* magazine interview, Olivier named John Osborne's *The Entertainer* (which he had created on the London stage in 1957 and repeated in New York

prior to this film adaptation) as the performance of which he was most proud. Contrasting it with the "punishing roles of Shakespeare," he concluded: "I have an affinity with Archie Rice. It's what I really am. I'm not like Hamlet." An unusual admission perhaps, but *The Entertainer* offers, in its tragic central role, a formidable challenge for the actor courageous enough to hazard it. When, in 1976, Jack Lemmon played Archie Rice in a TV remake, one critic saluted that star's "nerve," but little else, concluding that Archie was, "of course, the creation and sole property of Laurence Olivier."

When he first began to read Osborne's unproduced play, Olivier visualized himself in the role of *Billy* Rice, Archie's elderly retired-vaudevillian father—until he finished the manuscript. Then, he later admitted, *Archie* Rice was a part he had to have. As conceived by Osborne, Archie's an over-the-hill song-and-dance man whose chief domain is the seedy music hall of an English seaside resort, where he performs his third-rate routines to half-empty houses. It's a shabby little world of noisy amusement piers, grubby rooming houses, and littered boardwalks, and Oswald Morris's cinematography finds a monochromatic beauty in the natural locations so thoroughly utilized by director Tony Richardson, who had collaborated with the same screenwriting team (John Osborne and Nigel Kneale) on his only previous film, *Look Back in Anger*. But while that 1959 drama remains a mixed artistic bag, *The Entertainer* stands solidly as a small gem, a minor masterpiece and a sterling monument to Olivier—a brilliant classical artist in his greatest contemporary role. If it weren't for his mercurial, probing, and multifaceted study of Archie Rice, the character could easily become an insufferable bore and an unmitigated heel. For there's little to admire about his not-quite-defeated failure of an embittered egotist, who cheats on his nagging, alcoholic wife and only manages to survive by conning everyone in sight. Wisecracks and vaudeville *shtick* are Archie's protection against encroaching reality, and if bedding an impressionable young beauty contestant (Shirley Ann Field) might net him financing for one of his tacky little extravaganzas, then Archie has charm to spare. His home life is miserable, and Osborne's scenes of family life—despite Archie's loving daughter, Jean (Joan Plowright, a year before becoming Lady Olivier)—are devastating studies in hatred and despair. "Life is a beastly mess," declares Archie as his empty world crumbles around him.

With good reason, it's often difficult to *find* Laurence Olivier, as we know him, in the rich guise of Archie Rice. Made up for his stage act, he quite disappears behind that greasepaint mask whose sunken eyes and mirthless, grinning mouth pave the way for an outrageous display of hammy showmanship and soft-shoe cli-

THE ENTERTAINER   As Archie Rice

152

chés, of grimacing facial expressions and fussy, nervous movements. And yet this cynical, hypocritical cad has his likable side, shining through that vain and hollow facade—which is what makes the character fascinating. His songs are awful (though expertly rendered) and his charm is utterly transparent. But Olivier's Archie can also move us when he confesses to his daughter that, amid those dreadful, stagey routines, he is "dead behind the eyes."

And *The Entertainer*'s supporting cast is equally fine, each in his or her own right: Joan Plowright offers a warm, intelligent portrait of Archie's best friend and daughter, Jean; Brenda de Banzie is pathetic and touching as the irritating wife Archie can barely tolerate any

longer; and Roger Livesey is moving as the retired-vaudevillian father Archie selfishly exploits. In lesser roles, two debuting movie actors of great future promise, Alan Bates and Albert Finney, have their moments as Archie's sons. But, in the final analysis, this is Olivier's show.

Nominated for his sixth Academy Award, Olivier lost this Oscar to Burt Lancaster's performance in *Elmer Gantry*.

OLIVIER:

"As with *Richard III*, the camera relished the intimate parts of Archie—and John Osborne wrote some more scenes to give the film of *The Entertainer* what it wanted, craved: more emotion. I think the film allowed John to

THE ENTERTAINER Archie in performance

THE ENTERTAINER   Archie does his stuff

himself is too shallow and cheap to be worth very much consideration or extensive sympathy. Mr. Olivier is nothing short of brilliant as he runs the monotonous scale of turns and tricks of his shoddy entertainer, singing banal songs, pumping out endless off-stage wheezes and oozing absurd synthetic charm."

Bosley Crowther in *The New York Times*

"In *The Entertainer* the smell of decay hangs over everything, decay and shabby misery. You watch with a sort of ghastly fascination as Olivier's third-rate music-hall performer sees his world break into gray crumbs at his feet. It does seem time to tender Osborne, Kneale and

show more of Archie Rice. I tuned up my stage performance, often changed it. I looked to the subtlety, the expressiveness, the reality of his mannerisms and accent (based on music-hall chums I'd lived with in theatrical digs, and artistes I'd seen in my youth), rehearsed the cheap music-hall flickers and flutters for the surfaces of the eyes, and made him dance expressively (at almost full theatrical throttle) and badly—which I achieved by dancing as well as I could! We all acted well in that picture, and Tony Richardson, the director, made the most of us and the medium."

CRITICS CIRCLE

"*The Entertainer* is primarily a devastating picture of a hollow, hypocritical heel and of the pitiful people around him who are drowned in his grubby vanity. The fellow

154

Richardson the respect their virile and individual and powerful work deserves. If the camera and much of the dialogue is strong, the acting, not only Olivier's, but Brenda de Banzie's, Joan Plowright's, Roger Livesey's and Shirley Ann Field's, is nothing less than brilliant."

Paul V. Beckley in *New York Herald-Tribune*

"Laurence Olivier here re-creates the role he played in John Osborne's play a couple of years ago, and a flawless piece of acting it is."

Brendan Gill in *The New Yorker*

THE ENTERTAINER With Joan Plowright

"The film errs in many ways, and at times the editing seems glaringly poor, but Olivier's performance gives it venomous excitement."

Pauline Kael in *5001 Nights at the Movies*

"John Osborne's play, considerably expanded for the screen, is as bitingly contemptuous of present-day Britain as ever; and Richardson, photographing against the piers and boardwalks of a third-rate seaside resort, and in a succession of shabby music-halls, provides natural settings that fully justify Osborne's contempt. A superb supporting cast has been assembled. But at the center, dominating everything, remains Olivier, singing, dancing, joking, quarrelling and breaking your heart. The seedy song-and-dance man with a jaunty grin and the hope of heaven fading from his eyes is a bravura role, a flashy

THE ENTERTAINER With Joan Plowright and Brenda de Banzie

155

gamut-spanner, and Olivier makes it one of the most exciting things ever put on celluloid."

Arthur Knight in *Saturday Review*

THE ENTERTAINER   With Roger Livesey

THE ENTERTAINER   Archie loses the backing on his new show

THE ENTERTAINER   With Shirley Ann Field

156

TERM OF TRIAL

1962

A Warner-Pathe release of a Romulus production

U.S. Distributor: Warner Bros. (1963)

CAST

Laurence Olivier *(Graham Weir)*; Simone Signoret *(Anna Weir)*; Sarah Miles *(Shirley Taylor)*; Hugh Griffith *(O'Hara)*; Terence Stamp *(Mitchell)*; Roland Culver *(Trowman)*; Frank Pettingell *(Ferguson)*; Thora Hird *(Mrs. Taylor)*; Dudley Foster *(Det. Sgt. Kiernan)*; Norman Bird *(Mr. Taylor)*; Newton Blick *(Prosecutor)*; Allan Cuthbertson *(Sylvan Jones)*; Nicholas Hannen *(Magistrate Sharp)*; Roy Holder *(Thompson)*; Barbara Ferris *(Joan)*; Rosamund Greenwood *(Constance)*; Lloyd Lamble *(Inspector Ullyat)*; Vanda Godsell *(Mrs. Thompson)*; Earl Cameron *(Chard)*; Clive Colin Bowler *(Collins)*; Ferdy Mayne *(The Italian)*.

CREDITS

Director-Screenwriter: Peter Glenville; *Producer*: James Woolf; *Associate Producer*: James Ware; *Based on the novel by* James Barlow; *Cinematographer*: Oswald Morris; *Editor*: James Clark; *Production Designer*: Wilfred Shingleton; *Art Director*: Anthony Woolard; *Set Decorator*: Peter James; *Music*: Jean-Michel Demase; *Costumes*: Beatrice Dawson; *Sound*: Charles Poulton and Leu Shilton; *Assistant Director*: Gerald O'Hara; *Running Time*: 130 minutes.

THE FILM

Peter Glenville, who had recently directed Olivier on-stage in *Becket*, now persuaded him to come to Ireland to accept the unlikely role of a downtrodden schoolmaster in Northern England, henpecked by his strong-willed, French-born wife (Simone Signoret) and victimized by a smitten student (Sarah Miles, in her screen debut) whose attentions he rejects on a school trip to Paris. But the humiliated girl retaliates by accusing him of indecent assault, and he's brought to court by her vindictive mother (Thora Hird), where he's tried and convicted. His impassioned courtroom plea for greater understanding moves his student to admit she lied. With the case dismissed, the schoolmaster is left to face his wife's contempt for the realization that he *wasn't* involved with his student; for then, she reasons, he at least would have behaved like other men. By assuring her that the girl's accusations *were* true, he subsequently becomes a man in his wife's eyes—and saves his crumbling marriage.

For their performances, Olivier and Miles won awards at 1962's Cork Film Festival.

OLIVIER:

"I'm not diffident about playing the ordinary man again, as I did with Simone Signoret and Sarah Miles in

TERM OF TRIAL   As Graham Weir

Term of Trial. Not boring myself. Getting closer to myself, perhaps. Not boring the audience. And learning all the time."

CRITICS CIRCLE

"It is an excellent story that fails to make its full effect principally because of the miscasting of Sir Laurence, who seems to have a taste for playing insignificant little men, but his noble looks, his commanding personality and his natural authority are against him. He can play a king, but he cannot play a mouse."

Thomas Wiseman in *London Daily Express*

"The schoolmaster hero of *Term of Trial* . . . offers this great player a framework for one of the finest portraits in his long, long gallery."

Paul Dehn in *The Daily Herald*

"If there is one role that Sir Laurence Olivier cannot play well, it is that of the little man. This pronunciamento—I'm afraid it sounds like that—is prompted by watching Olivier this week give a performance that reveals this cruel limitation to the finest tragic acting talent of his generation."

Alexander Walker in *The Evening Standard*

"A hero more afflicted than Lazarus and more humble and patient than Job is not likely to cut a dynamic or

157

TERM OF TRIAL   With
Simone Signoret

TERM OF TRIAL   With Simone Signoret and Sarah
Miles

TERM OF TRIAL   With Hugh
Griffith and players

captivating figure in a film, no matter how finely he is acted, even by Laurence Olivier. And that's why *Term of Trial* is not an exciting picture. The meek and shabby high school teacher that Mr. Olivier plays in this British rehash of *Blackboard Jungle*, with minor *Lolita* overtones, is a wistful and well-meaning fellow for whom your heart bleeds a drop or two as you watch him stoically enduring all sorts of troubles and woes. But he's just not enough of a person to make your blood run hot or cold."

Bosley Crowther in *The New York Times*

"It is Laurence Olivier's performance as the teacher that makes the picture worth seeing. In some recent films Olivier has seemed surly or partly anesthetized, and even in this one there are a few moments when he counts on impassivity to do too much for him. But in thick-rimmed glasses and old tweed jacket, he achieves the fundamental quality of a man grievously afflicted with compassion, who feels a little presumptuous at the size of his compassion and tries to hide it. His outburst at the trial cuts to the quick, a white-hot, bare-nerve revelation of agonized love."

Stanley Kauffmann in *The New Republic*

"Olivier's performance is gloomy, often deliberately dull, but it is minutely observed in detail and is never less than absorbing. Let it be put on record that he has one scene in the dock of a blazing theatrical intensity which, though it may be contrived, is boff thesping. His acting is always rewarding."

"Rich." in *Variety*

BUNNY LAKE IS MISSING   With Keir Dullea

BUNNY LAKE IS MISSING

1965

A Columbia Pictures release of a Wheel Productions film

CAST

Laurence Olivier (*Inspector Newhouse*); Carol Lynley (*Ann Lake*); Keir Dullea (*Steven Lake*); Martita Hunt (*Ada Ford*); Noël Coward (*Wilson*); Anna Massey (*Elvira Smollett*); Clive Revill (*Andrews*); Finlay Currie (*Dollmaker*); Lucie Mannheim (*Cook*); Richard Wattis (*Clerk in Shipping Office*); Adrienne Corri (*Dorothy*); Megs Jenkins (*Hospital Sister*); Victor Maddern (*Taxi Driver*); Delphi Lawrence (*First Mother*); Suzanne Neve (*Second Mother*); Kika Markham (*Nurse*); Jill Melford (*Teacher*); Damaris Hayman (*Daphne*); Patrick

BUNNY LAKE IS MISSING   With Carol Lynley

159

Jordan (*Policeman*); Jane Evers (*Policewoman*); Michael Wynne (*Rogers*); Bill Maxam (*Barman*); Tim Brinton (*Newscaster*); Fred Emney (*Man in Soho*); David Oxley (*Doctor*); John Forbes-Robertson (*Hospital Attendant*); The Zombies (*Themselves*); John Sharp (*Fingerprint Man*); Geoffrey Frederick (*Police Photographer*); Percy Herbert (*Policeman at Station*).

CREDITS

Producer-Director: Otto Preminger; *Associate Producer:* Martin C. Schute; *Screenwriters:* John and Penelope Mortimer; *Based on the novel* by Evelyn Piper; *Panavision Cinematographer:* Denys Coop; *Editor:* Peter Thornton; *Production Designer:* Don Ashton; *Set Decorators:* Elven Webb and Scott Slimon; *Music:* Paul Glass; *Special Effects:* Charles Staffell; *Costumes:* Hope Bryce; *Titles:* Saul Bass; *Running Time:* 107 minutes.

THE FILM

Very much in support of the movie's actual leading players, Carol Lynley and Keir Dullea, Olivier nevertheless receives top billing as Inspector Newhouse, the Scotland Yard man assigned to investigate the alleged disappearance from a London nursery school of four-year-old Bunny Lake. Although her unwed American mother Ann (Lynley) claims to have left the child there only a short time earlier, apparently no one at the school can recall her. Ann is aided in her frantic search by her possessive brother Steven (Dullea), whose relationship to his sister occasionally appears to be more that of a *husband*.

BUNNY LAKE IS MISSING   With Carol Lynley and Keir Dullea

Although missing from much of this psychological mystery thriller's plot development, Olivier's character reappears in time to participate in the unusual denouement.

Shot entirely in England with a largely British cast, *Bunny Lake Is Missing* varied considerably from the novel it was based on, because producer-director Otto Preminger sought to avoid clichéd plot twists. Its production professionally reunited Olivier and Noël Coward for the first time since their 1930 stage hit, *Private Lives*.

OLIVIER:

"I played rather a little man in *Bunny Lake Is Missing*, probably bullied on to me by Otto Preminger—a real bully, who never stopped. Noël Coward and I didn't like the man much. Have a pleasant atmosphere on the set, and a director is in less need of a miracle."

CRITICS CIRCLE

"*Bunny Lake Is Missing* has surface interest and intermittent fascination, but it ultimately boils down to a routine game of psycho, psycho, who's got the psychosis. Noël Coward's spoof of an ultraesthete given to collecting whips and memorabilia of de Sade, and Martita Hunt's fascinating portrait of an aged kindergartner devoting her retirement to a study of children's fantasies hasn't much to do with Bunny Lake, but at least they are given a moment to perform. Laurence Olivier is not so fortunate in his downbeat, flat-toned role of investigator; any number of other gifted actors are given even shorter shrift than he, ranging from Clive Revill, wasted as his assistant, to Finlay Currie as a doting dollmaker, to Megs Jenkins, a one-line nurse."

Judith Crist in *New York Herald-Tribune*

"Olivier is the man to watch. Instead of rounding out the flattish character of the inspector, he sits like a paperweight on his own personality so that the character lies even flatter. Only a great actor dare make himself this small. It is a rare sight."

Alexander Walker in *The Evening Standard*

"To keep an eye on everyone, there is the man from Scotland Yard—dryly played by Sir Laurence Olivier, who seems bemused to find his king-sized talent tucked into so mundane a role."

Time magazine

"Getting Olivier to play a quiet, rather ordinary—but not commonplace—police inspector seems at first like hitching an Arabian stallion to a milk wagon. It is not.

Olivier doesn't give the part the smashing Old Vic treatment; no rolling consonants or reverberent vowels. He cannot still the intensity, however. That commands attention and respect. It underlines the rationality of his role in the midst of trickery, conflict and muddle."

The Hollywood Reporter

OTHELLO

1965

An Eagle Lion Films Ltd. release of a B.H.E. production

U.S. Distributor: Warner Bros. (1966)

CAST

Laurence Olivier *(Othello)*; Frank Finlay *(Iago)*; Maggie Smith *(Desdemona)*; Joyce Redman *(Emilia)*; Derek Jacobi *(Cassio)*; Robert Lang *(Roderigo)*; Anthony Nicholls *(Brabantio)*; Harry Lomax *(Duke of Venice)*; Sheila Reid *(Bianca)*; Michael Turner *(Gratiano)*; Kenneth Mackintosh *(Lodovico)*; Edward Hardwicke *(Montano)*; Roy Holder *(Clown)*; David Hargreaves and Malcolm Terris *(Senate Officers)*; Terence Knapp *(Duke's Officer)*; Keith Marsh *(Senator)*; Tom Kempinski *(Sailor)*; Nicholas Edmett *(Messenger)*; William Hobbs and Trevor Martin *(Cypriot Officers)*.

CREDITS

Director: Stuart Burge; *Producers:* Anthony Havelock-Allan and John Brabourne; *Associate Producer:* Richard Goodwin; *Based on* John Dexter's National Theatre production; *From the play by* William Shakespeare; *Panavision-Technicolor Cinematographer:* Geoffrey Unsworth; *Editor:* Richard Marden; *Production Designer:* Jocelyn Herbert; *Music:* Richard Hampton; *Sound:* John Cox and Dickie Bird; *Assistant Director:* Christopher Dryhurst; *Running Time:* 166 minutes.

THE FILM

For a goodly portion of his distinguished stage career, Olivier studiously avoided the role of Othello. In 1938, he portrayed Iago to Ralph Richardson's Moor in an unsuccessful Tyrone Guthrie production of the Shakespearean classic at the Old Vic. But he had little desire to essay Othello himself, calling the role "a terrible study and a monstrous, monstrous burden for the actor." It was critic Kenneth Tynan, then serving in a text-advisory capacity to Olivier's National Theatre Company, who persuaded him to tackle the part, in celebration of Shakespeare's Quatercentenary.

This film version of the National's production of *Othello* represents a straightforward, studio-bound movie record of the stage play. It was shot during three weeks in the summer of 1965, without recourse to exterior settings or the location photography customarily used to establish an exotic locale. Nor were any cuts made; this *Othello* runs just fourteen minutes short of three hours. In the U.S., it opened as a reserved-seat, advanced-price attraction, playing simultaneously in a great number of theaters—for four performances only. Nevertheless, it won a great deal of critical acclaim, as well as Academy Award nominations for Olivier, Frank Finlay's Iago, Maggie Smith's Desdemona, and Joyce Redman, in the supporting role of Emilia.

Shakespeare's classic tale of jealousy, deception and multiple vengeance first reached the screen in a 1908 Vitagraph silent one-reeler, directed by W.V. Ranous with a long-forgotten cast. A second silent adaptation came from Germany in 1923, featuring Emil Jannings as the Moor, Lya de Putti as the fair Desdemona, and Werner Krauss as treacherous Iago. The play was not filmed again until 1951, when Orson Welles produced, directed, and starred in a frequently powerful version, partly shot in Morocco amidst strikingly cinematic backgrounds. His costars were the little-known Suzanne Cloutier and Micheal MacLiammoir. In 1955, the Soviet Mosfilm Studio produced a lavishly effective *Othello*, starring actor-director Sergei Bondarchuk. And more recently, there was Franco Zeffirelli's acclaimed 1986 opera-film preserving Placido Domingo's masterful stage portrayal of Verdi's *Otello*.

Olivier's *Othello* may not be the definitive film of Shakespeare's tragedy, but it does contain a great deal of theatrical power and, as a record of one of that actor's greatest stage triumphs, it is invaluable.

Producers Anthony Havelock-Allan and John Brabourne had hoped to re-create on film the National Theatre's *Othello*, with all of its theatrical impact and atmosphere. But, of course, the irreconcilable differences of the two media make this quite impossible. And, while some of Olivier's onstage electricity is necessarily lost, the subtleties of Frank Finlay's quietly cunning, coldly cerebral Iago performance are strengthened by the techniques of film, rendering the conflict between Othello and his crafty chief lieutenant all the more explosive.

Olivier's characterization and physical makeup stirred a certain amount of critical controversy, with his artful use of black-face, blunted features, and close-cropped, inky hair. Most reviewers, however, were able to bypass obvious potshots and recognize Olivier's brilliantly original conception of a neurotic contemporary-type man, saddled with paranoid concerns, racial sensitivities, and, with regard to his Caucasian wife, a figure of powerful sexuality. Maggie Smith makes of his Desdemona a vibrant woman, responding to Othello's attentions with warmth and passion.

161

Stuart Burge's direction, adapting John Dexter's National Theatre production to the cameras, shows evidence of his efforts to avoid the static look of a photographed play, though he appears overly fond of giant close-ups. Olivier's *Othello* remains somewhat less towering a film than his Shakespearean masterpieces *Hamlet*, *Henry V*, and *Richard III*, but it is nevertheless a great performance, judiciously preserved.

OLIVIER:

"Films based on obvious stage origins sometimes misfire. Stuart Burge directed the film of the National's *Othello*, and he did it marvelously, within its limited concept. Alas, my performance was tired. I mistimed effects. Somehow, I was lacking in confidence and full vitality; perhaps, subconsciously, I was being gnawed by the question: 'Why aren't we making a full-blown Shakespeare film of this?' Certainly I regret that now."

CRITICS CIRCLE

"Sir Laurence has created an entirely new Moor of Venice in a revolutionary and remarkably contemporary concept of body and soul. Gone is the near-stereotype of the dark-skinned hero, the noble savage victimized by evil intrigue and his own emotion; we have done with the agony of the innocent. We have instead a modern man, riddled with neuroses, a manic-depressive skirting the edges of paranoia, led—by the very tensions of the military life—to excesses, his nerves honed to super-sensitivity by his race-consciousness, his pride polished to brittle brilliance by his achievements, his total insecurity evidenced in the super-assurance of his stride, his quick lapse into humility before his superiors, his self-conscious bonhomie with his officers, his dominating sexuality with his wife. And this Olivier has embodied in almost minstrel-show make-up, so that we meet Othello as a pitch-black figure, flashing teeth and crimson mouth slashing the shiny ebony of his face—a slightly effete figure in his hour of relaxation, flourishing a scarlet rose as his thoughts linger on love. This is the jolt, then, of the black-face tragedian—but I, for one, find it a powerful effect. Here are the dull graying tones of torment, here the greenish cast of ugly violence, the warm taupes of self-realization and despair. Accomplished through both make-up and lighting, these are ideal for the cam-

OTHELLO   With Maggie Smith and players

163

OTHELLO   With Frank Finlay

era, which explores every nuance in a detail never available to the audience eye in the best seat in the living theater. I cannot imagine that this Othello was as effective on stage, at least in visual terms, for the camera seems to penetrate to his very soul in every close-up."

Judith Crist in *New York Herald-Tribune*

"As theatre, this filmed version of *Othello* should be seen by every lover of fine acting. As proper use of film, however, it is inferior to Laurence Olivier's previous Shakespearean efforts. . . . However excellent, this is a filmed play. What, then, makes *Othello* so important? First and foremost, to see and hear Olivier. To see him create the tormented soul who 'loved not wisely, but too well.' To hear, as the ear is regaled by his incredible feat of turning the richly-embroidered lines into understandable conversation. Olivier combines the many faceted characteristics of Othello into a single, remarkable human being. . . . Need another reason for seeing *Othello*? To stake a claim for the future of having witnessed one of the great performances of our time. Olivier is surrounded

by a generally excellent company that, in a few instances, captures something of his magic."

"Robe." in *Variety*

"The center of interest is Laurence Olivier's performance as the Moor. This is acting of a virtuosity that is rare even in the theater now. Watching it like this, it is important to remember that Olivier knows the difference between stage and cinema as well as any man alive. We have proof elsewhere of his compatibility with the camera, and we need look back no further than his junket-eater in *Bunny Lake Is Missing* for a reminder of his talent for underplaying. Here it is as if the camera were an interloper. The actor repeats his stage performance, which was already placed in relief and seems more now. What we see is not a performance that works on film, but an X-ray of theatrical technique. As such it is beyond valuation, because the technique in itself is superlative. An uncommonly privileged view of a great actor at work."

Gordon Gow in *Films and Filming*

164

OTHELLO With Maggie Smith

"This *Othello* thankfully brought to the screen almost whole and pure is as brilliant and beautifully modeled a version as one would wish to see . . . For here is acting of enormous skill and passion. As is well known by now, Olivier has taken Shakespeare's 'black' description of the Moor of Venice as implying 'blackamoor,' for otherwise Othello would have been of mixed Arab and Berber ancestry. So he has dyed his body to the darkest of hues, reddened the inner portions of his lips for a broadening effect and crinkled his hair, and to these stereotyped physical characteristics of a Negro he has added a deeper, huskier voice tone than is his usual, and bodily movements that are, again, not his own, but those of certain Negroes he has presumably studied. Olivier has quite obviously done this in order to make clearer the essential nature of Othello as a man of bravery, nobility, and simplicity whose very lack of guile and cunning enable him to be destroyed by the sophisticated and scheming Iago. Rigorous integrity of artistic purpose was Olivier's aim, but there are those who are going to be made unhappy by what might seem an undue emphasis on racial characteristics, and the suggestion (is it Shakespeare's or Olivier's?) of a certain residual primitivism in Othello's psyche. Very little has been done to make this Othello cinematic (as was not the case with Olivier's *Hamlet* and *Richard III*), and, as a result, we have the play itself, benefiting hugely from the use of close-ups, discreet in its shifting of scene, a living proof that theater and film can serve each other and serve us all."

Hollis Alpert in *Saturday Review*

KHARTOUM

1966

A United Artists release of a Julian Blaustein production

CAST

Charlton Heston (*General Charles "Chinese" Gordon*); Laurence Olivier (*The Mahdi*); Richard Johnson (*Col. J.D.H. Stewart*); Ralph Richardson (*Prime Minister Gladstone*); Alexander Knox (*Sir Evelyn Baring*); Johnny Sekka (*Khaleel*); Michael Hordern (*Lord Granville*); Zia Mohyeddin (*Zobeir Pasha*); Marne Maitland (*Sheikh Osman*); Nigel Green (*General Wolseley*); Hugh Williams (*Lord Hartington*); Douglas Wilmer (*The Khalifa Abdullah*); Edward Underdown (*Colonel Hicks*); Alec Mango (*Bordeini Bey*); George Pastell (*Giriagis Bey*); Peter Arne (*Major Kitchener*); Alan Tilvern (*Awaan*); Michael Anthony (*Herbin*); Jerome Willis (*Frank Power*); Leila (*The Dancer*); Ronald Leigh-Hunt (*Lord Northbrook*); Ralph Michael (*Sir Charles Dilke*).

166

CREDITS

Director: Basil Dearden; *Producer:* Julian Blaustein; *Screenwriter:* Robert Ardrey; *Technicolor Cinematographer:* Ted Scaife; *Second-Unit Photography:* Harry Waxman; *Editor:* Fergus McDonnell; *Art Director:* John Howell; *Music:* Frank Cordell; *Second-Unit Director:* Yakima Canutt; *Prologue-scenes director:* Eliot Elisofen; *Special Effects:* Richard Parker; *Production Supervisor:* Charles Orme; *Running Time:* 134 minutes.

THE FILM

In the 1883 Sudan, a British general and 10,000 untrained Egyptian troops are wiped out by a fanatic Arab religious leader known as the Mahdi (Laurence Olivier), prompting Prime Minister Gladstone (Ralph Richardson) to send Britain's national hero Gen. Charles "Chi-

OTHELLO   With Maggie Smith

nese" Gordon (Charlton Heston) there to evacuate 13,000 troops and civilians from Khartoum—and contend with the Mahdi. But Gordon isn't given sufficient support by Gladstone, who disbelieves the seriousness of the situation. Later, he sends Gen. Wolseley (Nigel Green) and 7,000 men to save Gordon, but not Khartoum—which Gordon refuses to abandon. Eventually, refusing to bow to the Mahdi and his hordes, Gordon is killed and Khartoum falls.

OLIVIER:

"Immediately after *Othello,* I played the Mahdi in *Khartoum.* In epic pictures there's not much time for deep characterization—sometimes the dialogue can be anybody's—and you have to rely very strongly on the pictorial effect. Every epic film has its flamboyant part—usually played by Peter Ustinov. The secret is to play the part up to the audience's expectation of it—a healthy tradition from Shakespeare to Westerns and Mae West—and the real amusement is the little extra. A great deal more extra, if it's real. We all loved Charles Laughton for his big performances. It's given me a lot of fun being part of that cinema tradition."

CRITICS CIRCLE

"On the face of it, this is the best historical spectacle in some time. It is certainly the most intelligent, with a highly literate script and some excellent, undemonstrative acting. Yet somehow, in spite of Charlton Heston's intelligent performance, one is left at the end with the feeling of having passed through a not particularly interesting history lesson. A spectacular should be remembered for the way it looks: what one remembers here is Heston's performance—a carefully rounded study, suggesting depth and complexity, and never slipping into caricature. In contrast, Laurence Olivier's Mahdi is strangely weak. Made up in variable degrees of black, his tongue between his teeth, Olivier so strives after intonation that what should be an immense character is no character at all."

"D.W." in *Monthly Film Bulletin*

"Olivier, playing the Mahdi, is excellent in creating audience terror of a zealot who sincerely believes that a mass slaughter is Divine Will, while projecting respect and compassion for his equally-religious adversary, Heston. The role calls for Olivier to have a darkened face, relative physical immobility and heavily-garbed body. Thus, through eyes and voice only, his impact is all the more noteworthy."

"Murf." in *Variety*

KHARTOUM   As The Mahdi

KHARTOUM   With Charlton Heston

KHARTOUM   As The Mahdi

"The role of the Mahdi is so impressively and eloquently played by a dark-stained Sir Laurence Olivier, wearing a gleaming white burnoose and addressing his seething cohorts and General Gordon in beautifully chiseled words, that it is not surprising that he puts the gold-braided figure of Mr. Heston's Chinese Gordon in the shade."

Bosley Crowther in *The New York Times*

"The only important drawback of the film, in fact, is the role of the Mahdi and the way it is played by Sir Laurence Olivier: we are given a formidable display of eye-rolling and lip-licking, a weird Peter Sellers Oriental accent and a valiant but unsuccessful attempt to disguise Sir Laurence's all-too-English features with false hair and green lipstick. But no feeling of a real man ever comes over. Perhaps it is the difference between stage and film acting; no doubt Sir Laurence could act rings around Mr. Heston at the National Theatre, but here, as in that earlier and apparently just as unfair contest between Sir Laurence and Marilyn Monroe in *The Prince and the Showgirl*, there remains no doubt either about whose shadow has more substance on the silver screen."

The Times of London

ROMEO AND JULIET

1968

A Paramount Pictures release of a British Home Entertainments Production, in association with Verona Productions and Dino De Laurentiis Cinematografica

CAST

Olivia Hussey *(Juliet)*; Leonard Whiting *(Romeo)*; Milo O'Shea *(Friar Lawrence)*; Michael York *(Tybalt)*; John McEnery *(Mercutio)*; Pat Heywood *(Nurse)*; Robert Stephens *(Prince of Verona)*; Natasha Parry *(Lady Capulet)*; Keith Skinner *(Balthazar)*; Richard Warwick *(Gregory)*; Dyson Lovell *(Sampson)*; Ugo Barbone *(Abraham)*; Bruce Robinson *(Benvolio)*; Paul Hardwick *(Lord Capulet)*; Antonio Pierfederici *(Lord Montague,* with voice dubbed by Laurence Olivier); Esmeralda Ruspoli *(Lady Montague)*; Robert Bisacco *(Count Paris)*; Roy Holder *(Peter)*; Aldo Miranda *(Friar John)*; Dario Tanzini *(Page to Tybalt)*.

CREDITS

Director: Franco Zeffirelli; *Producers:* Anthony Havelock-Allan and John Brabourne; *Associate Producer:* Richard Goodwin; *Screenwriters:* Franco Brusati and Masolino D'Amico, *adapted from the play by* William Shakespeare; *Technicolor Cinematographer:* Pasquale De San-

tis; *Editor:* Reginald Mills; *Production Designer:* Renzo Mongiardino; *Art Director:* Luciano Puccini; *Set Decorator:* Christine Edzard; *Costumes:* Danilo Donati; *Music:* Nino Rota; *Lyrics:* Eugene Walter; *Prologue and Epilogue Spoken by* Laurence Olivier (uncredited); *Running Time:* 152 minutes.

THE FILM

Franco Zeffirelli followed his lusty 1967 Richard Burton-Elizabeth Taylor movie version of *The Taming of the Shrew* with Shakespeare's timeless romantic drama, *Romeo and Juliet*, utilizing a cast of little-known players and—in the title roles—two teenagers reflecting the actual ages of the classic characters they portrayed: Leonard Whiting and Olivia Hussey.

When Zeffirelli showed a rough draft of the script to his friend Olivier, the latter asked to be a part of the enterprise—with the proviso that his name not be used on either the credits or publicity. Thus, he spoke the film's prologue and epilogue, as well as dubbing for Italian actor Antonio Pierfederici (who played Lord Montague)—and even supplying shouts in the crowd scenes.

CRITICS CIRCLE

"If this *Romeo and Juliet* had been produced in 1956, there might have been no need for [the stage production

ROMEO AND JULIET   Olivia Hussey and Leonard Whiting

of] *West Side Story* the following year. It is a dangerous game, rewriting Shakespeare, but *Romeo and Juliet* proves that it can be played and won. An even greater risk was to give the leading roles to a pair of youthful unknowns with virtually no acting experience: Juliet is a tremulous 15-year-old, Olivia Hussey; Romeo is Leonard Whiting, 17. Both look their parts and read their lines with a sensitivity far beyond the limitations of their age. Visually, Shakespeare has never been better realized—and seldom has he had so sensitive a collaborator."

Time magazine

"Because these kids are authentic teen-agers, just as Shakespeare had envisaged them, they take on a vitality and poignance that no middle-aged actor could project. This *Romeo and Juliet*, sumptuously mounted, excitingly imagined, lives on the truth of its characters rather than on simply the splendor of its lines. Somehow, I think Shakespeare would have preferred it that way."

Arthur Knight in *Saturday Review*

"It is a trifle ironic that the only voice which seems able to take the measure of Shakespeare should be the one without a face—Laurence Olivier, who speaks the prologue and epilogue."

Eric Shorter in the *Daily Telegraph*

THE SHOES OF THE FISHERMAN   As Piotr Ilyich Kamenev

THE SHOES OF THE FISHERMAN

1968

A Metro-Goldwyn-Mayer release of a George Englund production

THE SHOES OF THE FISHERMAN   With Oskar Werner, Clive Revill, and Anthony Quinn

CAST

Anthony Quinn *(Kiril Lakota)*; Laurence Olivier *(Piotr Ilyich Kamenev)*; Oskar Werner *(Fr. David Telemond)*; David Janssen *(George Faber)*; Vittorio De Sica *(Cardinal Rinaldi)*; Leo McKern *(Cardinal Leone)*; John Gielgud *(The Elder Pope)*; Barbara Jefford *(Dr. Ruth Faber)*; Rosemarie Dexter *(Chiara)*; Frank Finlay *(Igor Bounin)*; Burt Kwouk *(Peng)*; Arnoldo Foa *(Gelasio)*; Paul Rogers *(Augustinian)*; George Pravda *(Gorshenin)*; Clive Revill *(Vucovich)*; Niall MacGinnis *(Capuchin Monk)*; Marne Maitland *(Cardinal Rahamani)*; Isa Miranda *(The Marchesa)*; George Harper *(Brian)*; Leopoldo Trieste *(Dying Man's Friend)*; Jean Rougeul *(Dominican)*; Peter Copley and Arthur Howard *(English Cardinals)*; Alfred Thomas *(Negro Cardinal)*; Dom Moor *(Polish Cardinal)*; John Frederick *(American Cardinal)*.

CREDITS

Director: Michael Anderson; *Producer:* George Englund; *Screenwriters:* John Patrick, James Kennaway, and (uncredited) Morris L. West; *Based on the novel by* Morris L. West; *Panavision-Metrocolor*

171

THE SHOES OF THE FISHERMAN   With Anthony Quinn and Burt Kwouk

THE SHOES OF THE FISHERMAN   With Anthony Quinn

Cinematographer: Erwin Hillier; *Editor:* Ernest Walter; *Art Director:* Edward Carfagno; *Set Decorator:* Arrigo Breschi; *Music:* Alex North; *Production Supervisor:* Stanley Goldsmith; *Costumes:* Orietta Nasalli-Rocca; *Sound:* Kurt Doubravsky; *Running Time:* 157 minutes.

THE FILM

Morris L. West's best-seller about a Russian ex-labor camp prisoner who becomes Pontiff of the Roman Catholic Church, and is designated to solve the world's complex political problems where its leaders have failed, was brought to the screen as a star-studded, epic-length entertainment that was criticized for its sluggish pace and its implausibility. Although West had adapted his novel, other writers became involved in the project, and West later requested that his screenwriting credit be removed. Although cast in a sizable role, Laurence Olivier was accorded special, single-frame billing at the bottom of the cast list. The project, which required the actor's presence in Rome for three weeks in 1967 while he recovered from cancer treatments, served to reunite Olivier with Anthony Quinn, his old *Becket* stage colleague. *The Shoes of the Fisherman* was not released in the United Kingdom until 1972.

OLIVIER:

"I had to do cameo roles for the sake of my health, the balance of my professional life, the balance of my social life—and my bank account. Working with friends. Working for friends. I did a sort of double act with Frank Finlay in that film where my friend Anthony Quinn wears *The Shoes of the Fisherman.*"

CRITICS CIRCLE

"*The Shoes of the Fisherman* is a multimillion-dollar Hollywood Reverential that will probably do for the papacy what *The Sound of Music* did for family chorales. Of course, Quinn and Olivier and Werner go through their paces properly. But not all the pomp and circumstance and endless cliches about love and loneliness, nor all the pseudo-realism and scenic schmaltz can gloss over the basic pedantry and simple-mindedness of the theme. It's a Hollywood Reverential all right—mostly Hollywood and little true reverence."

Judith Crist in *New York* magazine

"Lord Olivier strolls through his role as the Russian Premier who once imprisoned Quinn for 20 years—but I suppose it pays the rent."

Sue Freeman in *London Daily Express*

"A most timely narrative. Quinn's performance is excellent. Olivier, along with Frank Finlay and Clive Revill, are superior in projecting not unsympathetic Russian politicians."

"Murf." in *Variety*

OH! WHAT A LOVELY WAR

1969

A Paramount Pictures release of an Accord production

OH! WHAT A LOVELY WAR As Sir John French

CAST

John Mills *(Field-Marshal Sir Douglas Haig)*; Dirk Bogarde *(Stephen)*; Phyllis Calvert *(Lady Haig)*; Jean-Pierre Cassel *(French Colonel)*; John Clements *(Gen. von Moltke)*; John Gielgud *(Count Leopold von Berchtold)*; Jack Hawkins *(Emperor Franz Joseph)*; Ian Holm *(President Poincare)*; Kenneth More *(Kaiser Wilhelm II)*; Ralph Richardson *(Sir Edward Grey)*; Laurence Olivier *(Sir John French)*; Michael Redgrave *(Gen. Sir Henry Wilson)*; Vanessa Redgrave *(Sylvia Pankhurst)*; Maggie Smith *(Music Hall Star)*; Susannah York *(Eleanor)*; John Rae *(Grandpa)*; Mary Winbush *(Mother)*; Corin Redgrave *(Bertie)*; Maurice Roeves *(George)*; Paul Shelley *(Jack)*; Malcolm McFee *(Freddie)*; Colin Farrell *(Harry)*; Paul Daneman *(Tsar Nicholas II)*; Pia Colombo *(French Singer)*; Christian Doermer *(Fritz)*; Joe Melia *(Photographer/Poppyman)*; Cecil Parker *(Rich Man in Limousine)*; Robert Flemyng *(Staff Major in Gassed Trench)*; Nanette Newman and Juliet Mills *(Nurses at Station)*; David Lodge *(Recruiting Sergeant)*; Meriel Forbes *(Lady Grey)*; Guy Middleton *(Gen. Sir William Robertson)*; Natasha Parry *(Sir William's Lady)*; Isabel Dean *(Sir John French's Lady)*; Vincent Ball *(Australian Soldier)*; Edward Fox, Geoffrey Davies, and Anthony Ainley *(Aides)*; Norman Bird *(Training Sergeant)*; Gerald Sim *(Chaplain)*.

CREDITS

Director: Richard Attenborough; *Producers:* Brian Duffy and Richard Attenborough; *Associate Producer:* Mack Davidson; *Screenwriter:* Len Deighton (uncredited); *From the musical play by* Joan Littlewood and Members of Her Theatre Workshop; *Panavision-Technicolor Cinematographer:* Gerry Turpin; *Editor:* Kevin Connor; *Production Designer:* Don Ashton; *Art Director:* Harry White; *Set Decorator:* Peter

James; *Music Adaptor/Arranger:* Alfred Ralston; *Choreographer:* Eleanor Fazan; *Costumes:* Anthony Mendelson; *Running Time:* 144 minutes. (U.S. version edited to 132 minutes.)

THE FILM

World War I as a classy musical revue, playing on the boardwalk at England's Brighton Beach? That's the conceit used as a framework for this lavishly expanded version of what was, in 1960, a BBC-radio special by Charles Hilton entitled *The Long Long Trail.* Adapted for the stage by Joan Littlewood and retitled *Oh! What a Lovely War,* it became one of London's hits of 1963. This screen expansion was accomplished by spy-novelist Len Deighton *(The Ipcress File),* who was originally Richard Attenborough's coproducer on the project. Eventually, Deighton withdrew his participation, requesting that his name be removed from the movie's credits. His reason—that Attenborough's handling of the material "should have been tougher"—obviously holds reference to the metamorphosis of the angry stage version's satiric savagery into a gentler, expensively opulent piece of "popular entertainment." What had once been a sharply tuned and daringly original stage musical had now become, in the opinion of some critics, a star-studded audio-visual marshmallow to succeed *The Sound of Music.* Those of this opinion missed much of the point. True, the film's producers hoped for a commercial success—and employed "name" actors and colorful production values to attain that end. But *Oh! What a Lovely War* is nonetheless powerful, either as trenchant antiwar satire or as an outstanding example of the filmmaking art.

Its debuting director, Richard Attenborough, already highly respected as an actor, was helped in his initial directorial project by a great number of his famed colleagues, who agreed to defer salaries to play cameo roles. But even with that much industry support, *Oh! What a Lovely War* represents a formidable sort of "first film." Its structure is immensely complex, depending for its effectiveness on a clever juxtaposition of period songs, historical reenactments, and blackout sketches as that Brighton pier, in 1914, flashes an electric sign announcing World War I and selling tickets for the "ever popular War Game—complete with songs, battles, and a few jokes." The public is even kept regularly apprised of the body count until, at the end in 1918, the scoreboard registers a tally of nine million casualties. The movie's final shot, as the helicopter-borne camera rises to reveal seemingly endless thousands of graves marked with white crosses, is a shattering panorama that even the film's detractors have to admire.

OLIVIER:

"Richard Attenborough asked me to do Field-Marshal French in his brilliant directing debut *Oh! What a Lovely*

War, which was a bright couple of days in Brighton—which might have been the trouble with the film, where the songs didn't have the same eerie effect that they had in the theatre."

CRITICS CIRCLE

"Richard Attenborough . . . has chosen to make a big, elaborate, sometimes realistic film whose elephantine physical proportions and often brilliant all-star cast simply overwhelms the material with a surfeit of good intentions. Some of the sketches, vignettes and songs are absolutely superb, especially early in the film before a certain monotony sets in. Chief among these is a music-hall number in which Maggie Smith sings a raucous, deliberately naughty recruiting song, "I'll Make a Man of You." In this short interlude, the film achieves the precarious balance it seeks between satire, nostalgia and ghastly humor. Also fine are . . . the vignettes that spread throughout with Laurence Olivier, John Mills and Michael Redgrave as staff officers who might have been conceived by Punch, but whose lines are often recorded history."

Vincent Canby in *The New York Times*

"John Mills as Field-Marshall Haig has a principal role, and after him come awesome names in cameo parts:

174

Sir Ralph Richardson as Sir Edward Grey, Britain's chief diplomat; Jack Hawkins as Emperor Franz Josef; Sir Laurence Olivier, Sir John Gielgud, Kenneth More, Vanessa Redgrave as a suffragette (inevitably). *Oh! What a Lovely War* is so honorable, important and moving a piece of film that it seems niggling to say that it misses (narrowly) being fully the masterpiece it might have been. But I hope it is high praise to note that a first-time director undertook a monumentally difficult and forbidding task and did very nearly achieve his masterpiece."

Charles Champlin in *The Los Angeles Times*

"It is not merely at this point the best film of 1969, but an outstanding film for all time. Attenborough has brought to it the impeccable taste and professionalism that have been the hallmarks of his acting career. Celebrities and dignitaries are portrayed by the crème de la crème of England's acting profession; the result is not the usual cameo-studded spectacular, but a unique star-spangled spectacle across which comets flash—here Olivier as the mumblingly blimpish Sir John French of the liquorish eye; there Gielgud, a wily Von Berchtold, manipulating Jack Hawkins as the silent, droop-lidded Kaiser; now Maggie Smith, raucous and insidious as a Lilith of the music hall—and hovering over all, reveling in the game and personal consultations with God, John Mills as Haig, supreme commander of the butchery that claims nine million casualties."

Judith Crist in *New York* magazine

"Olivier is superbly smooth, amusing, properly stuffy as Sir John French, who loses his command of British forces to an upstart, who 'has something to do with whiskey,' Sir Douglas Haig."

Wanda Hale in New York *Daily News*

BATTLE OF BRITAIN

1969

A United Artists release of a Spitfire production

CAST

Harry Andrews *(Senior Civil Servant)*; Michael Caine *(Sqn. Ldr. Canfield)*; Trevor Howard *(Air Vice-Marshal Keith Park)*; Curt Jurgens *(Baron von Richter)*; Kenneth More *(Group Capt. Baker)*; Laurence

175

BATTLE OF BRITAIN   As Sir Hugh Dowding

Olivier (*Air Chief Marshal Sir Hugh Dowding*); Christopher Plummer (*Sqn. Ldr. Colin Harvey*); Michael Redgrave (*Air Vice-Marshal Evill*); Ralph Richardson (*British Minister in Switzerland*); Robert Shaw (*Sqn. Ldr. Skipper*); Susannah York (*Section Officer Maggie Harvey*); Ian McShane (*Sgt. Pilot Andy*); Patrick Wymark (*Air Vice-Marshal Trafford Leigh-Mallory*); Nigel Patrick (*Group Capt. Hope*); Michael Bates (*Warrant Officer Warrick*); Isla Blair (*Andy's Wife*); John Bascomb (*Farmer*); Tom Chatto (*Willoughby's Asst. Controller*); James Cosmo (*Jamie*); Robert Flemyng (*Wing Commander Willoughby*); Barry Foster (*Sqn. Ldr. Edwards*); Edward Fox (*Pilot Officer Archie*); W.G. Foxley (*Sqn. Ldr. Evans*); David Griffin (*Sgt. Pilot Chris*); Jack Gwillim (*Senior Air Staff Officer*); Myles Hoyle (*Peter*); Duncan Lamont (*Flt. Sgt. Arthur*); Sarah Lawson (*Skipper's Wife*); Mark Malicz (*Pasco*); Andre Maranne (*French N.C.O.*); Anthony Nicholls (*Minister*); Nicholas Pennell (*Simon*); Andrzej Scibor (*Ox*); Jean Wladon (*Jean-Jacques*); Wilfred van Aacken (*Gen. Osterkamp*); Karl Otto Alberty (*Jeschonnek*); Alexander Allerson (*Major Brandt*); Dietrich Frauboes (*Feldmarschall Milch*); Alf Jungermann (*Brandt's Navigator*); Peter Hager (*Feldmarschall Kesselring*); Wolf Harnish (*Gen. Fink*); Reinhard Horras (*Bruno*); Helmut Kircher (*Boehm*); Paul Neuhaus (*Maj. Foehn*); Malte Petzel (*Col. Beppo Schmid*); Manfred Redde-

mann (*Maj. Falke*); Hein Riess (*Reichsmarschall Goering*); Rolf Stiefel (*Adolf Hitler*).

CREDITS

Director: Guy Hamilton; *Producers:* Harry Saltzman and S. Benjamin Fisz; *Associate Producer:* John Palmer; *Screenwriters:* James Kennaway and William Greatorex; *Based partly on the book* The Narrow Margin *by* Derek Wood and Derek Dempster; *Panavision-Technicolor Cinematographer:* Freddie Young; *Second-Unit Photographer:* Bob Huke; *Aerial Photographers:* Skeets Kelly and John Jordan; *Editor:* Bert Bates; *Supervising Art Director:* Maurice Carter; *Art Directors:* Bert Davey, Jack Maxsted, William Hutchinson and Gil Parrondo; *Music:* Ron Goodwin; *"Battle in the Air" theme:* William Walton; *Aerial/Second-Unit Director:* David Bracknell; *Special Effects:* Cliff Richardson, Glen Robinson, Wally Veevers and Ray Caple; *Running Time:* 131 minutes.

THE FILM

This spectacular docudrama celebrating the Royal Air

BATTLE OF BRITAIN   With Michael Redgrave

Force and Britain's defense of her homeland in World War II utilized a stellar alphabetically-listed cast (many in cameo parts), headed by Michael Caine, Christopher Plummer, Kenneth More, and Susannah York in the meatier roles. As Sir Hugh Dowding, whose tactics were instrumental in bringing down Hitler's Luftwaffe, Olivier makes the most of a supporting part.

Because of its patriotic subject matter, many of England's best actors willingly participated at far less than their customary salaries. Olivier, who had been paid $250,000 for just eight day's work on *Khartoum*, accepted a mere $20,000 for *Battle of Britain*.

OLIVIER:

"I was awfully thrilled, naturally. I had admired him very much. It was Lord Dowding who stopped our aircraft going straight across to France when Churchill was filled with thoughts of our great allies. Acting isn't really a question of 'being,' as long as you think right and give roughly the right sort of appearance of a character, it ought to turn out very real."

CRITICS CIRCLE

"*Battle of Britain* is a homage to those airmen who, in 1940, broke the back of the threatened Nazi invasion. It is also one of those all-star non-movies, of a somewhat lower order than *The Longest Day*, that attempt to recapitulate history, but add nothing to one's understanding. . . . Guy Hamilton, whose most stylish claim to fame is *Goldfinger*, hasn't so much directed the film as marshaled it. The aerial combat footage is, however, fine. There's an accidental irony in the appearance of *Battle of Britain* at this particular moment, just two weeks after the opening here of the satirical *Oh! What a Lovely War*, six of whose stars play more or less the same sort of roles in the new film."

Vincent Canby in *The New York Times*

"Only Sir Laurence Olivier is memorable, but then Sir Hugh Dowding is the only really written character, a dry, sad man who commands belief. Otherwise, it is a long, slow pull. Plane spotters will have a field day, but I'm not sure about less dedicated mortals."

John Russell Taylor in *The Times* of London

"Laurence Olivier here portrays Dowding with a selfless austerity and an outspoken bluntness that I found convincing and winning. Olivier's Dowding is an unrelievedly worried, but also a competent man. It's a masterly performance."

Edward Jablonski in *Films in Review*

THE DANCE OF DEATH

1969

A Paramount Pictures release of a B.H.E./National Theatre Company presentation

(*U.S. release: 1979*)

CAST

Laurence Olivier (*Edgar*); Geraldine McEwan (*Alice*); Robert Lang (*Kurt*); Janina Faye (*Judith*); Malcolm Reynolds (*Allan*); Carolyn Jones (*Jenny*); Maggie Riley (*Kristin*); Peter Penry-Jones (*The Lieutenant*); Jeanne Watts (*An Old Woman*); Frederick Pyne, Barry James, and David Ryall (*Sentries*).

THE DANCE OF DEATH   As Edgar

THE DANCE OF DEATH   With Robert Lang

THE DANCE OF DEATH   With Geraldine McEwan

CREDITS

Director: David Giles; *Producer:* John Brabourne; *Associate Producer:* Richard Goodwin; *Screenwriter:* C.D. Locock; *Based on the play by* August Strindberg; *Technicolor Cinematographer:* Geoffrey Unsworth; *Editor:* Reginald Mills; *Art Director:* Herbert Smith; *Set Decorator:* Helen Thomas; *Costumes:* Amy C. Binney; *Sound:* John Aldred; *Production Manager:* Elisabeth Woodthorpe; *Running Time:* 149 minutes.

THE FILM

Long before Edward Albee realized a Broadway hit with his corrosive comedy-drama *Who's Afraid of Virginia Woolf?* Sweden's August Strindberg made his mark with similar material in a morbid 1901 stage drama he called *The Dance of Death.* In an old fortress on a remote Swedish island, a friendless, unhappily married couple named Alice and Edgar celebrate the verge of their twenty-fifth anniversary by continuing the acrimonious skirmishes that have apparently sustained their precarious relationship. The arrival of Alice's cousin Kurt—appointed quarantine officer for the island—provides a welcome new focal point for their battles. But it is Edgar's daughter Judith, already promised in marriage to an elderly general, who unsettles everything by falling in love

with Kurt's son Allan. The shock of that revelation causes Edgar to suffer a fatal stroke, and Alice is left to ponder whether her resultant emotional state is due to actual love for the husband she long thought she hated.

Based on Britain's National Theatre Company version of the classic play, *The Dance of Death* was "opened up" for the screen sufficiently to qualify as a bona-fide *movie.* But its subject matter remained what most film distributors term "non-commercial," and it took this production a decade to reach U.S. cinemas.

OLIVIER:

"I found *The Dance of Death* by Strindberg a pretty claustrophobic piece in which you can't open out too much, unlike *Miss Julie.* Strindberg is *veritas,* perfectly straight forward, no undercurrent, no sub-text, no sneaky underneath thought that he is either subconsciously unaware of or is hiding to himself. The part of Strindberg's Edgar is a big one—intense and emotional—and if occasionally I appear to go over the top, that didn't ruin the performance or discount the screen's potential to contain a big performance. You have to follow the rhythms, the death-dance rhythms of the play. My feelings for the part were right. I swam along with the other actors, especially

THE DANCE OF DEATH   With Robert Lang and Geraldine McEwan

179

Geraldine McEwan, my leading lady. Any flaws, put down to professional misjudgment in a profession where the watchword should not be caution."

CRITICS CIRCLE

"It is surely perverse to take a performance pitched in purely theatrical proportions and to record it, virtually without adaptation or modulation, for a medium which depends on intimacy and subtlety for its effect. The result, inevitably, is distorted, unbalanced, hopelessly 'out of true.' Huge close-ups reveal the smallest mechanics and calculations of every performance (and the stilted inadequacy of some of the support). Microphones amplify each word with no apparent attempt at balance, so that everyone seems to be shouting his head off—particularly disastrous in the case of Olivier, who uses a staccato military bark that shatters the eardrums. Knowing what a superb film actor Olivier can be, one regrets more than ever that this extraordinary performance should have been committed to celluloid as a travesty of itself."

Brenda Davies in *Monthly Film Bulletin*

"Lord Olivier's performance in the film never fails to be entertaining, nor is it lacking in charm. But it is, if anything, *too* charming, especially since Geraldine McEwan plays Alice as such an unrelieved shrew. Miss McEwan is giving a stage performance in front of a movie camera, which greatly magnifies its flaws, and she winds up seeming not just a poor foil but a disproportionate one."

Janet Maslin in *The New York Times*

"One of Laurence Olivier's greatest performances— perhaps his greatest—has been encapsulated in a tin can for posterity."

Penelope Mortimer in *The Observer*

"Sir Laurence's performance is dismaying to a degree one would not have thought possible. It is a performance which is compounded of every showoffy gimmick he has ever picked up; he never stops winking, as it were, at the audience; and it is not surprising that he is therefore totally unconvincing."

Richard Roud in *The Guardian*

"Every time we single out the feature that makes Olivier a marvel—his lion eyes or the voice or the way it seizes on a phrase—he alters it or casts it off in some new role, and is greater than ever. It is no special asset, it is the devilish audacity and courage of this man. What is extraordinary is inside, and what is even more extraordinary

is his determination to give it outer force. He has never leveled off; he goes on soaring."

Pauline Kael in *The New Yorker*

THREE SISTERS
1970

A Lion International Films release of an Alan Clore Films/British Lion production

U.S. Distributor: American Film Theatre (1974)

CAST

Jeanne Watts *(Olga)*; Joan Plowright *(Masha)*; Louise Purnell *(Irina)*; Derek Jacobi *(Andrei)*; Sheila Reid *(Natasha)*; Kenneth Mackintosh *(Kulighin)*; Daphne Heard *(Anfissa)*; Harry Lomax *(Ferrapont)*; Ronald Pickup *(Tusenbach)*; Laurence Olivier *(Chebutikin)*; Frank Wylie *(Solloni)*; Alan Bates *(Vershinin)*; Richard Kay *(Fedotik)*; David Belcher *(Rode)*; Judy Wilson *(Serving Maid)*; Mary Griffiths *(Housemaid)*; George Selway *(Orderly)*; David Munro, Alan Adams, and Robert Walker *(Officers)*.

CREDITS

Director: Laurence Olivier; *Co-Director:* John Sichel; *Executive Producer:* Alan Clore; *Producer:* John Goldstone; *Associate Producers:* Timothy Burrill and James C. Katz; *Playwright:* Anton Chekhov, *translation by* Moura Budberg; *Eastman Colour Cinematographer:* Geoffrey Unsworth; *Editor:* Jack Harris; *Production Designer:* Josef Svoboda; *Art Director:* Bill Hutchinson; *Music:* William Walton; *Costumes:* Beatrice Dawson; *Running Time:* 165 minutes.

THE FILM

For this only slightly "opened-up" filming of his National Theatre production of the Chekhov classic, Olivier also took on the important role of Chebutikin, the alcoholic old doctor, which Paul Curran had played in the N.T. stage version. This was to help insure a better box-office reception for the film, as was the casting of Alan Bates in the important part of Colonel Vershinin.

Originally released in Britain in 1970, *Three Sisters* took four years to reach U.S. audiences—and then only under the auspices of the American Film Theatre's subscription series. It contained Olivier's first film directing since 1957's *The Prince and the Showgirl*.

OLIVIER:

"Several theatre productions of mine were made into films, including *The Three Sisters*, based on a beautiful production from the National with a marvellous cast. It was a celebration of the acting, rather than a thoroughly

THREE SISTERS   As Chebutikin

THREE SISTERS   With Derek Jacobi and Joan Plowright

conceived filmic version of the play. That would have been a mammoth task for which we had neither time nor money.

"I had a couple of 'visual' sequences, such as Irina's dream of a better future in Moscow, and the camera seemed to like Chekhov's dialogue and his shifts of mood. I had little to do with the screenplay, which made it not-a-director's film in my book."

CRITICS CIRCLE

"Once again we are faced with a neither-film-nor-play production, but it is, in Moura Budberg's liberal but satisfying translation and under Olivier's semicinematic direction, one at very least to fascinate devotees of the play. The movie-oriented will find this 165-minute-plus-intermission version almost unbearably static, its few filmic concessions involving sporadic close-ups, Irina's dream of life in Moscow and Tusenbach's foreflash of his fatal duel with Solloni. . . . Olivier, whose direction seems to ebb and flow toward granting both cinema and stage their due, has himself a ball with the role of Chebutikin, the old doctor who is all character."

Judith Crist in *New York* magazine

"It remains a most elegant and important production of the Chekhov classic, as well as marking a welcome return to film direction, after a lengthy hiatus, of Laurence Olivier. Despite the lush physical trappings, it's the performances which ultimately attract, and there's a splendid assortment. Olivier, of course, is vastly enjoyable as Chebutikin; Joan Plowright, totally in command as Masha; and Alan Bates, an impressively dosed Vershinin. What cannot be faulted is the overall quality of the production down to the minutest detail, and the rich and lasting contribution it makes in firming a permanent record, for future consultation, discussion and enjoyment of another stage gem."

"Hawk." in *Variety*

"Chekhov becomes the screen better than most playwrights. His plays are cinematic."

Alexander Walker in *The Evening Standard*

"Many of the performances, among them Olivier's as Chebutikin, are to be admired—but [the production] does not belong to the cinema."

Dilys Powell in *London Sunday Times*

NICHOLAS AND ALEXANDRA

1971

A Columbia Pictures release of a Horizon Films production

CAST

Michael Jayston *(Tsar Nicholas II)*; Janet Suzman *(Alexandra)*; Laurence Olivier *(Count Witte)*; Michael Redgrave *(Sazonov)*; Jack Hawkins *(Count Fredericks)*; Harry Andrews *(Grand Duke Nicholas)*; Irene Worth *(Queen Mother Marie Fedorovna)*; Ian Holm *(Yakoviev)*; Tom Baker *(Rasputin)*; Alexander Knox *(American Ambassador Root)*; Roy Dotrice *(General Alexeiev)*; Curt Jurgens *(German Consul Sklarz)*; Alan Webb *(Yurovsky)*; John Wood *(Col. Kobykinsky)*; Timothy West *(Dr. Botkin)*; Roderic Noble *(Alexis)*; Fiona Fullerton *(Anastasia)*; Ania Marson *(Olga)*; Lynne Frederick *(Tatiana)*; Candace Glendenning *(Marie)*; Katherine Schofield *(Tegleva)*; Jean-Claude Drouot *(Gilliard)*; John Hallam *(Nagorny)*; Guy Rolfe *(Dr. Fedorov)*; Eric Porter *(Stolypin)*; Maurice Denham *(Kokovtsov)*; Ralph Truman *(Rodzianko)*; Gordon Gostelow *(Guchkov)*; John McEnery *(Kerensky)*; Michael Bryant *(Lenin)*; Vivian Pickles *(Mme. Krupskaya)*; Brian Cox *(Trotsky)*; James Hazeldine *(Stalin)*; Stephen Greif *(Martov)*; Steven Berkoff *(Pankratov)*; Eric Chapman *(Plekhanov)*; Leon Lissek *(Avadeyev)*; David Giles *(Goloshchekin)*; Martin Potter *(Prince Yussoupov)*; Richard Warwick *(Grand Duke Dmitry)*; Vernon Dobtcheff *(Dr. Lazovert)*; Ralph Neville *(British Ambassador Buchanan)*; Jorge Rigaud *(French Ambassador Paleologue)*; Julian Glover *(Gapon)*; John Shrapnel *(Petya)*; Diana Quick *(Sonya)*; John Forbes Robertson *(Col. Voikov)*; Alan Dalton *(Flautist)*; David Baxter *(Young Bolshevik)*.

CREDITS

Director: Franklin J. Schaffner; *Producer:* Sam Spiegel; *Associate Producer:* Andrew Donnally; *Screenwriter:* James Goldman; *Based on the book by* Robert K. Massie; *Additional Dialogue:* Edward Bond; *Eastman Color Cinematographer:* Freddie Young; *Second-Unit Photographer:* Manuel Berenguer; *Editor:* Ernest Walter; *Production Designer/Second-Unit Director:* John Box; *Art Directors:* Jack Maxsted, Ernest Archer and Gil Parrondo; *Set Decorator:* Vernon Dixon; *Music:* Richard Rodney Bennett; *Special Effects:* Eddie Fowlie; *Costumes:* Yvonne Blake and Antonio Castillo; *Running Time:* 183 minutes.

THE FILM

Robert K. Massie's best-selling biography on the last of the Romanovs—covering the first eighteen years of this century, from the marriage of Tsar Nicholas II and the Empress Alexandra to their execution by an impromptu Bolshevik firing squad—fascinated producer Sam Spiegel, and he bought the screen rights to it in 1968, initially announcing that George Stevens would direct. But pre-production problems and differences of opinion regarding concept and casting saw Stevens depart the project, followed by a succession of distinguished others (An-

NICHOLAS AND
ALEXANDRA As
Count Witte

NICHOLAS AND ALEXANDRA   Michael Jayston and Janet Suzman

thony Harvey, Charles Jarrott, and Joseph L. Mankiewicz) before the assignment finally went to Franklin J.
Schaffner. Ultimately, the critics concurred that *Nicholas and Alexandra* was a handsome and spectacular production, but there was widespread disagreement as to its
value as either entertainment or history.

Olivier's role offers him only a couple of brief but
telling scenes as Count Witte, the strong-minded old
adviser to Tsar Nicholas.

Nicholas and Alexandra garnered Academy Awards for
its art direction, set decoration, and costume design.

OLIVIER:

"Franklin Schaffner, who directed *Nicholas and Alexandra*, was having a bit of a go at Michael Jayston, who
played Nicholas: 'Make him weaker!' So Michael, one of
our finest young actors, tried to make him weaker, but it
just looked like weak acting. Then we noticed his eyes
watered when he acted anger—just something he could
do, lucky man, a marvellous gift. You could hardly do
better than that as a symbol of weakness."

CRITICS CIRCLE

"With his latest production, Sam Spiegel comes
up with a rarity: the intimate epic, a film which unusually and courageously avoids most of the usual trappings
and grants few of the concessions of the genre in
telling the fascinating story of the downfall of the
Romanovs. . . . Michael Jayston makes a most believable Nicholas, while Janet Suzman is also just right in
the perhaps more difficult role of the Empress. There are
notable contributions also from such cast luminaries as
Laurence Olivier, Irene Worth and John McEnery,
merely three names picked from an equally deserving
roster."

"Hawk." in *Variety*

"*Nicholas and Alexandra* is as obsequiously respectful
as if it had been made about living monarchs who might
graciously consent to attend the first performance. In
minor roles, Laurence Olivier, Harry Andrews and Alan
Webb show their professional stature, but Irene Worth,
like Janet Suzman, is forced to show hers mainly by the
regal assurance with which she wears her gowns."

Pauline Kael in *The New Yorker*

"Only Sir Laurence Olivier manages to pierce the pantomime by inventing details of performance that trick us
into feeling for a moment."

Gavin Millar in *The Listener*

"The brilliant gem in the mosaic is Laurence Olivier.
So great was his facial makeup as Count Witte, I had to
take a second look into his sad eyes to recognize this
greatest of all actors. As the president of the council of

185

ministers, he advises the Tsar against war with Germany. Olivier's cultivated voice is his weapon, soft and purring, raised and ringing in pleading his cause."

Wanda Hale in New York *Daily News*

LADY CAROLINE LAMB

1972

A United Artists release of a GEC/Pulsar Productions-Vides Cinematografica-Tomorrow Enterprises coproduction

CAST

Sarah Miles *(Lady Caroline Lamb)*; Jon Finch *(William Lamb)*; Richard Chamberlain *(Lord George Gordon Byron)*; John Mills *(Tory Leader Canning)*; Margaret Leighton *(Lady Melbourne)*; Pamela Brown *(Lady Bessborough)*; Silvia Monti *(Miss Milbanke)*; Ralph Richardson *(The King)*; Laurence Olivier *(The Duke of Wellington)*; Michael Wilding *(Lord Holland)*; Peter Bull *(Government Minister)*; Charles Carson *(Mr. Potter)*; Sonia Dresdel *(Lady Pont)*; Nicholas Field *(St. John)*; Felicity Gibson *(Girl in Blue)*; Robert Harris *(Apothecary)*; Richard Hurndall *(Radical Member)*; Paddy Joyce *(Irish Housekeeper)*; Bernard Kay *(Benson)*; Janet Key *(Miss Fairfax)*; Mario Maranzana *(Coachman)*; Robert Mill *(Wellington's Aide-de-Camp)*; Norman Mitchell *(Restaurant Functionary)*; John Moffatt *(Murray)*; Trevor Peacock *(Agent)*; Maureen Pryor *(Mrs. Buller)*; Fanny Rowe *(Lady Holland)*; Stephen Sheppard *(Buckham)*; Roy Stewart *(Black Pug)*; Ralph Truman *(Admiral)*; Preston Lockwood *(First Partner)*; John Rapley *(Second Partner)*; Ivor Slater *(Chatsworth Domo)*.

CREDITS

Director-Screenwriter: Robert Bolt; *Executive Producer:* Franco Cristaldi; *Producer:* Fernando Ghia; *Associate Producer:* Bernard Williams; *Eastman Colour Cinematographer:* Oswald Morris; *Second-Unit Photographer:* Paddy Carey; *Editor:* Norman Savage; *Art Director:* Carmen Dillon; *Set Decorator:* Vernon Dixon; *Music:* Richard Rodney Bennett; *Costumes:* David Walker; *Assistant Director:* David Tringham; *Running Time:* 123 minutes.

THE FILM

Historical subject matter had long held great interest for playwright/screenwriter Robert Bolt (*A Man for All Seasons, Lawrence of Arabia*). *Lady Caroline Lamb*, which, like *Ryan's Daughter*, was designed as a vehicle for his actress-wife Sarah Miles, marked his own directorial debut. But its artistic liberties with history were roundly aired by the critics, who seemed to take special delight in publishing their erudition, at Bolt's expense.

For Olivier, who employed a hawkish putty nose for his cameo impersonation of the Duke of Wellington, it

LADY CAROLINE LAMB   As The Duke of Wellington

was one more "guest role" in a star-studded costume special, accepted more for the money than any particular artistic satisfaction. The actor omits any mention of *Lady Caroline Lamb* in either of his biographical volumes.

CRITICS CIRCLE

"Anybody out there want to make a movie about Lady Caroline Lamb, that madcap outrageous society matron of the Regency period who had a two-month affair with Lord Byron and made a lifework of it thereafter to earn herself a spot in the histories of both literature and scandal? Shades of all the schmaltz of *That Hamilton Woman*—complete with the Duke of Wellington and George IV and balls and page boys and glittering chandeliers. . . . Robert Bolt has written and directed a movie called *Lady Caroline Lamb* and indeed Sarah Miles bears that name in the course of his penny-dreadful plotting. It's replete with chandeliers and pages and absolutely delicious moments provided by Sir Laurence Olivier as the plain-spoken Wellington; Sir Ralph Richardson as the slow-spoken George, and, in larger portrait, Marg-

LADY CAROLINE LAMB   With Sarah Miles

aret Leighton as Caroline's shrewdly antagonistic
mother-in-law, Lady Melbourne."

Judith Crist in *New York* magazine

"The real pros, John Mills, Laurence Olivier, Ralph
Richardson and Margaret Leighton are more fun to
watch—Olivier simply marvelous as the Duke of Wellington who is given a drinking evening and a night between the sheets with the Lady Caroline."

Wanda Hale in New York *Daily News*

"Laurence Olivier's brief appearance as the Duke of
Wellington is a beautifully witty and rounded characterization that is worth the price of admission in itself."

Philip French in *The Times* of London

"Evidently a little like the historical figure herself,
Lady Caroline Lamb is beautiful but dumb. Sarah Miles
acts with great intensity and Bolt (her husband) has favored her with immense close-ups, not always flattering

LADY CAROLINE LAMB   Sarah Miles and Richard
Chamberlain

187

and indeed often ghoulishly green. But there is always less there than meets the eye or the ear, and she is engaging neither as a romantic convention nor as her true and truly minor historical self. Given a basically unyielding situation, the acting is splendid in a grand and florid way. Laurence Olivier in a false nose is plain spoken and world-weary as the Duke of Wellington."

Charles Champlin in the *Los Angeles Times*

SLEUTH

1972

A 20th Century-Fox release of a Palomar Pictures production

CAST

Laurence Olivier *(Andrew Wyke)*; Michael Caine *(Milo Tindle)*; Alec Cawthorne *(Inspector Doppler)*; Eve Channing *(Marguerite)*; John Matthews *(Sgt. Tarrant)*; Teddy Martin *(Constable Higgins)*; Karen Monfort-Jones *(Teva)*.

CREDITS

Director: Joseph L. Mankiewicz; *Executive Producer:* Edgar J. Scherick; *Producer:* Morton Gottlieb; *Associate Producer:* David Misslemas; *Screenwriter:* Anthony Shaffer, *based on his stage play; Deluxe Color Cinematographer:* Oswald Morris; *Editor:* Richard Marden; *Production Designer:* Ken Adam; *Art Director:* Peter Lamont; *Set Decorator:* John Jarvis; *Music:* John Addison; *Costumes:* John Furniss; *Sound:* John Mitchell; *Assistant Director:* Kip Gowans; Running Time: 139 minutes.

THE FILM

With its small cast and elaborate, prop-cluttered set, Anthony Shaffer's brilliantly tricky, Tony-winning mystery thriller achieved hit status on both London and New York stages in 1970, continuing to draw audiences long after the release of its excellent 1972 film version. In this, the last movie to be directed by Joseph L. Mankiewicz, Laurence Olivier and Michael Caine play an ingenious game of cat and mouse, now ridiculous, then deadly. Olivier portrays a popular, blue-blooded, mystery novelist named Andrew Wyke, who invites to his English country estate a nouveau-riche young beauty shop owner, Milo Tindle (Caine), whom Andrew knows to be romantically involved with his wife, Marguerite. Subsequently, the ill-matched rivals become conspirators in an unlikely theft scheme. Or so Milo believes. What he fails to realize is how skilled his cunning opponent is as a master player of games. Wyke soon finds Tindle his equal

188

SLEUTH   As Andrew Wyke

in game-playing as they participate in a fascinating succession of moves and countermoves in a classic test of one-upmanship that culminates in a multi-twist finale that cannot fairly be revealed here.

Both Caine and Olivier garnered Oscar nominations for *Sleuth*, but the winner was Marlon Brando for *The Godfather*. However, for this performance, Olivier was named 1972's Best Actor by the New York Film Critics.

SLEUTH   With Michael Caine

SLEUTH   With Michael Caine

SLEUTH   With Alec Cawthorne

189

SLEUTH With Michael Caine

OLIVIER:

"Time, strength and the opportunity to do a full-length film part arrived with *Sleuth*—an amusing script by Anthony Shaffer, from his stage play. The making of *Sleuth* was, for me, tinged with nostalgia and hope for the future. The part was big and good enough to test my powers to amuse on a sustained level. Michael Caine was an absolute delight in *Sleuth* (except he didn't like rehearsing—I went through my lines with the continuity girl). The camera loves him just as much as we who work with him do. He has the true personality of a star, and in *Sleuth*—in particular the scene on the staircase—he showed deep and difficult emotion."

CRITICS CIRCLE

"*Sleuth* is not only a whodunit but a whodunwhat, none of which probably would be tolerable for a minute in a production less wittily acted, directed and set. . . . To witness Olivier at work is to behold a one-man revue of theatrical excesses—all marvelous. He minces. He bellows. He does exotic things with his tongue. He leaps around as if possessed by the spirit of Errol Flynn in Flynn's early Warner Brothers days. Olivier's Andrew is hugely funny and extravagant, and Caine's low-born beautician-on-the-make is a perfectly unstable mixture of fury and foolishness. Equally memo-

rable are the members of the supporting cast—Karen Monfort-Jones as Olivier's mistress, and Alec Cawthorne as a police inspector who takes a dim view of Andrew's fictional sleuth, St. John Lord Merridewe."

Vincent Canby in *The New York Times*

"This is a fastidious, acrobatically cunning and invigoratingly well-acted thriller. It gently parodies the puzzles of what has come to be known as the golden age of detective fiction at the same time that it cannily manipulates them. . . . Of late, Olivier's movie activity has been confined to playing a variety of cameos in top-heavy histories like *Nicholas and Alexandra*. It is good to see him again in a role of size, if not of substance, and he makes wonderful support of it. His face is a study in split-second metamorphoses. He does so much with it so fast that sometimes, in a close-up, he gives the impression of a multiple exposure. Caine seems not in the least daunted by acting with a legend incarnate. To say that he matches Olivier in every way is to pay him the highest of compliments."

Jay Cocks in *Time* magazine

"*Sleuth* is consummate artistry, a suspense teaser and a chuckle evoker with every line of verbal duelling between

190

an English snob and an Italian of emigrant parents who is trying hard to be an English snob. . . . We get further proof that Olivier is the greatest actor of our lifetime. And proof that Michael Caine, in an excellent role under Mankiewicz's guidance, can rise to the proffered challenge."

Wanda Hale in New York *Daily News*

"Joseph L. Mankiewicz's film version of *Sleuth* is terrific. Anthony Shaffer's topnotch screenplay of his legit hit provides Laurence Olivier and especially Michael Caine with their best roles in years. Hailed as a major suspenser by playgoers and legit critics, the story operates on many intellectual and physical levels to provide a broader mixture of terror, sophistication and sardonic humor."

"Murf." in *Variety*

"Wyke is not only wealthy, urbane, a connoisseur of mechanical toys and a master of the sardonic epigram; he also provides Laurence Olivier with the best comedy role of his film career."

Felix Barker in *The London Evening News*

THE REHEARSAL

1974

Never Released

CAST

Melina Mercouri, Laurence Olivier, Maximilian Schell, Arthur Miller, Lillian Hellman.

CREDITS

Director-Screenwriter: Jules Dassin; *Producers:* Jules Dassin and Melina Mercouri; *Music:* Mikis Theodorakis; *Running Time:* 90 minutes.

THE FILM

A professed labor of love for director Jules Dassin and his actress-wife, Melina Mercouri—before she left acting to become Greece's Minister of Culture—this little-known (if not altogether forgotten) motion picture is a semidocumentary that Dassin described to *New York Times* screen-news editor A.H. Weiler as a dramatization and re-creation of the student-worker uprising in Athens in November 1973, against the ruling military junta that resulted in a number of deaths and hundreds of wounded. With Mercouri featured, *The Rehearsal* was said by Dassin to have had "the volunteer services of some famous people and a group of about sixty local actors, Greek-American students and technicians."

Filmed in London, Olivier read a poem by the Greek Nobel Laureate, George Seferis, while Maximilian Schell, Arthur Miller, and Lillian Hellman were photographed in similar readings elsewhere. As Dassin told Weiler in April of 1974, "I've lived and worked there for years. I feel I'm part of them and the cause they're fighting for." He further expressed his intention of having the feature ready for a showing at that year's Cannes Festival in May. But the junta fell, and with it the film's *raison d'etre*.

In the Olivier motion picture canon, *The Rehearsal* has become so obscure that it isn't even mentioned in Anthony Holden's otherwise comprehensive 1988 biography of the actor.

THE REHEARSAL

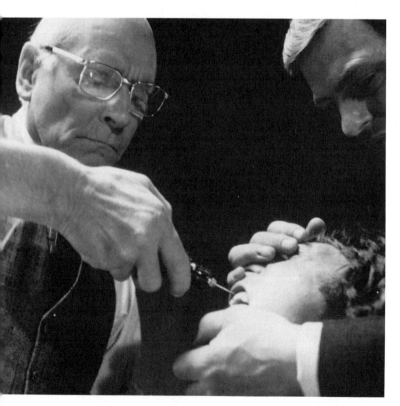

MARATHON MAN   As Dr. Christian Szell

MARATHON MAN   With Dustin Hoffman and Richard Bright

MARATHON MAN

1976

A *Paramount Picture*

CAST

Dustin Hoffman (*Babe Levy*); Laurence Olivier (*Dr. Christian Szell*); Roy Scheider (*Doc Levy*); William Devane (*Janeway*); Marthe Keller (*Elsa*); Fritz Weaver (*Prof. Biesenthal*); Richard Bright (*Karl*); Marc Lawrence (*Erhard*); Allen Joseph (*Babe's Father*); Tito Goya (*Melendez*); Ben Dova (*Szell's Brother*); Lou Gilbert (*Rosenbaum*); Jacques Marin (*LeClerc*); James Wing Woo (*Chen*); Nicole Deslauriers (*Nicole*); Lotta Andor-Palfi (*Old Lady on 47th Street*); Lionel Pina, Church, Tricoche, Jaime Tirelli, and Wilfredo Hernandez (*Street Gang*); Harry Goz, Michael Vale, Fred Stuthman, and Lee Steele (*Jewelry Salesmen*); William Martel (*Bank Guard*); Glenn Robards and Ric Carrott (*Plainclothesmen*); Alma Beltran (*Laundress*); Daniel Nuñez, Tona Peña, and Chuy Franco (*Guards in Uruguay*); Billy Kearns and Sally Wilson (*Tourist Couple*); Tom Ellis (*TV Announcer*); Bryant Fraser (*Young Photographer*); George Dega (*Hotel Valet*); Gene Bori (*French Doctor*); Annette Claudier (*Nurse*); Roger Etienne (*Headwaiter*); Ray Serra (*Truck Driver*); John Garson, Charlott Thyssen, and Estelle Omens (*Bystanders*); Madge Kennedy (*Lady in Bank*); Jeff Palladini (*Babe as a Boy*); Scott Price (*Doc as a Boy*).

CREDITS

Director: John Schlesinger; *Producers:* Robert Evans and Sidney Beckerman; *Associate Producer:* George Justin; *Screenwriter:* William Goldman, *based on his novel; Metrocolor Cinematographer:* Conrad Hall; *Special Photography:* Garrett Brown; *Editor:* Jim Clark; *Production Designer:* Richard MacDonald; *Art Director:* Jack De Shields; *Set Decorator:* George Gaines; *Music:* Michael Small; *Special Effects:* Richard E. Johnson and Charles Spurgeon; *Costumes:* Robert De Mora; *Sound:* David Ronne; *Assistant Directors:* Howard W. Koch, Jr., Burtt Harris, and William Saint John; *Running Time:* 125 minutes.

THE FILM

Of his many Academy Award-nominated film performances, *Marathan Man* offered Laurence Olivier his first entry in the category of Best *Supporting* Actor, despite the size of his meaty role. *Marathan Man* reflected the faith its director, John Schlesinger, had in the distinguished actor, despite the still-frail condition caused by his serious recent illness. At the movie's rehearsal stage, Olivier was cruelly challenged by its high-priced star, Dustin Hoffman, to an exhausting bout of ad-lib improvisation, which screenwriter William Goldman has attributed to "Hoffman's need to put himself on at least an equal footing with this sick old man."

Unlike anything Olivier previously portrayed on the screen, *Marathan Man* cast him as a sadistic Nazi named Szell, whose concentration-camp experiments

MARATHON MAN   With Dustin Hoffman

and the diamonds obtained from his victims have made him the wealthiest of hunted war criminals. What brings Szell to New York City from the safety of his Uruguayan hideout is the demise of his brother—keeper of those gems. There, fate puts him up against Babe Levy (Hoffman), a student and a marathon contender, whose older brother Doc (Roy Scheider) provides the connection that thrusts Babe into dangerous encounters with Szell. Audiences who have seen this well-fashioned thriller are not likely to forget, in particular, one harrowing scene in which Babe is subjected to dental torture by Szell, whose repeated demand to know "Is it safe?" only serves to bewilder his hapless captor.

OLIVIER:

"After getting home, when I had left my bed and begun going out and taking the air, some encouraging hints of professional activity appeared. By the end of May, John Schlesinger was telephoning to talk about *Marathon Man*. To a mere man and a career man at that, there is nothing so revivifying as the bewitching appearance of opportunity, and I have always regarded John as my restorer of life; through him I felt that life, real life, was starting again and I seemed to breathe nothing but oxygen. This new breath carried me through some twenty films from 1975 to 1981."

CRITICS CIRCLE

"Lord Olivier, one of the great ornaments of the English-speaking theater and cinema, helps to make John Schlesinger's *Marathon Man* a film that you won't want to miss, given a strong stomach for bloodshed and graphic torture that includes dental interference of an especially unpleasant sort. . . . In addition to Lord Olivier's superb performance, *Marathon Man* has several other superior things going for it: Dustin Hoffman as a moody, guilt-ridden, upper-West Side New Yorker, a haunted innocent obsessed with running, pursued by an unknown evil; Roy Scheider and William Devane as members of some sort of super-super Central Intelligence Agency, and the direction of Mr. Schlesinger, who has made a most elegant, bizarre, rococo melodrama out of material that, when you think about it, makes hardly any sense at all."

Vincent Canby in *The New York Times*

"The performing and direction are so superb, the suspense and mood so intense, that few may bother to ponder what the story is all about. The murky, hardly credible plot, scripted by William Goldman from his novel, falls into the category of violent secret-agent machinations. The terror grows particularly horrendous because it engulfs an innocent in familiar surroundings. You may not believe the suppositions, but the suspense nails you to the seat. . . . Lord Laurence Olivier, a master at turning every part he does into a unique experience, brings remarkable individuality to the malevolent role of the conniving Nazi villain Szell."

William Wolf in *Cue* magazine

193

"Olivier gives an A-budget version of what George Zucco did in hundreds of formula programmers."

"Murf." in *Variety*

"Only Olivier, trapped in the role of the proverbially cartoonish Nazi, washes out of the film—and he's more than compensated for by Hoffman, who's simply extraordinary. If only out of self-preservation, Hoffman seems to have dug deeper into himself than he has since he worked with Schlesinger previously in *Midnight Cowboy:* his Babe fairly well bursts with grief and panic."

Frank Rich in *New York Post*

"A psychological thriller of excruciating intensity, with Dustin Hoffman, as a student enmeshed in his brother's double-agent activities, and Laurence Olivier as the White Angel of Auschwitz, unforgettable."

Judith Crist in *TV Guide*

"The most satisfying element is the work of Olivier, one of the few who turn acting into one of the great humane professions of Western civilization. It's wonderful to see how Olivier invests everything he does, no matter how small a role, with the same care, preparation and resourcefulness that he gives to *Othello* or *Long Day's Journey into Night.* Olivier shows us that a great actor is the sculptor of his self, turning his body into a sign, a symbol, and a force that jolts us into a higher consciousness."

Newsweek

THE SEVEN-PER-CENT SOLUTION

1976

A Universal Picture

CAST

Nicol Williamson *(Sherlock Holmes)*; Alan Arkin *(Sigmund Freud)*; Robert Duvall *(Dr. Watson)*; Vanessa Redgrave *(Lola Deveraux)*; Lau-

MARATHON MAN   With Dustin Hoffman

rence Olivier *(Prof. Moriarty)*; Joel Grey *(Lowenstein)*; Samantha Eggar *(Mary Watson)*; Jeremy Kemp *(Baron von Leinsdorf)*; Charles Gray *(Mycroft Holmes)*; Georgia Brown *(Mrs. Freud)*; Regine *(Madame)*; Anna Quayle *(Freda)*; Jill Townsend *(Mrs. Holmes)*; John Bird *(Berger)*; Alison Leggatt *(Mrs. Hudson)*; Frederick Jaeger *(Marker)*; Erik Chitty *(Butler)*; Jack May *(Dr. Schultz)*; Gertan Klauber *(Pasha)*; Leon Greene *(Squire Holmes)*; Michael Blagdon *(Young Holmes)*; Ashley House *(Young Freud)*; Sheila Shand Gibbs *(Nun)*; Erich Padalewsky *(Station Master)*; John Hill *(Train Engineer)*.

CREDITS

Producer-Director: Herbert Ross; *Executive Producers:* Arlene Sellers and Alex Winitsky; *Associate Producer:* Stanley O'Toole; *Production Associate:* Howard Jeffrey; *Screenwriter:* Nicholas Meyer; *Based on his novel derived from characters created by* Arthur Conan Doyle; *Technicolor Cinematographer:* Oswald Morris; *Second-Unit Photographer:* Alex Thomson; *Editors:* William Reynolds and Chris Barnes; *Production Designer:* Ken Adam; *Art Director:* Peter Lamont; *Set Decorator:* Peter James; *Music:* John Addison; *Song:* "The Madame's Song" *by* Stephen Sondheim, *sung by* Regine; *Sound:* Cyril Swern; *Costumes:* Alan Barrett; *Running Time:* 113 minutes.

THE FILM

Following a bout with life-threatening illness, Olivier returned to take on yet another small supporting role—as the master criminal Prof. Moriarty, a sometime nemesis of the legendary detective Sherlock Holmes—in Nicholas Meyer's own adaptation of his best-selling novel. In this non-traditional Holmes yarn, Nicol Williamson portrays a cocaine-addicted Sherlock, who's aided by none other than Sigmund Freud (impersonated by Alan Arkin) in solving the case of a kidnapped actress (Vanessa Redgrave).

CRITICS CIRCLE

"It's an adventure tale told with a deliciously light tongue-in-cheekiness. The plotting is so ingenious, so perfectly in keeping with the Holmes we all know and love, that it's almost as if a whole new Conan Doyle manuscript has suddenly turned up in a trunk somewhere. And the cast is flawless—as one might expect just looking at the names. But they have been asked by director Herbert Ross to perform what is probably the most difficult feat in the actor's handbook, to walk the tightwire line between melodramatics and stylized comedy. (The very thing that Billy Wilder failed to bring off in *The Private Life of Sherlock Holmes* by playing everything too straight, and that undermined Gene Wilder's *The Adventure of Sherlock Holmes' Smarter Brother* because he played it too broadly.) As that arch-villain Moriarty, Olivier is correctly ambiguous."

Arthur Knight in *The Hollywood Reporter*

"Laurence Olivier is marvelous as Professor Moriarty,

THE SEVEN-PER-CENT SOLUTION   As Professor Moriarty

THE SEVEN-PER-CENT SOLUTION

an extremely tentative, timid old fellow to be such a tycoon of crime."

Vincent Canby in *The New York Times*

195

THE SEVEN-PER-CENT SOLUTION   Robert Duvall, Nicol Williamson, and Alan Arkin

"The actors seem to be having an actor's holiday. And Olivier, who couldn't rise above the material in *Marathon Man*, is in tremendous high form. His Moriarty, a prissy, complaining old pedagogue who feels persecuted by Holmes, is performed with the covert wit that is his specialty. It's not a big part, but this Moriarty—his face expressing injury to the verge of tears—is amusingly dislikable, a Dickensian monster."

Pauline Kael in *The New Yorker*

"His Professor Moriarty is the most memorable feature in this curious combination of fact and fictitious fiction. As Holmes' nemesis Moriarty, Olivier gives a performance of majestically comic and alarming proportions."

Margaret Hinxman in *London Daily Mail*

A BRIDGE TOO FAR

1977

A United Artists Picture

CAST

Dirk Bogarde (*Lt. Gen. Frederick Browning*); James Caan (*Staff Sgt. Eddie Dohun*); Michael Caine (*Lt. Col. J.O.E. Vandeleur*); Sean Connery (*Maj. Gen. Robert Urquhart*); Edward Fox (*Lt. Gen. Brian Horrocks*); Elliott Gould (*Col. Bobby Stout*); Gene Hackman (*Maj. Gen. Stanislaw Sosabowski*); Anthony Hopkins (*Lt. Col. John Frost*); Hardy Kruger (*Maj. Gen. Ludwig*); Laurence Olivier (*Dr. Spaander*); Ryan O'Neal (*Brig. Gen. James M. Gavin*); Robert Redford (*Maj. Julian Cook*); Maximilian Schell (*Lt. Gen. Wilhelm Bittrich*); Liv Ullmann (*Kate ter Horst*); Arthur Hill (*Tough Colonel*); Wolfgang Preiss (*Field Marshal Gerd von Rundstedt*); Siem Vroom (*Underground Leader*); Marlies Van Alcmaer (*His Wife*); Eric Van't Wout (*Their Son*); Mary Smithuysen (*Old Dutch Lady*); Hans Croiset (*Hans, Her Son*); Nicholas Campbell (*Capt. Glass*); Christopher Good (*Maj. Carlyle*); Keith Drinkel (*Lt. Cornish*); Peter Faber (*Capt. Harry Bestebreurtje*); Hans von Borsody (*Gen. Blumentritt*); Josephine Peeper (*Cafe Waitress*); Paul Maxwell (*Maj. Gen. Maxwell Taylor*); Walter Kohut (*Field Marshal Model*); Hartmut Becker (*German Sentry*); Frank Grimes (*Maj. Fuller*); Jeremy Kemp (*RAF Briefing Officer*); Donald Pickering (*Lt. Col. Mackenzie*); Donald Douglas (*Brig. Lathbury*); Peter Settelen (*Lt. Cole*); Stephen Moore (*Maj. Steele*); Michael Byrne (*Lt. Col. Giles Vandeleur*); Paul Copley (*Pvt. Wicks*); Gerald Sim (*Col. Sims*); Harry Ditson (*U.S. Private*); Erik Chitty (*Organist*); Brian Hawksley (*Vicar*); Colin Farrell (*Corp. Hancock*); Norman Gregory (*Pvt. Morgan*); Alun Armstrong (*Corp. Davies*); Anthony Milner (*Pvt. Dodds*); Barry McCarthy (*Pvt. Clark*); Ben Cross (*Trooper Binns*); Denholm Elliott (*RAF Met. Officer*); John Ratzenberger (*U.S. Lieutenant*); John Stride (*Grenadier Guards Major*).

CREDITS

Director: Richard Attenborough; *Producers:* Joseph E. Levine and Richard P. Levine; *Coproducer:* Michael Stanley-Evans; *Associate Pro-*

A BRIDGE TOO FAR   As Dr. Spaander

A BRIDGE TOO FAR   With Liv Ullmann and players

ducer: John Palmer; *Second-Unit Director:* Sidney Hayers; *Screen-writer:* William Goldman; *Based on the book by* Cornelius Ryan; *Panavision-Technicolor Cinematographer:* Geoffrey Unsworth; *Second-Unit Photographer:* Harry Waxman; *Aerial Photographer:* Robin Browne; *Editor:* Antony Gibbs; *Production Designer:* Terence Marsh; *Art Directors:* Roy Stannard, Stuart Craig and Alan Tomkins; *Set Decorator:* Peter Howitt; *Music:* John Addison; *Costumes:* Anthony Mendleson; *Special Effects:* Wally Veevers and John Richardson; *Production Consultant:* Gabriel Katzka; *Technical Adviser:* Kathryn Morgan Ryan; *Running Time:* 175 minutes.

THE FILM

The extravagant Joseph E. Levine harbored every hope that *A Bridge Too Far*—based on Cornelius Ryan's best-selling book about "Operation Market-Garden," the disastrous 1944 military maneuver in which an airdrop was botched by Allied troops behind German lines in Holland—would be his penultimate motion picture. Expensive and studded with names of popular male stars (Liv Ullmann was the sole distaff exception), this nearly-three-hour World War II epic was quite overwhelmed by its technical logistics and its sprawling overproduction. It had been hoped to equal the greatness of producer Darryl F. Zanuck's crowning achievement, *The Longest Day.* It didn't.

For Laurence Olivier, it offered yet another in his long stream of foreign-accented cameos—this time as a courageous Dutch doctor who attended the injured and the dying in a makeshift hospital in the luxurious home of a benevolent local woman (Ullmann).

A BRIDGE TOO FAR   With Liv Ullmann

197

"The movie is massive, shapeless, often unexpectedly moving, confusing, sad, vivid and very, very long. . . . Unlike *The Longest Day*, which recalled one of the Allies' most stunning victories, *A Bridge Too Far* recalls one of their most tragic and costly defeats. If one doesn't quite grasp the import of this film, it's because, after a couple of hours, scenes of tanks, buildings and bridges being blown up, of shells exploding, of soldiers being mutilated and of their carnage are all pretty much alike, no matter who ultimately wins the day. Missing is some point of view more particular (and more historical) than the idea that war is hell.

"Anthony Hopkins is fine as the British officer assigned to capture the bridge at Arnhem. James Caan stars in a furiously effective episode about a sergeant who forces a doctor, at gunpoint, to operate on his wounded captain. Laurence Olivier and Liv Ullmann give recognizable emotions to Dutch civilians caught in the crossfire, and Edward Fox is quietly but brilliantly funny as a gung-ho British officer."

Vincent Canby in *The New York Times*

"*A Bridge Too Far* is a reel too long. For another thing, it is both confused and historically gap-toothed, despite its legion of military and special advisers. Laurence Olivier and Liv Ullmann are given parts they could accomplish on their heads."

Derek Malcolm in *The Guardian*

THE GENTLEMAN TRAMP

1978

A Marvin Films release of a Tinc Productions Corp. picture

CREDITS

Director-Writer-Editor: Richard Patterson; *Producer:* Bert Schneider; *Associate Producer:* Artie Ross; *Music:* Charles Chaplin; *Narrators:* Walter Matthau, Laurence Olivier, and Jack Lemmon; *Running Time:* 80 minutes.

THE FILM

An authorized profile of comedian Charlie Chaplin (1889–1977), this film was accompanied by the informa-

tion that "every frame, from rough cut to final version, has been checked and approved personally by Charles Chaplin." Including newsreel footage, as well as clips from his movies, the documentary also contained supplementary material by cinematographer Nestor Almendros.

"Like all authorized biographies, it's somewhat too pious for its own good. There's an attempt to recapitulate highlights of Chaplin's life—both good times and bad—with newsreel footage, as well as with still photographs, some of which are accompanied by lofty quotations from Chaplin's book, *My Autobiography*. The quotations, read by Laurence Olivier, come off worse on film than they do on the printed page."

Vincent Canby in *The New York Times*

"This must-see movie has captured the quintessence of the artist and his art. It provides invaluable highlights from 17 Chaplin films, and puts them into the context of his life and times."

Judith Crist

THE GENTLEMAN TRAMP

"The life, loves and hard times of actor/director/comic genius Charlie Chaplin are explored in *The Gentleman Tramp*, an uneven and ultimately disappointing documentary. Most of the time it does more to confuse than enlighten. Perhaps the reason for the superficial treatment of Chaplin's life is because Chaplin himself approved the docu shortly before he died. . . . What made [it] worth watching were some priceless excerpts from Chaplin classics. But even this enjoyment is spoiled by sloppy production. As the clips are shown, Laurence Olivier and Jack Lemmon read from books by Chaplin and his son. But the reading adds nothing to the clips and serves as an unnecessary distraction."

"Kev." in *Variety*

THE BETSY

1978

An Allied Artists Release of a Harold Robbins International/Allied Artists production

CAST

Laurence Olivier *(Loren Hardeman, Sr., "Number One")*; Robert Duvall *(Loren Hardeman III)*; Katharine Ross *(Sally Hardeman)*; Tommy Lee Jones *(Angelo Perino)*; Jane Alexander *(Alicia Hardeman)*;

THE BETSY   With Paul Rudd

THE BETSY   With Katharine Ross

199

THE BETSY   As the elderly Loren Hardeman, Sr.

THE BETSY With
Tommy Lee Jones

Lesley-Anne Down (*Lady Roberta Ayres*); Joseph Wiseman (*Jake Weinstein*); Kathleen Beller (*Betsy Hardeman*); Edward Herrmann (*Dan Weyman*); Paul Rudd (*Loren Hardeman, Jr.*); Roy Poole (*John Duncan*); Richard Venture (*Mark Sampson*); Titos Vandis (*Angelo Luigi Perino*); Clifford David (*Joe Warren*); Inga Swenson (*Mrs. Craddock*); Whitney Blake (*Elizabeth Hardeman*); Carol Williard (*Roxanne*); Read Morgan (*Donald*); Charlie Fields (*Loren III, as a Boy*); Robert Phalen (*Man*); Nick Czmyr (*Bellhop*); Norman Palmer, Fred Carney, Maury Cooper, and Russell Porter (*Board Members*); Teri Ralston (*Hotel Clerk*); Warney H. Ruhl (*Security Guard*); Patrick J. Monks (*Helicopter Pilot*); William Roerick (*Secretary of Commerce*); William B. Cain (*Butler*); Edward C. Higgins (*Chauffeur*); Mary Petrie (*Nurse*); H. August Kuehl (*Male Guest*); Robert Hawkins (*Retired Man*); Sadie Hawkins (*Retired Woman*); Anthony Steere (*Car Driver*).

CREDITS

Director: Daniel Petrie; *Executive Producer*: Emanuel L. Wolf; *Producer*: Robert R. Weston; *Associate Producer*: Jack Grossberg; *Screenwriters*: Walter Bernstein and William Bast; *Based on the novel by* Harold Robbins; *Technicolor Cinematographer*: Mario Tosi; *Editor*: Rita Roland; *Production Designer*: Herman A. Blumenthal; *Set Decorators*: James Payne and Sal Blydenburgh; *Music*: John Barry; *Costumes*: Dorothy Jeakins, Orpha Barry, and Darryl Athone; *Special Effects*: Greg Auer; *Running Time*: 125 minutes.

THE FILM

Harold Robbins's steamy best-seller of love, lust and corporate intrigue within several generations of an auto-rich Midwestern family is the sort of multicharacter, time-spanning narrative that has become familiar fodder in more recent years to those who follow TV miniseries (frequently deriving from the works of authors like Judith Krantz and Jackie Collins). As a movie, *The Betsy* has all the attributes of these potboilers, plus occasional snatches of nudity and softcore sex. Its cast is studded with familiar names, many of whose roles are too skimpy for a proper showcase of talent. But among those who come off best are the three male leads—Tommy Lee Jones, Robert Duvall, and Laurence Olivier. At seventy, Olivier not only does an impressive job of portraying a still-feisty old patriarch, but is also able to convince audiences that he is a man in his forties in flashback scenes. However, his efforts at a Midwestern accent are so far-ranging that one is always aware that this actor is using vocal tones foreign to his natural speech patterns. With top billing and many scenes—including the chance at sexy romantic segments—the answer to why Sir Laurence Olivier would accept a role that some would consider beneath his talents and distinguished career is obvious; not only did he need the money to help support his second family, but he has admitted to relishing both the stretch and the challenge.

OLIVIER:

"You can say what you like about the film, but it was very enjoyable to do. It was a filthily vulgar part, the most

200

awful character I've ever played in my life, and I enjoyed it highly. It took four hours for makeup to make me look ninety; it only took two hours for the forty part of it."

CRITICS CIRCLE

"Through a series of flashbacks, Olivier ages from 40 to 90. Complete with midwest accent, he's on target, maybe too much so. Ditto for Robert Duvall, as his grandson and current president of the auto company, Jane Alexander as Duvall's wife and Katharine Ross as Olivier's daughter-in-law and lover. Tommy Lee Jones as a daredevil race driver hired by Olivier to build the dream car plays his role with a mixture of edginess and offhandedness—a combination of Burt Reynolds and Harvey Keitel. His style—it's got a sense of humor and a campy quality to it—seems more to the point. It's almost trashy."

"Hege." in *Variety*

"The direction by Daniel Petrie and the screenplay by Walter Bernstein and William Bast produce a structure of action and reminiscence that resembles a grotesque parody of *Godfather II*. Laurence Olivier as crusty old Loren Hardeman, Sr., lustful auto tycoon extraordinary, does most of the reminiscing as he relives in flashback such lurid high points of his existence as his bedding down of a new maid on the night of his son's wedding. (The spectacle of Sir Laurence, the lion of acting, cavorting on the screen like an old goat is a bit of breathtaking sacrilege that will undoubtedly sell tickets.)"

Andrew Sarris in *The Village Voice*

"Laurence Olivier, who plays the superabundantly sexed patriarch of an automobile dynasty, stands out with startling boldness, and one begins to perceive the secret of his greatness: Laurence Olivier dares to be foolish. He doesn't protect himself; he just goes right out there and takes the risks. In *The Betsy*, he keeps on acting after everyone else has given up. They all wilt and die, and there he is, supplying energy to his scenes, working up a Scottish-Midwestern accent, giving tautness to his flabby lines. He must be doing it for himself—for the sheer love of testing himself as an actor. The lines destroy the other performers; you see the sheepish faces and the dead fall of the words. How does Olivier manage to speak so that we absorb the sense without having the idiot dialogue ring in our ears? Partly by distracting us with his accent . . . and partly by using the big, harsh voice he has developed in recent years, as if in defiance of natural processes, to blast through the film's largo style."

Pauline Kael in *The New Yorker*

"Laurence Olivier, as the auto magnate, spends the entire picture searching for the proper American accent and trying to master a Midwestern twang. At times, he sounds like a cross between Walter Brennan and Billy Carter. And yet he also insists upon pronouncing the word "car" like a Bostonian. What makes this movie especially painful is that it exposes this brilliant actor at his very worst in a performance totally out of control."

Kathleen Carroll in *New York Daily News*

"God bless Laurence Olivier. And God only knows what the incomparable actor of the Western world is doing in a piece of hilarious idiocy like *The Betsy*. Taking away a zillion dollars, one hopes. This is no cameo role; the great septuagenarian is playing the lead. And lead he does, in the greatest put-on performance you've ever seen. Having plumbed the depths of Shakespeare and Chekhov, Olivier has little trouble proving the nooks and crannies of Harold Robbins, from whose best seller this farrago was farragoed."

Jack Kroll in *Newsweek*

THE BOYS FROM BRAZIL

1978

*A 20th Century-Fox release of a
Producer Circle production*

CAST

Gregory Peck (*Dr. Josef Mengele*); Laurence Olivier (*Ezra Lieberman*); James Mason (*Eduard Seibert*); Lilli Palmer (*Esther Lieberman*); Uta Hagen (*Frieda Maloney*); Steven Guttenberg (*Barry Kohler*); Denholm Elliott (*Sidney Beynon*); Rosemary Harris (*Mrs. Doring*); John Dehner (*Henry Wheelock*); John Rubinstein (*David Bennett*); Anne Meara (*Mrs. Curry*); Jeremy Black (*Jack Curry/Simon Harrington/Erich Doring/Bobby Wheelock*); Bruno Ganz (*Prof. Bruckner*); Walter Gotell (*Mundt*); David Hurst (*Strasser*); Wolfgang Preiss (*Lofquist*); Michael Gough (*Mr. Harrington*); Joachim Hansen (*Fassler*); Guy Dumont (*Hessen*); Carl Duering (*Trausteiner*); Linda Hayden (*Nancy*); Richard Marner (*Doring*); Georg Marischka (*Gunther*); Gunter Meisner (*Farnbach*); Prunella Scales (*Mrs. Harrington*); Paul Faustino Saldanha (*Ismael*); Jurgen Anderson (*Kleist*); Mervyn Nelson (*Stroop*); David Brandon (*Schmidt*); Monica Gearson (*Gertrud*); Wolf Kahler (*Schwimmer*); Gerti Gordon (*Berthe*); Guida De Carlo (*Blonde Woman*).

THE BOYS FROM BRAZIL   As Ezra Lieberman

THE BOYS FROM BRAZIL   With Gregory Peck

CREDITS

Director: Franklin J. Schaffner; *Executive Producer:* Robert Fryer; *Producers:* Martin Richards and Stanley O'Toole; *Screenwriter:* Heywood Gould; *Based on the novel by* Ira Levin; *Panavision-DeLuxe Color Cinematographer:* Henri Decaë; *Editor:* Robert Swink; *Production Designer:* Gil Parrondo; *Art Directors:* Peter Lamont and Steve Hendrickson; *Set Decorator:* Vernon Dixon; *Music:* Jerry Goldsmith; *Song:* "We're Home Again" *by* Jerry Goldsmith and Hal Shaper, *performed by* Elaine Paige; *Costumes:* Anthony Mendleson; *Special Effects:* Roy Whybrow; *Technical Adviser:* Dr. Derek Bromhall; *Running Time:* 123 minutes.

THE FILM

Ira Levin's best-seller was a surefire bet for the screen, with its theme of cloning babies who will grow up into Hitlers, while pitting a Viennese-Jewish Nazi hunter against the ruthless war criminal Josef Mengele (formerly the notorious Auschwitz "Angel of Death"), who's involved in genetic experiments from his Brazilian jungle retreat.

The film offered Olivier, as Ezra Lieberman (patterned after the real-life Simon Wiesenthal), a sharp contrast to the sadistic Nazi from South America that he had portrayed two years earlier in *Marathon Man*—and equally radical a change of traditional character for Gregory Peck, cast as Mengele (who, if still alive, has yet to surface).

Olivier, who received his eleventh Academy Award nomination for this role, tied with *Coming Home*'s Jon Voight (who took home the Oscar) for the National Board of Review's 1978 Best Actor citation.

CRITICS CIRCLE

"With two excellent antagonists in Gregory Peck and Lord Laurence Olivier, *The Boys from Brazil* presents a gripping, suspenseful drama for nearly all of its two hours—then lets go at the end and falls into a heap. In a fine shift from his usual roles, Peck plays the evil Josef Mengele, a real-life character who murdered thousands of Jews, including many children, carrying out bizarre genetic experiments at Auschwitz in Poland. Olivier, slipping completely into the role of an elderly Jewish gentleman, is the Nazi hunter who brings him to bay- . . . . What they are and whence they came are plausibly developed in Haywood Gould's script, and director Franklin J. Schaffner builds the threatening menace well. Eventually, Peck and Olivier come face to face, however, in a bloody sequence that turns silly as Peck keeps pouring bullets into the old man, who still manages to carry on a conversation. Worse still, though, is the last scene in the hospital, where Olivier totally loses his determined concerns, and Schaffner and Gould lose the whole point of Levin's book."

"Har." in *Variety*

THE BOYS FROM BRAZIL   With Lilli Palmer

THE BOYS FROM BRAZIL   With Anne Meara and Jeremy Black

"The movie's meat is the bravura acting of Laurence Olivier, Gregory Peck and James Mason. Fresh from a thoughtful, underrated portrayal of Douglas MacArthur, Peck throws his characteristic decorum to the dogs and plays Mengele as a monstrous, ranting genius of moral idiocy. Olivier's ironic, subtle acting as usual has a thousand nuances."

Jack Kroll in *Newsday*

"Olivier relishes playing the old Jew. Wise and crusty, frail of frame but stout of heart, Lieberman is one of those movie character roles that the great actor visibly enjoys doing and that one cannot help enjoying along with him."

Richard Schickel in *Time* magazine

"Given a Mengele portrayed as a stiffly made-up, monstrous machine, Gregory Peck scarcely has to act at all; Laurence Olivier, on the other hand, employs a dismaying barrage of 'Jewish' tics and mannerisms (this double casting against type may have been an effort to avoid confusion with Olivier's own Mengele-inspired character in *Marathon Man*).

Richard Combs in *Monthly Film Bulletin*

A LITTLE ROMANCE

1979

*An Orion-Warner Bros. release of a
Pan Arts-Trinacra coproduction*

CAST

Laurence Olivier *(Julius Edmond Santorin)*; Thelonious Bernard *(Daniel)*; Diane Lane *(Lauren King)*; Arthur Hill *(Richard King)*; Sally Kellerman *(Kay King)*; Broderick Crawford *(Himself)*; David Dukes *(George de Marco)*; Andrew Duncan *(Bob Duryea)*; Claudette Sutherland *(Janet Duryea)*; Graham Fletcher-Cook *(Londet)*; Ashby Semple *(Natalie Woodstein)*; Claude Brosset *(Michel Michon)*; Jacques Maury *(Inspector Leclerc)*; Anna Massey *(Ms. Siegel)*; Peter Maloney *(Martin)*; Dominique Lavanant *(Mme. Cormier)*; Mike Marshall *(First Assistant Director)*; Michel Bardinet *(French Ambassador)*; Alain David Gabison *(French Representative)*; Isabelle Duby *(Monique)*; Jeffrey Carey *(Make-Up Man)*; John Pepper *(Second Assistant Director)*; Denise Glaser *(Woman Critic)*; Jeanne Herviale *(Woman in Metro)*; Carlo Lastricati *(Tour Guide)*; Judith Mullen *(Secretary)*; Philippe Brigaud *(Theatre Manager)*; Lucienne Legrand *(Cashier)*.

CREDITS

Director: George Roy Hill; *Executive Producer:* Patrick Kelley; *Producers:* Yves Rousset-Rouard and Robert L. Crawford; *Screenwriter:*

Allan Burns; *Based on the novel* **E = MC2 Mon Amour** *by* Patrick Cauvin; *Technicolor Cinematographer:* Pierre William Glenn; *Editors:* William Reynolds and Claudine Bouche; *Production Designer:* Henry Bumstead; *Art Directors:* Francois De Lamothe and Marino Calvadore; *Set Decorators:* Robert Christides, Jean Colin, and Jacques Quinternet; *Music:* Georges Delerue; *Costumes:* Rosine Delamare and Jeannine Vergne; *Running Time:* 108 minutes.

THE FILM

Orion Pictures, before becoming a major force in the Hollywood film firmament, had an auspicious start with this delightful little comedy-drama about adolescent love against a European backdrop. It was distributed by Warner Bros. Orion now releases its own films.

As the movie's top-billed player, Laurence Olivier took on a role that drew inevitable critical comparisons with the parts that had, until his death seven years earlier, been the exclusive domain of the elderly French charmer, Maurice Chevalier. Of the two youngsters por-

traying the film's protagonists, Thelonius Bernard seems to have disappeared, while Diane Lane has developed into a young adult actress as much acclaimed for her looks as for her ability—especially in the award-winning 1989 television miniseries *Lonesome Dove*. But perhaps director George Roy Hill was the party most deserving of A *Little Romance*'s pleasantly unexpected reception. Without his delicate balancing of the story's poignancy with its humor, the end results would never have pleased so many critics, as well as moviegoers. Of its two Oscar nominations (screenplay and music), A *Little Romance* took home a statuette for Georges Delerue's lilting score.

CRITICS CIRCLE

"A *Little Romance* is quite the most original and delightful script in ages, and the film George Roy Hill has made from it is positively enchanting. The acting is superb, and the children are exciting and mature discover-

A LITTLE ROMANCE   As Julius Edmond Santorin

A LITTLE ROMANCE

205

A LITTLE ROMANCE

A LITTLE ROMANCE   With Thelonius Bernard and Diane Lane

ies who just happen to be trapped in teenage disguise for the moment. I have a notion we'll be hearing and seeing a great deal more from Thelonious Bernard and Diane Lane. Laurence Olivier, in his 60th motion picture, plays the old roué with appliqued layers of wit, charm and virtuoso artistry. Olivier's battles with serious illness in recent days leave him no worse for wear. He looks fit and feisty and even did some of his own stuntwork in the film, including a strenuous uphill bike race."

Rex Reed in New York *Daily News*

"One of the consistent joys of '70s moviegoing has been Laurence Olivier's game, witty performances in otherwise terrible films. Even junk like *The Betsy* and *The Boys From Brazil* became memorable in his hands. Who could forget his parody of a Midwestern accent in the former or his rapturous cigarette smoking in the latter? Olivier is such a sly devil that he could make his Oscar acceptance speech, a riotous stream of sheer poppycock, sound as though it were a Shakespearean soliloquy. In *A Little Romance*, Olivier has another crusty character: a suave old coot of a Frenchman who plays

fairy godfather to a pair of star-crossed lovers who are just thirteen. He is in delightful fettle and creates one classic bit, a gasping fit while reading a newspaper. Yet this is one latter-day Olivier film that has more going for it than its star."

Jay Cocks in *Time* magazine

"The grim thing in *A Little Romance* is the sight of Laurence Olivier coming as close to making a spectacle of himself as he ever has in his screen career. Mr. Olivier plays the Maurice Chevalier role, a role in which even Mr. Chevalier finally became tiresome. Mr. Olivier is never tiresome—sometimes he is quite funny—but he does seem desperate. As an elderly, extremely soft-hearted, French pickpocket who befriends the young lovers, Mr. Olivier is required to be not much more than cute. Because this clearly doesn't interest him, he gives the busiest, most lip-smacking, most eyeball-rolling performance of his career, outdoing even his impersonation of a West Indian Othello some years ago."

Vincent Canby in *The New York Times*

"Olivier gives himself, and us, the fun of which he is uniquely capable. His tongue seems to be lolling in his cheek like a hot spaniel's, as it often does when he is calling with ease on his genius and working at the top of his form. The man played by Sir Laurence speaks to the children's heart. The performance is sauced with the peculiar daintiness that Olivier brings to mischievously trivial parts. He endows this one with some of the debonair alertness he gives to Restoration comedy. The film is fortunate to have him; perhaps most of all fortunate for his importation of implicit centuries of European learning and merriment."

Penelope Gilliat in *The New Yorker*

DRACULA

1979

A Universal Picture

CAST

Frank Langella *(Count Dracula)*; Laurence Olivier *(Abraham Van Helsing)*; Donald Pleasence *(Jack Seward)*; Kate Nelligan *(Lucy Seward)*; Trevor Eve *(Jonathan Harker)*; Jan Francis *(Mina Van Helsing)*; Janine Duvitski *(Annie)*; Tony Haygarth *(Renfield)*; Teddy Turner *(Swales)*; Sylveste McCoy *(Walter)*; Kristine Howarth *(Mrs. Galloway)*; Joe Belcher *(Tom Hindley)*; Ted Carroll *(Scarborough Sailor)*; Frank Birch *(Harbourmaster)*; Gabor Vernon *(Captain of "Demeter")*; Frank Henson *("Demeter" Sailor)*; Peter Wallis *(Priest)*.

CREDITS

Director: John Badham; *Executive Producer:* Marvin E. Mirisch; *Producer:* Walter Mirisch; *Associate Producer:* Tom Pevsner; *Second-Unit Director:* Gerry Gavigan; *Screenwriter:* W.D. Richter; *Based on the play by* Hamilton Deane and John L. Balderston, *from the novel by* Bram Stoker; *Panavision-Technicolor Cinematographer:* Gilbert Taylor; *Additional Photography:* Leslie Dear and Harry Oakes; *Editor:* John Bloom; *Production Designer:* Peter Murton; *Art Director:* Brian Ackland-Snow; *Set Decorator:* Peter Young; *Music:* John Williams; *Costumes:* Julie Harris; *Visual Consultant:* Maurice Binder; *Special Effects:* Albert Whitlock and Roy Arbogast; *Sound:* Robin Gregory and Gerry Humphries; *Running Time:* 109 minutes.

THE FILM

Bram Stoker's 1897 Gothic novel about a compelling vampire named Count Dracula was dramatized as a play in 1927 by Hamilton Deane and John L. Balderston, who not only staged his work in London, but also played Dr. Van Helsing, the Dutch medical specialist who proves the count's nemesis, ultimately stopping his evil influence by driving a wooden stake through the vampire's heart.

On stage and screen, Hungarian-born Bela Lugosi was, of course, the first actor to make a name for himself as Dracula in the early 1930s, followed decades later by England's Christopher Lee. More recently, the more romantic and mellifluous-voiced Frank Langella brought a new sensuality to the character in a Tony-winning 1977 Broadway revival notable for Edward Gorey's inventive black-and-white sets and costumes.

The present movie remake of *Dracula* retained Langella's Byronic concept of the vampire count, but little else, replacing Gorey's stage designs with opulent and picturesque Gothic trappings. Director John Badham had no desire to reproduce the play, so Langella arrived in Cornwall, England (where *Dracula* was shot), faced with not only a new concept of the story, but also an entirely new cast. Of Olivier, he had only words of praise: "The thing about him that's pretty wonderful is that when we were on the set together there was no such thing as the legend, the reputation, the past. There was only the moment, how we work this moment and 'Oh, dear boy, what do you think we should do about this?' and 'Oh, my God, will you help me out?'—all those wonderful things he does to make you feel relaxed."

Thanks largely to Frank Langella's earlier Broadway triumph in the role—and the story's new romantic appeal to women—the 1979 *Dracula* again enjoyed hit status as a motion picture. (In late 1991, Francis Ford Coppola began filming yet another version of *Dracula*.)

CRITICS CIRCLE

"Mr. Langella is still playing Dracula as the compleat ladykiller, a dashing and romantic figure who just happens to have one little kink. This works beautifully in those portions of the film that aspire to elegance, and a lot less well when [director John] Badham switches abruptly from glamor to ghoulishness. Mr. Langella creates a Dracula who's seductive rather than scary, only to have Mr. Badham periodically spice up the movie with graphic horror tricks that undermine the performance. . . . The Van Helsing character has been drawn more deeply into the story to accommodate Laurence Olivier, who is supposed to be Dutch but sounds much as he did in *Marathon Man* and *The Boys From Brazil*. Lord Olivier and Mr. Langella meet primarily for action scenes, which are the forte of neither. Lord Olivier has some delightful moments with Donald Pleasence, though, as each plays the father of a beautiful young woman with nasty-looking puncture marks on her neck."

Janet Maslin in *The New York Times*

DRACULA   As Abraham Van Helsing

208

DRACULA With
Frank Langella

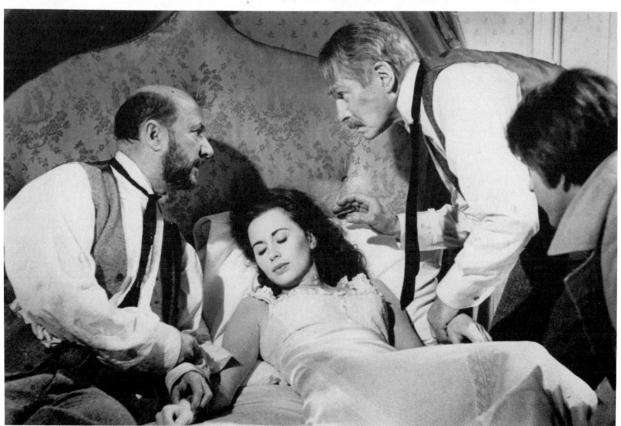

DRACULA With Donald Pleasence, Kate Nelligan and Trevor Eve

DRACULA   With Donald Pleasence

"A staple in film lineups the past few years has been Laurence Olivier. He can now be seen mingling politely with the cast of *Dracula*, where he serves humbly as a Dutch doctor whose daughter has gone to her own death at the teeth of the popular fiend and who is conversant with the defensive application of garlic, crucifixes, yew stakes and daylight. Having chosen to establish himself in the film as a straight man, Olivier defers to the calculated flamboyance of Frank Langella in the title role, and also to Donald Pleasence, who takes nice advantage of his own opportunities in a more accommodating character part."

Susan Lardner in *The New Yorker*

"The bad news is that Dracula is getting a bit long in the tooth, if you'll pardon the pun. Langella's Dracula is more sexy than malevolent. The film is awfully corny, and ambiguous, too. It's fun to hear Olivier, with his hammy Dutch accent, ask: 'Did you ever hear of vurvul-

ves?' But enough is enough and, in the end, I think this poor old vampire deserves a long rest."

Rex Reed in New York *Daily News*

THE JAZZ SINGER

1980

An Associated Film Distribution release of a Jerry Leider production

CAST

Neil Diamond *(Yussel Rabinovitch/"Jess Robin")*; Laurence Olivier *(Cantor Rabinovitch)*; Lucie Arnaz *(Molly Bell)*; Catlin Adams *(Rivka Rabinovitch)*; Franklyn Ajaye *(Bubba)*; Paul Nicholas *(Keith Lennox)*; Sully Boyar *(Eddie Gibbs)*; Mike Kellin *(Leo)*; James Booth *(Paul

Rossini); Luther Waters *(Teddy)*; Oren Waters *(Mel)*; Rod Gist *(Timmy)*; Walter Janowitz *(Rabbi Birnbaum)*; Janet Brandt *(Aunt Tillie)*; John Witherspoon *(M.C. at Cinderella Club)*; Dale Robinette *(Tommy)*; David Coburn *(Bar Mitzvah Boy)*; Judy Gibson *(Peg)*; Hank Garrett *(Police Sergeant)*; Ernie Hudson *(Heckler)*; James Karen *(Barney Callahan)*; Tim Herbert *(First Technician)*; Ed Jahnke *(Guard)*; Hugh Gillin *(Texas Bartender)*; Jill Jaress *(Cowgirl)*; Victor Paul *(Irate Driver)*; Cantor Uri Frenkel *(Cantor)*; Rex Cutter *(Semi Driver)*; Mike Pasternak *(Zany Gray)*; Sandy Helberg *(Sound Engineer)*; Brion James *(Man in Bar)*; Douglas Nigh *(Second Technician)*.

CREDITS

Director: Richard Fleischer; *Producer:* Jerry Leider; *Associate Producer:* Joel Morwood; *Screenwriter:* Herbert Baker; *Based on the play by* Samson Raphaelson; *Adaptation:* Stephen H. Foreman; *DeLuxe Color Cinematographer:* Isidore Mankofsky; *Editors:* Frank J. Urioste and Maury Winetrobe; *Production Designer:* Harry Horner; *Art Director:* Spencer Deverill; *Set Designers:* Christopher Horner and Mark Poll; *Set Decorators:* Ruby Levitt and Robert deVestel; *Costumes:* Albert Wolsky, Bill Whitten, James W. Tyson, Bruce Ericksen, and Margaret Thorin; *Music:* Bob Gaudio and Leonard Rosenman; *Songs:* "You

THE JAZZ SINGER   As Cantor Rabinovitch

Baby," "Jerusalem," "America," and "My Name Is Yussel" by Neil Diamond and Gilbert Becaud; "Hello Again" by Neil Diamond and Alan Lindgren; "Amazed and Confused" by Neil Diamond and Richard Bennett; "Acapulco" by Neil Diamond and Doug Rhone; "Hine Mah Tove" and "Havah Nagilah" (trad.) adapted by Neil Diamond; "Adon Olom" and "Kol Nidre" (trad.) adapted by Neil Diamond and Uri Frenkel; "Shabbat Shalom" (trad.) adapted by Uri Frenkel; "Heysur Bulgar" (trad.) arranged by Klezmorim Band; *Choreographer:* Don McKayle; *Running Time:* 115 minutes.

THE FILM

Samson Raphaelson's sentimental old stage play about the cantor's son who chooses show business over the synagogue—eventually returning to his father's calling—began as a hit 1925 Broadway vehicle for George Jessel, before going on to greater fame as a 1927 silent film that boasted revolutionary chunks of dialogue and songs, sung and acted by Al Jolson. In 1953, a second film version starred Danny Thomas, followed in 1959 by Jerry Lewis's television adaptation, and this (and, many critics hoped, *final*) remake, designed around pop singer Neil Diamond. Actually, this version was made *twice:* Diamond

THE JAZZ SINGER   As Cantor Rabinovitch

apparently was disenchanted with the original director Sidney J. Furie's cut, and had Richard Fleischer brought in to begin anew. Olivier was reported to be agreeable to do his part all over again and get a second salary.

For a singing actor, the lure of this legendary story was understandable. But for an acting *singer* like Diamond, the failure of the effort was sufficient to confine him thereafter to the more comfortable areas of the concert stage and the recording studio. By 1980, it appeared that moviegoers (all except for Diamond's staunchest fans) had little interest in the "jazz-singing" predicament of a rabbi's son. Nor did the supporting presence of an acting talent of the stature of Laurence Olivier's help matters; his performance was much criticized for its ethnic excesses, and—as was now frequently the case—he had accepted the role for the money and the adventure of the enterprise.

OLIVIER:

"It was damned embarrassing enough to do once. But then they switched directors and asked me to go through the whole silly thing again. That made it doubly embarrassing. It's trash."

CRITICS CIRCLE

"Of all the things that the world needs now, another remake of Samson Raphaelson's hoary chestnut, *The Jazz Singer*, is probably the least pressing. Obviously, the impulse behind this production was to capitalize on the soaring popularity of Neil Diamond's husky baritone. Even so, one marvels that nobody could come up with material less riddled with clichés and anticlimaxes. It's as if the movie got trapped in a time warp; its attitudes are of the past, its look is of the present. And seldom the twain shall meet.

"As to performances, Neil Diamond has to be the greatest nonactor of our day. He's dynamic enough when onstage doing his songs, but left to his own resources, it's Liberace time. He just smiles a lot. It's not pleasant to report that, as the cantor, Laurence Olivier is hardly better. His is a surface interpretation of the role, a practiced combination of shrugs and accents, but emotional as a smoked sturgeon. And if Olivier is smoked sturgeon, then Lucie Arnaz, the *shiksa* who promotes Diamond's career, is strictly a lox. . . . Better it should have been a rock concert."

Arthur Knight in *The Hollywood Reporter*

"*The Jazz Singer* lives again, but it's fighting a severe case of anemia. Laurence Olivier is the father who just wants to continue the family tradition of raising an endless line of cantors. Don't blame Olivier for taking on the role of this stodgy stick-in-the-mud. Just be grateful we can continue to enjoy his presence on screen in whatever he chooses to do."

Ernest Leogrande in New York *Daily News*

"Using his Old World Jewish accent for the fourth time in recent years, Lord Laurence Olivier, as the elderly cantor, seems to take the job of acting a lot more seriously than anyone else around him, which places his scenes on a completely different level of intensity. . . . The unanswered $64,000 question is, what is jazz to Neil Diamond and Neil Diamond to jazz? Old title has nothing to do with music on display here and would seem meaningless to modern audiences."

"Cart." in *Variety*

"If pure fluke—song and bits of dialogue—had not made 1927's *The Jazz Singer* a milestone movie, it would have been forgotten as just another period schmaltzer, as simpleminded as Samson Raphaelson's original play. This 1980 version offers Neil Diamond as the cantor's son seeking show-biz fame. It's for Diamond's fans. The rest of us will find his dramatic debut as ludicrous as Laurence Olivier's portrait of his dialect-laden daddy. The movie, looking like an animated series of cut-rate album covers, is devoid of either contemporary relevance or taste. You don't have to be Jewish to despise it—but it helps."

Judith Crist in *TV Guide*

INCHON

1981

An MGM/UA release of a One Way production

INCHON   As General Douglas MacArthur

CAST

Laurence Olivier (*Gen. Douglas MacArthur*); Jacqueline Bisset (*Barbara Hallsworth*); Ben Gazzara (*Maj. Frank Hallsworth*); Toshiro Mifune (*Saito-San*); Richard Roundtree (*Sgt. August Henderson*); David Janssen (*David Field*); Nam Goon Won (*Park*); Gabriele Ferzetti (*Turkish Brigadier*); Rex Reed (*Longfellow*); Sabine Sun (*Marguerite*); Dorothy James (*Jean McArthur*); Karen Kahn (*Lim*); Lydia

213

INCHON The General reflects on a bust of Julius Caesar

Lei (*Mila*); James Callahan (*Gen. Almond*); Anthony Dawson (*Gen. Collins*); Rion Morgan (*Pipe Journalist*); Peter Burton (*Adm. Sherman*); John Pochna (*Lt. Alexander Haig*); William Dupree (*Turkish Sergeant*); Grace Chan (*Ah Cheu*); Nak Hoon Lee (*Jimmy*); Kwang Nam Yang (*President Rhee*); Il Woong (*North Korean Commissar*); Mickey Knox (*Adm. Doyle*).

CREDITS

Director: Terence Young; *Producer:* Mitsuharu Ishii; *Associate Producer:* Matsusaburo Sakaguchi; *Screenwriters:* Robin Moore and Laird Koenig; *Original Story:* Robin Moore and Paul Savage; *Color Cinematographer:* Bruce Surtees; *Editor:* Gene Milford; *Art Directors:* Shigekazu Ikuno and Pierluigi Basile; *Music:* Jerry Goldsmith; *Special Advisor on Korean Matters:* Sun Myung Moon; *Original Running Time:* 140 minutes; *General Release Running Time:* 105 minutes.

THE FILM

Because of the circumstances surrounding its controversial production, the force of its critical lambasting upon release, and its subsequent complete disappearance (yet to be seen on TV, it also remains unavailable on videocassette), *Inchon* has thus become the most obscure of all Laurence Olivier's later movies. With the notorious Rev. Sun Myung Moon and his Unification Church behind the project, in collaboration with his friend, the wealthy Japanese newspaper publisher Mitsuharu Ishii, *Inchon* was some three years in production at a cost of a reported $48 to $50 million. It was Ishii who was inspired by the historical incident of Gen. Douglas MacArthur's surprise landing at Inchon in 1950, amid the Korean War. When *Inchon* was filming in 1979, the Rev. Moon's involvement was adamantly denied; on the release print, he is simply credited as being "special adviser." In May 1981, *Inchon* was given a one-time-only showing in Washington, D.C., in its full 140-minute original version. Subsequently, for general release in the U.S. and Canada (it has not, to date, been shown in Britain), the film was cut to 105 minutes by MGM/UA. Its total U.S.-Canadian gross is said to have been a miserable $1.9 million.

Considering Olivier's ongoing health problems in his later years, *Inchon*'s location shooting could not have been an easy one for him. Indeed, with his role seemingly completed, he returned to England before it was found that he was required for one last important shot. Loath to return to Korea, Olivier was able to film that final scene in Rome where, against a cheap backdrop, he recited (as MacArthur) the Lord's Prayer. Always addicted to working with different accents, the actor had taken pains to track down old recordings of MacArthur's voice, and was intrigued with their inconsistencies—and of how his vowel sounds varied.

Among those left on the cutting-room floor in the edited version were film journalist (and sometime-performer) Rex Reed and David Janssen, who had since died of a heart attack at fifty.

214

OLIVIER:

(Interviewed during production)

"People ask me why I'm playing in this picture. The answer is simple. Money, dear boy. I'm like vintage wine. You have to drink me quickly before I turn sour. I'm almost used up now and I can feel the end coming. That's why I'm taking money now. I've got nothing to leave my family but the money I can make from films. Nothing is beneath me if it pays well. I've earned the right to damn well grab whatever I can get in the time I've got left."

CRITICS CIRCLE

"*Inchon* is a hysterical historical epic, somewhat less offensive than *The Green Berets* and far funnier. It's the Rev. Sun Myung Moon's tribute to the late Gen. Douglas MacArthur and the 1950 United Nations amphibious operation by which the general outflanked the North Korean invaders of South Korea. . . . According to the film's publicity material, Mr. Moon 'took an intense personal interest' in the movie and suggested further shooting from time to time, 'a bit of advice which caused the production to return to Korea three times, Rome twice and Los Angeles twice.' Vanity productions aren't easy, nor do they come cheap. *Inchon* looks like the most expensive B-movie ever made. However, it does have its compensations, all of them provided by the great Laurence Olivier who, as General MacArthur, provides the kind of outrageous performance that cannot be demurely described. It is without price. Wearing ghastly Douglas MacArthur makeup that has the effect of making him look like an Oriental actor playing an Occidental, Lord Olivier appears to have had himself a ball. He sends up the film and his employers with such zest—and so politely—that there must have been no way he could be decently restrained. His eyeballs roll up under heavy lids as he's conning the general staff with mock humility. When he catches a glimpse of a bust of Julius Caesar in his office, he does the sort of flinch affected by W. C. Fields on colliding with a small, disgusting child."

Vincent Canby in *The New York Times*

"Its main attraction is watching Sir Laurence Olivier strut around as MacArthur, using a carefully spoken flat American accent and with hair and eyebrows dyed an unnatural dark brown, the hair plastered across his head in a baldness-concealing sweep. Complete with hair, frown, corncob pipe and stiff walk, Olivier does resemble MacArthur, but not realistically. It's like watching Archie Rice do a vaudeville turn in *The Entertainer*."

Ernest Leogrande in New York *Daily News*

"*Inchon* is the worst movie ever made. . . A dog to

begin with, an eternity of desperate cutting and splicing have reduced *Inchon* to a rancid gumbo of fake piety and cynical violence—the kind of dumb, passive violence in which you put a bunch of guys in a jeep or a tank and blow them to kingdom come. But the real violence is that visited upon every professional connected with the film. Saddest of all is Laurence Olivier. Can this really be the greatest living actor, with his ghastly waxworks makeup, speaking in an ear-grating travesty of an 'American' accent? At one awful moment, Olivier has to look at a bust

CLASH OF THE TITANS   With Susan Fleetwood, Ursula Andress, Pat Roach, Jack Gwillim, Claire Bloom and Maggie Smith

of Caesar; he does so with a mournful, embarrassed gaze, as if to say, 'They got you cleanly with daggers, Julius, but they got me with a lousy million-and-a-quarter bucks.' "

Jack Kroll in Newsweek

CLASH OF THE TITANS

1981

A United Artists release of a
Metro-Goldwyn-Mayer Picture

CAST

Laurence Olivier *(Zeus)*; Harry Hamlin *(Perseus)*; Claire Bloom *(Hera)*; Judi Bowker *(Andromeda)*; Maggie Smith *(Thetis)*; Ursula Andress *(Aphrodite)*; Burgess Meredith *(Ammon)*; Jack Gwillim *(Poseidon)*; Susan Fleetwood *(Athena)*; Sian Phillips *(Cassiopeia)*; Pat Roach *(Hephaestus)*; Flora Robson, Freda Jackson, and Anna Manahan *(Stygian Witches)*; Tim Pigott-Smith *(Thallo)*; Neil McCarthy *(Calibos)*; Donald Houston *(Acrisius)*; Vida Taylor *(Danae)*; Harry Jones *(Huntsman)*.

CREDITS

Director: Desmond Davis; *Producers:* Charles H. Schneer and Ray Harryhausen; *Associate Producer:* John Palmer; *Screenwriter:* Beverley Cross; *Dynarama-Metrocolor Cinematographer:* Ted Moore; *Underwater/Aerial Cameraman:* Egil S. Woxholt; *Editor:* Timothy Gee; *Production Designer:* Frank White; *Art Directors:* Don Picton, Peter Howitt, Giorgio Desideri and Fernando Gonzalez; *Set Dresser:* Harry Cordwell; *Music:* Laurence Rosenthal; *Costumes:* Emma Porteus; *Special Effects:* Ray Harryhausen, Jim Danforth, and Steven Archer; *Special Miniatures:* Cliff Culley; *Running Time:* 118 minutes.

THE FILM

Greek mythology, the special effects monsters of animation wizard Ray Harryhausen, and a cast headed by some of Britain's most distinguished actors were the main elements designed to attract audiences to this juvenile adventure fantasy in which Laurence Olivier received top billing as the God Zeus, with muscular young Harry Hamlin as his mortal son Perseus. Long in production, due to the specifics of special effects animation and photography, *Clash of the Titans* failed to live up to expectations, especially for those Harryhausen followers who expected their king of animation to top his motion picture achievements of the early 1960s *(The Mysterious Island, Jason and the Argonauts)*.

CRITICS CIRCLE

"The sad fact is that Harryhausen's stop-frame animation techniques, serviceable enough when he was apprenticing with Willis O'Brien on *Mighty Joe Young*, now seem not only antiquated but primitive. They produce no sense of wonder. We don't even wonder how they were created, the techniques are so painfully obvious. It's strictly a 'painting by the numbers' approach to mythology, lacking in style, grace or urgency. Even so, there are heroics on the grand scale, and detailed with

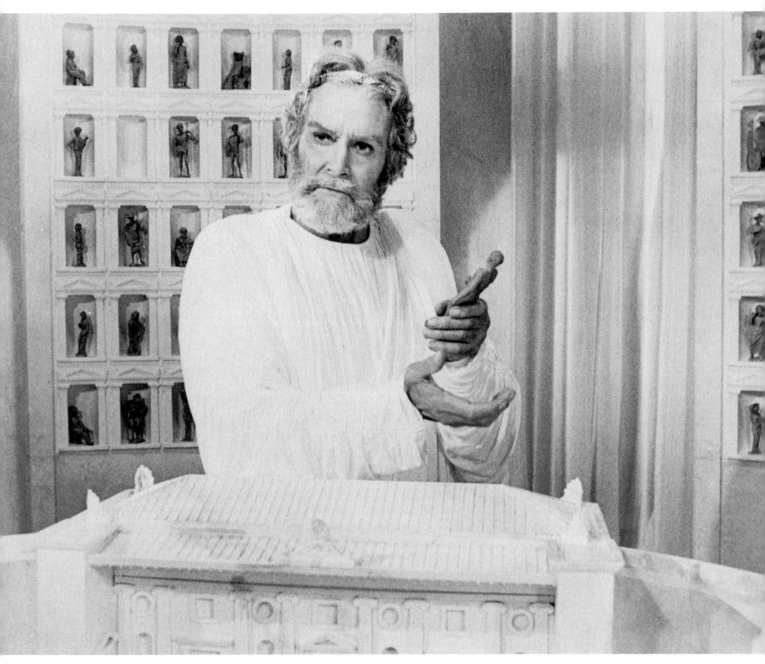

CLASH OF THE TITANS   As Zeus

considerable gusto both by Beverley Cross's screenplay and Desmond Davis's broad direction of the action passages. Davis grows notably stiffer whenever he approaches Olympus, however, no doubt in deference to all those Gods—although both Cross and Olivier seem to be deriving a bit of ironic fun from the notion of Zeus's meddling with human destinies. But then we return to Harryhausen's uninspired animations . . . and one has the feeling that he's seeing the reissue of a movie made

40 years ago. Sometimes it's better to live with the memories."

Arthur Knight in *The Hollywood Reporter*

"Lord Olivier, Miss Smith, Miss Andress and Miss Bloom come and go so rapidly you might think you dreamed them. Mr. Hamlin and Miss Bowker are appropriately vapid, and Mr. Meredith is sonorously credible as a playwright-friend of Perseus. The film is principally concerned with its cataclysms and its monsters—animated puppets—which are less convincing than interesting as examples of the real cinema art of special effects. Beverley Cross wrote the screenplay that, for the most part, avoids the facetious, and Desmond Davis directed it efficiently."

Vincent Canby in *The New York Times*

"Conceived in 1976, filmed at Pinewood and various Mediterranean locations in 1979, and finally packaged with Ray Harryhausen's Dynamation sequences for re-

lease in 1981, *Clash of the Titans* looks even older than this history might suggest. . . . The script entombs the characters in flat, feeble dialogue, though the performers, from Olivier downwards, make little effort to free themselves."

Geoff Brown in *Monthly Film Bulletin*

"MGM's *Clash of the Titans* is an unbearable bore of a film that will probably put to sleep the few adults stuck taking the kids to it. Watching acclaimed actors like Laurence Olivier, Maggie Smith and Claire Bloom wandering through the clouds in long white gowns as Greek

CLASH OF THE TITANS   Harry Hamlin and Judi Bowker

gods is funny enough. But when they start to utter the stylized dialog about what they're going to do to the mortals on the earth below, one wants to look to the Gods for help. It's obvious that something went wrong somewhere in the making of this picture, and hopefully all of the talent will go on to bigger and better things."

"Berg." in Variety

THE BOUNTY

1984

An Orion Pictures release of a Dino De Laurentiis production

CAST

Mel Gibson *(Fletcher Christian)*; Anthony Hopkins *(Lt. William Bligh)*; Laurence Olivier *(Adm. Hood)*; Edward Fox *(Capt. Greetham)*; Daniel Day-Lewis *(John Fryer)*; Bernard Hill *(Cole)*; Philip Davis *(Young)*; Liam Neeson *(Churchill)*; Wi Kuki Kaa *(King Tynah)*; Tevaite Vernette *(Mauatua)*; Philip Martin Brown *(Adams)*; Simon Chandler *(Nelson)*; Malcolm Terris *(Dr. Huggan)*; Simon Adams *(Heywood)*; John Sessions *(Smith)*; Andrew Wilde *(McCoy)*; Neil Morrissey *(Quintal)*; Richard Graham *(Mills)*; Dexter Fletcher *(Ellison)*; Pete Lee-Wilson *(Purcell)*; John Gadsby *(Norton)*; Brendan Conroy *(Lamb)*; Barry Dransfield *(Blind Fiddler)*; Steve Fletcher *(Valentine)*; Jack May *(Prosecuting Captain)*; Mary Kauila *(Queen Tynah)*; Sharon Bower *(Mrs. Bligh)*; Tavana *(King Tynah's Councillor)*.

CREDITS

Director: Roger Donaldson; *Producer:* Bernard Williams; *Screenwriter:* Robert Bolt; *Based on the book* **Captain Bligh and Mr. Christian** *by* Richard Hough; *Technicolor Cinematographer:* Arthur Ibbetson; *Second-Unit Photographer:* Douglas Milsome; *Model Photographer:* Leslie Dear; *Editors:* Tony Lawson and Barrie Vince; *Production Designer:* John Graysmark; *Art Director:* Tony Reading; *Set Decorators:* Bob Cartwright and Louise Carrigan; *Music:* Vangelis; *Costumes:* John Bloomfield; *Special Effects:* John Stears; *Historical Adviser:* Stephen Walters; *Running Time:* 130 minutes.

THE FILM

Although not a direct remake of either the 1935 *Mutiny on the Bounty* or its 1962 successor, *The Bounty*, nevertheless, does deal with the celebrated mutiny aboard His Majesty's armed vessel Bounty in 1789. But this is a revisionist telling of the incident, deriving not from the Nordhoff-Hall book, but from Richard Hough's 1972 volume, *Captain Bligh and Mr. Christian*. Origi-

THE BOUNTY   Liam Neeson, Anthony Hopkins, Philip Davis, Mel Gibson, and Dexter Fletcher

THE BOUNTY   As Admiral Hood

nally, David Lean was to have directed this project—when it was slated to be two separate movies, *The Lawbreakers* and *The Long Arm*, recounting for the first time the entire "Bounty" saga. But the revered British director moved on to other projects, and producer Dino De Laurentiis (having already gone to the expense of constructing a replica ship) decided to condense Robert Bolt's two-part script into one feature film, engaging Roger Donaldson (the New Zealand director of *Sleeping Dogs* and *Smash Palace*), who filmed on location in Tahiti and Moorea.

For Olivier, who looks particularly frail in his brief scenes, this was yet another cameo role, accepted for the money . . . and, of course, adding prestige to the film's credits.

CRITICS CIRCLE

"Using as its source the Richard Hough book, *The Bounty* means to be a far more historically accurate version of the great sea saga that rocked the British Admiralty toward the end of the 18th century. *The Bounty*, which stars Mel Gibson as Fletcher Christian and Anthony Hopkins as Bligh, attempts to rehabilitate Bligh's reputation, at least up to a point, and to discover in Christian a far more troubled, more complicated identity than has been seen before. That seems like a good idea, but the evidence on the screen proves that one fools around with legendary characters, even historically inaccurate ones, at some peril. . . . In addition to Mr. Hopkins and Mr. Gibson, one of our best new young actors, a lot of very good people are involved in this venture. However, nothing in the film really works. Prominent in the supporting cast are Laurence Olivier, seen briefly as a majestic Admiral Hood, the senior officer in charge of Bligh's court-martial, and Edward Fox, who looks elegantly high-toned and cross as the prosecuting officer."

Vincent Canby in *The New York Times*

THE BOUNTY   With Anthony Hopkins and players

THE JIGSAW MAN   As Sir Gerald Scaith

"What this *Bounty* is really about is the better-late-than-never vindication of Bligh. The film is framed by his trial, during which he must explain to a court-martial headed by Sir Laurence Olivier and Edward Fox how he happened to lose his ship. Whether they will condemn him as a monster or an incompetent or commend him for doing his best under adverse circumstances is the dramatic crux of the picture. Yet most of the movie takes place on the open sea, not in a courtroom, the result being a splendidly realized adventure that lacks a dramatic center."

Eleanor Ringel in *The Atlanta Constitution*

"This is a sprawling, complicated, and enthralling canvas, lustily directed by New Zealand's celebrated young Roger Donaldson and vigorously acted by a fine cast that includes Laurence Olivier as Admiral Hood, chief judge in Bligh's court-martial. The men of the Bounty, even the natives, are first-rate. But in the end it is really Anthony Hopkins who dominates the film. His is a galvanized performance of fierce determination and

pride bordering on cruelty and even covert insanity. Dino De Laurentiis has spared no expense, and the result is a richly satisfying adventure yarn that delivers all it promises—and more."

Rex Reed in *New York Post*

THE JIGSAW MAN

1984

A United Film Distribution release of an Evangrove Production

CAST

Michael Caine *(Sir Philip Kimberley/Kuzminsky)*; Laurence Olivier *(Adm. Sir Gerald Scaith)*; Susan George *(Penny)*; Robert Powell *(Jamie)*; Charles Gray *(Sir James Charley)*; Michael Medwin *(Milroy)*; Anthony Shaw *(Matthews)*; Maureen Bennett *(Susan)*; Patrick Dawson

THE JIGSAW MAN   Michael Caine

(Ginger); Juliet Nissen (Miss Fortescue); David Kelly (Cameron); Peter Burton (Douglas); Maggie Rennie (Pauline); Peggy Marshall (Polly); David Allister (Sgt. Lloyd); P.G. Stephens (Driver); Richard Borthwick (Plainclothesman); Vladek Sheybal (Gen. Zorin); Matthew Scurfield and Robert Austin (KGB Men).

CREDITS

Director: Terence Young; Executive Producer: Mahmud A. Sipra; Producer: S. Benjamin Fisz; Co-Producer: Robert Porter; Associate Producer: Ron Carr; Screenwriter: Jo Eisinger; Based on the novel by Dorothea Bennett; Eastmancolor Cinematographer: Freddie Francis; Editors: Peter Hunt, Alan Strachen, and Derek Trigg; Production Designer: Michael Stringer; Art Director: John Roberts; Music: John Cameron; Running Time: 91 minutes.

THE FILM

Reuniting Laurence Olivier and Michael Caine undoubtedly seemed like a good idea twelve years after *Sleuth*—especially in a Cold War spy thriller like Dorothea Bennett's novel *The Jigsaw Man*. But its script and direction were hardly on a par with *Sleuth*, and there were other problems, as well. Not only did financing difficulties put a temporary halt to the film in mid-production, but Olivier's deteriorating health (he collapsed during location shooting on London's Thames embankment) limited his availability for filming. All of which

THE JIGSAW MAN   Michael Caine and Susan George

224

might account for unexplained "holes" in the script, such as the confusingly brief flashback scene in which—in shadowy lighting—a younger-looking Olivier shares a brief romantic moment with Susan George (who plays Caine's daughter Penny), apparently doubling here as her own mother, Annabelle.

In the title role, Caine plays a Russia-defected Englishman in his early sixties who's given age-reducing facial surgery and is dispatched back to Britain on a spy mission that puts him into a cat-and-mouse game with his former boss, intelligence officer Olivier, while also involving George and her agent-lover Robert Powell.

The film was released by a small independent distributor with tightened purse strings, and publicity materials (these pages reflect the few photos released for publication) were skimpy. And neither the critics nor the public were overly impressed; The Jigsaw Man disappeared quickly from sight.

CRITICS CIRCLE

"With bursts of choler and sly wit, Laurence Olivier provides a zesty centerpiece for The Jigsaw Man, the latest in a long line of British thrillers to trade on spies, moles, double agents, defections, betrayed lovers and the long, cold war between the K.G.B. and M.I. 6. Although the main line of the story is clear enough, truncated subplots involving homosexual lovers, old animosities, off-screen events and peripheral characters occasionally confuse matters in a way that suggests that director Terence Young was trying to preserve too much of his source material (a novel written by his wife, Dorothea Bennett). . . . Nevertheless, with so many seasoned professionals involved, The Jigsaw Man, once it gets going, moves briskly through spy literature's familiar landscape of move and countermove, enlivened by the vigor and variety of Mr. Olivier's performance."

Lawrence Van Gelder in The New York Times

"There are huge chunks of script someone forgot to include in the finished product and the acting is, well, less than inspired. Laurence Olivier, as the present Secret Service head, just looks uncomfortable throughout. All in all, Jigsaw Man is a puzzle that stubbornly refuses to form a complete picture."

Hank Gallo in New York Daily News

"Complex, yet inane, the spy-versus-spy shenanigans of this trouble-plagued production don't add up to very much on either the artistic or commercial ledgers. Caine and Olivier's reteaming a decade after Sleuth is far from magical, and the supporting players have thankless roles. Technical work is competent but far from inspired."

"Klad." in Variety

"Having worked together 12 years ago in the dynamic and suspenseful Sleuth, Olivier and Caine throw away the acting books and simply ham it up. They're pros and at this stage of the game can get away with anything . . . even murder. The problem lies with Jo Eisinger's less-than-adequate screenplay. In this case, it appears that too many red herrings have spoiled an otherwise tasty broth. But one will not be bored with The Jigsaw Man as long as Olivier and Caine are in control. This one's a ham's delight."

Mitch Neuhauser in The Film Journal

WILD GEESE II

1985

A Thorn-EMI Presentation of a
Frontier Film production

U.S. Distributor: Universal Pictures

CAST

Scott Glenn (John Haddad); Barbara Carrera (Kathy Lucas); Edward Fox (Alex Faulkner); Laurence Olivier (Rudolf Hess); Robert Webber (Robert McCann); Robert Freitag (Heinrich Stroebling); Kenneth Haigh (Col. Reed-Henry); Stratford Johns (Mustapha El Ali); Derek Thompson (Hourigan); Paul Antrim (Murphy); John Terry (Michael Lukas); Ingrid Pitt (Hooker); Patrick Stewart (Russian General); Michael Harbour (KGB Man); David Lumsden (Joseph Khoury); Frederick Warder (Jamil Khoury); Malcolm Jamieson (Pierre Helou); Billy Boyle (Devenish); David Sullivan (EBC Commentator); Dan Van Husen (Stroebling's Driver); James Monaghan (First Heavy); Michael Büttner (Second Heavy); Herbert Chwoika (Ali's Man); Carl Price (British Corporal); Ronald Nitschke (East German Soldier); Wilfried Gronau (Immigration Official); Shaun Lawton (Intelligence Man); Peter Kybart (Hunter); Amelie zur Muhlen (Russian Woman); Gabriele Kastner (East German Tour Guide); Tom Deiniger and the "La Vie en Rose" Ensemble (Nightclub Artists).

CREDITS

Director: Peter Hunt; Executive Producer: Chris Chrisafis; Producer: Euan Lloyd; Co-Producer: A. Eric Scotini; Second-Unit Director: James Devis; Screenwriter: Reginald Rose; Based on the Novel The Square Circle by David Carney; Technicolor Cinematographer: Michael Reed; Editor: Keith Palmer; Production Designer: Syd Cain; Art Director: Peter Williams; Set Decorator: Don Mingaye; Costumes: Diane Holmes; Music: Roy Budd; "Berliner Luft" by Paul Lincke, performed by the Musikkorps der Polizei Berlin; "Say You'll Be Mine" by Roy Budd, performed by Peter Hoffmann; Running time: 125 minutes.

THE FILM

The Wild Geese was an entertaining and successful 1978 British-made action tale starring Richard Burton,

WILD GEESE II   As Rudolph Hess

Roger Moore, and Richard Harris, about a group of mercenaries who rescue a kidnapped African leader. Seven years later, there followed this sequel, which bears a dedication to Burton, who had died before he could recreate his original character of Alex Faulkner, here portrayed by Edward Fox. Released in Britain in mid-

226

1985, *Wild Geese II* had its initial U.S. release that October in Denver and Salt Lake City, where it racked up a dismal $31,000 in forty-eight theaters in three days. Americans anxious to see this one, therefore, would have to be content with buying or renting its Thorn EMI/HBO videocassette.

Again, Laurence Olivier had a cameo role, albeit a more pivotal one this time, as the nonagenarian Nazi leader Rudolf Hess, kidnap target of the movie's mercenary leader John Haddad (played by Scott Glenn). It would be Olivier's last role in a major theatrical motion picture.

CRITICS CIRCLE

"Edward Fox plays the Burton character, Colonel Faulkner, with comic zest. Unintentionally, perhaps, Laurence Olivier also extracts laughs from his Hess cameo. By contrast, Scott Glenn and Barbara Carrera take their parts more seriously than the script merits. Quiet opening scenes show that Peter Hunt can still direct with class, and the action scenes are competently staged. Other technical credits are fine."

"Japa." in *Variety*

"After a dauntingly clumsy start, in which the idea of Rudolf Hess as a television chat-show guest is contemplated with understandable incredulity by those assigned to extract him from Spandau, *Wild Geese II* settles down to the detours and coincidences of its narrative with a bland and cynical efficiency. Unlike its predecessor, this is a clandestine venture of espionage and betrayal in Harry Palmer territory, not far from the Berlin Wall. Confirming the pointlessness of the whole exercise, when Hess is at last engaged in conversation, he states with good reason that he is a relic with limited public appeal, neither desiring nor deserving freedom, and would like to be returned to his cell. Despite the mayhem expended on his rescue, nobody tries very hard to dissuade him, befriend him, film him, or interrogate him at least on matters of historical interest. He is just waved off back to internment like a favorite old uncle after a weekend with the family. The problem with Laurence Olivier in this role is that although—thanks mainly to the bushy eyebrows—he looks the part quite well, a sense of familiarity and affection attaches to his image which has nothing to do with Hitler's second-in-command."

Philip Strick in *Monthly Film Bulletin*

WAR REQUIEM

1989

An Anglo International Films release of a BBC-Libert Film Sales production

U.S. Release: 1990

CAST

Nathaniel Parker *(Wilfred Owen)*; Tilda Swinton *(Nurse)*; Laurence Olivier *(Old Soldier)*; Patricia Hayes *(Mother)*; Rohan McCullough *(Enemy's Mother)*; Nigel Terry *(Abraham)*; Owen Teale *(Unknown Soldier)*; Sean Bean *(German Soldier)*; Alex Jennings *(Blinded Soldier)*; Claire Davenport *(Charge Sister/Britannia)*; Spencer Leigh *(First Soldier)*; Milo Bell *(Second Soldier)*; Richard Stirling *(Third Soldier)*; Kim Kindersley *(Fourth Soldier)*; Stuart Turton *(Fifth Soldier)*; Lucinda Gane *(First Nurse)*; Beverly Seymour *(Second Nurse)*; Linda Spurrier *(Third Nurse)*; David Meyer *(Businessman)*.

CREDITS

Director: Derek Jarman; *Executive Producer*: John Kelleher; *Producer*: Don Boyd; *Associate Producer*: Chris Harrison; *Color Cinematographer*: Richard Greatrex; *Editors*: John Maybury and Rick Elgood; *Production Designer*: Lucy Morahan; *Art Directors*: Michael Carter and Annie Lapaz; *Costumes*: Linda Alderson; *Sound*: Garth Marshall; *Music*: "War Requiem" by Benjamin Britten, *performed by* the London Symphony Orchestra, *conducted by the composer, with soprano* Galina Vishnevskaya, *tenor* Peter Pears, *and baritone* Dietrich Fischer-Dieskau, *with* the Bach Choir, the London Symphony Orchestra Chorus, the Highgate School Choir *and* the Melos Ensemble; *Assistant Directors*: Sarah Swords, Mark Harrison, Marc Munden and Ian Francis; *Running Time*: 93 minutes.

THE FILM

Laurence Olivier's swan song, filmed when he was eighty-one in the autumn of 1988, was an unusual project, a visualization of Benjamin Britten's oratorio of the same name, as realized by the avant-garde British director Derek Jarman *(Sebastiane, The Tempest)*. Very much an "art film," it was financed through the BBC's Independent Planning Unit on a budget in the vicinity of $1.2 million, and intercut live-action footage with documentary stock from the Imperial War Museum.

Britten had written *War Requiem* for the May 1962 opening of the modern, new Coventry Cathedral, built adjacent to the old one (left a bombed-out shell by the Germans in World War II). A pacifist, Britten had intermingled the traditional Latin texts with the war poetry of Wilfred Owen.

Described by director Jarman as "the fastest-made movie in the history of the cinema," *War Requiem* was shot entirely on location in Darenth Park Hospital, which had served as a residential facility for the mentally ill until its closure a few months before filming began. Intended for cinemas, despite its BBC backing, *War Requiem* had brief theatrical runs both in Britain and the U.S., though it seems a more likely future candidate for Public Broadcasting.

The film's soundtrack is the 1963 recording of *War Requiem* that Britten himself conducted at London's Kingsway Hall, with the soloist voices of Galina Vishnevskaya, Peter Pears, and Dietrich Fischer-Dieskau.

CRITICS CIRCLE

"*War Requiem* has no dialog, though it opens with Laurence Olivier reciting Wilfred Owen's poem 'Strange Meeting.' Olivier—in a welcome return to the screen—also appears in a cameo as an old soldier tended by a young nurse, Tilda Swinton. Nathaniel Parker as tortured poet Owen and Swinton (a Jarman regular) as the nurse are excellent and made all the better by compassionate direction, plus evocative camerawork by Richard Greatrex."

"Adam." in *Variety*

"Derek Jarman's jarring *War Requiem* is an interesting piece of cinema, much in the way that the soundtrack, Benjamin Britten's oratorio by the same name, is an interesting piece of music. The Britten piece uses the darkly pacifist poetry of slain World War I soldier Wilfred Owen as an unlikely text for his religious requiem; Jarman's movie adds an extra, visual dimension. . . . There is no dialogue, save for a resonant reading of one of the poems by Sir Laurence Olivier in the great actor's final screen role as the Old Soldier, a memory device by which to begin a somber movie that says, in not so many words, that war is hell. . . . Olivier looks unbelievably frail—believably, in light of his recent death—in a wheelchair and lap blanket, with his voiceover eulogizing 'the pity of war, the pity war distilled.' "

Jami Bernard in *New York Post*

"Olivier's cameo appearance, his last work on film before his death, frames the visual element; he is an old soldier in a wheelchair fingering his medals, and the visions on the screen are his memory and reflections—including newsreel footage of World War I, an atomic explosion and scenes from Afghanistan and Vietnam. There are also personal scenes: Owen (Nathaniel Parker) killing and reflecting on death; an Unknown Soldier (Owen Teale) embodying the horror of life (and death) on the battlefield; a nurse (Tilda Swinton) who represents the compassion and powerlessness of those who observe but do not fight. They perform brilliantly in this violent, horrifying, ultimately inspiring film—an eloquent, complex and profoundly negative statement on war."

Joseph McLellan in *The Washington Post*

WAR REQUIEM   With Tilda Swinton

SHORTS
AND VOICE-ONLY
PERFORMANCES

1940—*Bundles for Britain*
1941—*Words for Battle*
1942—*George Cross Island*
1943—*The Volunteer*
　　—*Malta G C*
1944—*This Happy Breed* (feature)
1945—*Fighting Pilgrims*
1953—*A Queen Is Crowned* (feature)
1968—*Romeo and Juliet* (feature)
1975—*The Gentleman Tramp* (feature)

DRAMATIC TELEVISION
WORK

MACBETH   With Judith Anderson

232

Excerpts from
MACBETH
by William Shakespeare

Directed by George More O'Ferrall; *Produced by the* British Broadcasting Corporation; *Based on the 1937* Old Vic Theatre Production

CAST

Laurence Olivier *(Macbeth)*; Judith Anderson *(Lady Macbeth).*

No record exists of this early TV performance, made possible by Lilian Bayliss of the Old Vic, to whom the BBC paid £75 for everything, including actors, props and costumes.

JOHN GABRIEL BORKMAN

Directed by Caspar Wrede; *Live telecast of an Associated Television production of the play by* Henrik Ibsen; *Running Time:* 70 minutes.

CAST

Laurence Olivier *(John Gabriel Borkman)*; Irene Worth *(Ella Rentheim)*; Pamela Brown *(Gunhild Borkman)*; Maxine Audley *(Mrs. Fanny Wilton)*; George Relph *(Vilhelm Foldal)*; Anthony Valentine *(Erhart Borkman)*; Ann Castaldini *(Frida Foldal).*

THE PRODUCTION

Laurence Olivier's first full-scale TV performance was in the title role of this dark-textured Ibsen play. It drew widespread attention because of its star, whose inexperience with the medium did not help an ill-chosen vehicle with a novice director, Caspar Wrede. A subsequent survey of the ratings for this telecast indicated a large audience at the start, but a small one in the latter half. All told—a complete disaster. Olivier's explanation for the

JOHN GABRIEL BORKMAN   With Ann Castaldini

failure centered on the three-weeks rehearsal period having been inadequate.

CRITICS CIRCLE

"Olivier's Borkman displayed a series of characteristics rather than a continuous character; there was nothing arbitrary in the playing, but it tended to be episodic."

The London Times

233

THE MOON AND SIXPENCE

Directed by Robert Mulligan; *Produced for NBC Television by* David Susskind; *Teleplay by* S. Lee Pogostin, *from the novel by* W. Somerset Maugham; *Running Time*: 90 minutes.

CAST

Laurence Olivier *(Charles Strickland)*; Geraldine Fitzgerald *(Amy Strickland)*; Judith Anderson *(Tiare)*; Hume Cronyn *(Dirk Stroeve)*; Jessica Tandy *(Blanche Stroeve)*; Jean Marsh *(Ata)*; Cyril Cusack *(Dr. Coutras)*; Denholm Elliott *(The Writer)*; Murray Matheson *(MacAndrew)*.

THE PRODUCTION

This color taping of Maugham's 1919 fiction based on the life of French painter Paul Gauguin won Olivier his first Emmy for "Outstanding Single Performance by an Actor." (Lee J. Cobb previously had played the role of Strickland in a 1951 TV production of Maugham's novel.)

THE MOON AND SIXPENCE With Jessica Tandy and Hume Cronyn

CRITICS CIRCLE

"The closest thing to dramatic perfection ever known on television. Adjectives alone cannot describe the haunting beauty of *The Moon and Sixpence,* and particularly the performance by Sir Laurence Olivier, a towering craftsman, whose portrayal of the Gauguin-like hero had a brilliance and magnetism unmatched in the annals of TV. Olivier made the remarkable transition from a timid stockbroker to an imposing figure who was irreverent to all things but his paintings. This was not a likeable nor an admirable man, for he discarded people and conventions without so much as a twinge. But such was the force of Olivier's portrayal that, long before the end, the viewer was disarmed and engulfed."

Marie Torre in *New York Herald-Tribune*

1961

THE POWER AND THE GLORY

Directed by Marc Daniels; *Produced for CBS Television by* David Susskind; *Teleplay by* Dale Wasserman, *from the novel by* Graham Greene; *Photographed by* Alan Posage and Leo Farrenkopf; *Editors:* Sidney Meyers and Walter Hess; *Art Director:* Burr Smidt; *Music:* Laurence Rosenthal; *Running Time:* 98 minutes. (Released theatrically in Europe by Paramount Pictures)

CAST

Laurence Olivier *(The Priest)*; Julie Harris *(Maria)*; George C. Scott *(Police Lieutenant)*; Martin Gabel *(Police Chief)*; Roddy McDowall *(Mestizo)*; Cyril Cusack *(Tench)*; Keenan Wynn *(Cousin)*; Patty Duke *(Coral)*; Frank Conroy *(Padre José)*; Mildred Dunnock *(Spinster)*; Thomas Gomez *(Delgado)*; Fritz Weaver *(Schoolmaster)*; Tim O'Connor *(Gringo)*; Arthur Hughes *(Montez)*; Val Avery *(Sergeant)*; Mark Lenard *(Miguel)*; Jeremiah Morris *(Francisco)*; Leonardo Cimino and Louis Zorich *(Prisoners)*; Louis Sorin *(Old Man)*; Florence Stanley *(Farmer's Wife)*; Joanna Merlin *(Delgado's Wife)*; Linda Canby *(Brigida)*; Gerald Hiken and Dino Narizzano *(Red Shirts)*; Steve Curry *(Emilio)*; Martha Greenhouse *(José's Wife)*; Lou Antonio *(Vittorio)*; Roger DeKoven *(Corporal)*; Rose Gregorio *(Indian Woman)*.

THE PRODUCTION

Taped (and simultaneously filmed) as a $700,000 black-and-white TV spectacle, *The Power and the Glory* required forty massive sets and a cast of 151 actors. John Ford had filmed Graham Greene's novel in 1947 under

THE POWER AND THE GLORY   With Julie Harris

THE POWER AND THE GLORY   As The Priest

236

the title *The Fugitive*, with Henry Fonda as the alcoholic, tormented Mexican priest, pursued by a relentless police officer in an anti-Christian Latin American state. It later was staged in London with Paul Scofield in the lead and in the United States after that with Fritz Weaver starring. In this TV version, Weaver again appears but in another role.

CRITICS CIRCLE

"What makes it the year's most searing and significant TV drama is Olivier's masterful portrayal of a wayward Mexican priest who walks the way of a martyr."

Life magazine

"A fine, frequently moving performance. If only for the portrayals of Laurence Olivier and George C. Scott in

THE POWER AND THE GLORY   With George C. Scott

THE POWER AND THE GLORY   With Keenan Wynn

two extraordinary performances, the one counterpointing the other, it was well worth the viewing. Olivier's 'whiskey-priest' in essence brought to visual fulfillment the agonies and the ecstacies of a haunted, tormented soul seeking peace with himself and with God."

Variety

"Graham Greene's specific and uncompromising story of a dissolute priest was a major forward step for a mass medium traditionally skittish over controversial themes, most especially those of a religious nature. Sir Laurence's performance attained a stature and illumination in the concluding jail scene when the priest beseeches God's compassion. But for the main part of the two-hour work, it was disconcertingly studied and wanting in emotional electricity. As the priest's woman, Julie Harris in a few

minutes conveyed brilliantly the necessary qualities of humility, poignancy and degradation."

Jack Gould in *The New York Times*

"Apart from Laurence Olivier, who gives a magnetic performance as the priest, the rest of the cast figure briefly in dramatic highspots, rather than as unobtrusive links in the narrative chain."

The Daily Cinema

"*The Power and the Glory*, Dale Wasserman's adaptation of Graham Greene's novel, is TV's finest dramatic moment since Laurence Olivier did *The Moon and Sixpence*. Not quite coincidentally, Sir Laurence is in this one, too. The play is overwhelmingly Olivier's, and he glories in it. Present in every scene except a brief prologue, singled out in countless close-ups, Olivier very nearly reaches the actor's dream-state of absolute emotion absolutely disciplined, and he does it, as always, by playing every note of wry comedy he can find as counterpoint to the unfolding tragedy. Attention must be paid to this sort of excellence, on pain of having it disappear from television entirely."

Newsweek magazine

UNCLE VANYA

Directed by Stuart Burge; A British Home Entertainments production; *Based on the 1962* Chichester Festival Theatre *production, directed for the stage by* Laurence Olivier; *Translated by* Constance Garnett; *from the play by* Anton Chekhov; *Setting:* Sean Kenny; *Costumes:* Beatrice Dawson; *Music:* Alexis Chesnakov; *Running Time:* 112 minutes. (Released theatrically in the U.S. in 1977)

CAST

Laurence Olivier *(Mihail Lvovitch Astrov)*; Michael Redgrave *(Ivan Petrovitch Voynitsky/"Uncle Vanya")*; Joan Plowright *(Sofya Alexandrovna/"Sonya")*; Rosemary Harris *(Ilyena Andreyevna)*; Sybil Thorndike *(Marina Timofeyevna/"Nurse")*; Max Adrian *(Alexandr Vladimirovitch Serebryakov/"Professor")*; Lewis Casson *(Ilya Ilyitch Telyegin)*; Fay Compton *(Marya Vassilyevna Voynitsky/"Maman")*; Robert Long *(Yefim)*.

THE PRODUCTION

Made under difficult conditions that only allowed for one day of rehearsal and five shooting days, this was a "filmed record" of the successful all-star Chichester production. Olivier, who has called his colleague Michael Redgrave's acting "the definitively perfect Vanya of all time," considered the results too "rough-edged" for British consumption, permitting this *Uncle Vanya* to be seen only in the U.S. Of Olivier, director Stuart Burge later said, "I don't think he liked it very much."

CRITICS CIRCLE

"The production is neither a movie nor a play, but the sort of on-the-spot report that looks best on television. Stuart Burge, who directed the production for the screen, uses the kind of medium shots and close-ups most of the time that have the effect of isolating an individual actor

UNCLE VANYA With Rosemary Harris

238

UNCLE VANYA   With Joan Plowright

from his fellow players. Long shots, which would establish the physical and emotional relationships of the characters, are used so sparingly that it's impossible to judge accurately the effect of the ensemble acting. Mr. Redgrave and Mr. Olivier are splendid. The other actors don't always fare too well before a camera taking close-up shots of performances designed to be seen from a certain fixed distance. Keeping these things in mind, you should be able to enjoy this *Vanya* as one of the best readings of the play you're ever likely to hear."

Vincent Canby in *The New York Times* (1977)

"It is probably the best *Uncle Vanya* in English that we shall ever see. Dr. Astrov is played by Laurence Olivier with the hesitant rush that he particularly understands."

Pauline Kael in *The New Yorker*

1969

MALE OF THE SPECIES

Directed by Charles Jarrott; *Produced for Associated Television by* Cecil Clarke; *Written by* Alun Owen; *Running Time*: 90 minutes (commercials included).

CAST

Laurence Olivier (*Host/Narrator*); Sean Connery (*MacNeil*); Michael Caine (*Cornelius*); Paul Scofield (*Sir Emlyn Bowen*); Anna Calder-Marshall (*Mary MacNeil*); Katharine Blake (*Miss Saville*); Michael Bates (*Fred*); Geoffrey Chater (*Toby*).

THE PRODUCTION

Male of the Species is the American title for this package of three tied-together short stories revolving about three men in the life of an independent Scotswoman (Anna Calder-Marshall). Playwright Alun Owen tailored each story to a separate British male star—Sean Connery, Michael Caine, and Paul Scofield. In Britain, each of the separate stories (*Macneil; Cornelius* and *Emlyn*) was designed to be shown in half-hour segments on successive weeks. For both versions Laurence Olivier delivered its Introduction.

Male of the Species was an ATV British production to which all the stars involved donated their services to benefit the Combined Theatrical Charities Council. The result was a nearly $600,000 gift to the council for the rebuilding of Denville Hall, a home for retired actors and actresses.

CRITICS CIRCLE

"A skillful and absorbing little play. Miss Calder-Marshall's captivating performance was one level of interest, the separate contributions of the name male cast another, and the terse narration by Olivier still another. The narration which laced the segments together did not require an Olivier delivery, but it was quite a bonus that he did it."

Variety

1970

DAVID COPPERFIELD

Directed by Delbert Mann; An Omnibus production for NBC Television; *Produced by* Frederick H. Brogger; *Adapted by* Jack Pulman and Frederick H. Brogger, *from the novel by* Charles Dickens; *Photographed by* Ken Hodges; *Editor*: Peter Boita; *Art Director*: Alex Vetchinsky; *Costumes*: Anthony Mendleson; *Music*: Malcolm Arnold; *Running Time*: 118 minutes. (Released theatrically in Europe by 20th Century-Fox)

CAST

Robin Phillips (*David Copperfield*); Susan Hampshire (*Agnes Wickfield*); Edith Evans (*Aunt Betsey Trotwood*); Michael Redgrave (*Mr. Peggotty*); Ralph Richardson (*Mr. Micawber*); Wendy Hiller (*Mrs. Micawber*); Corin Redgrave (*Steerforth*); Pamela Franklin (*Dora*); Ron Moody (*Uriah Heep*); James Donald (*Mr. Murdstone*); Emlyn Williams (*Mr. Dick*); Laurence Olivier (*Mr. Creakle*); Richard Attenborough (*Mr. Tungay*); Megs Jenkins (*Clara Peggotty*); Anna Massey (*Jane Murdstone*); Cyril Cusack (*Barkis*); Nicholas Pennell (*Traddles*); Sinead Cusack (*Emily*); Andrew McCulloch (*Ham*); Isobel Black (*Clara Copperfield*); Donald Layne-Smith (*Mr. Wickfield*); James Hayter (*Porter*); Helen Cotterill (*Mary Ann*); Kim Craik (*Child Emily*); Alastair Mackenzie (*Child David*); Christopher Moran (*Boy Steerforth*); Jeffrey Chandler (*Boy Traddles*); Brian Tipping (*Boy*); Alison Blair (*Girl*); Liam Redmond (*Mr. Quinion*); Gordon Rollings (*Milkman*); George Woodbridge (*Vicar*); William Lyon Brown (*Doctor*); Christine Ozanne (*Midwife*); Phoebe Shaw (*Prostitute*); Robert Lankesheer (*Mr. Sharp*); Ann Stallybrass (*Martha*).

THE PRODUCTION

Charles Dickens's 1850 novel (reportedly his personal favorite of his works) had been the basis for several silent films, as well as the classic 1935 movie, directed for MGM by George Cukor. This all-star, British-made 1970 TV-movie utilized flashbacks to trace the adventures of young David (portrayed as an adult by Robin

DAVID COPPERFIELD With Richard
Attenborough

Phillips; as a child by Alastair Mackenzie) as he makes his way in Victorian England.

CRITICS CIRCLE

"The story is jerkily and bitterly related, mainly in flashbacks, but the constant return to the brooding, self-pitying Copperfield makes for a melancholy drag. The performance presumably demanded of Robin Phillips by [director Delbert] Mann is so downbeat and lacking in spunk that it kills its own objective. It also means that through constant flashbacks few of Dickens' wonderful array of characters gets much opportunity to develop their roles and, in some cases, have only a minute or so to register. Notably, Laurence Olivier, as the schoolmaster Creakle, and Richard Attenborough, as his cringing, one-legged assistant, Tungay. Their brilliant, brief appearances light up the screen in about 60 seconds flat. Then they disappear."

"Rich." in *Variety*

"Laurence Olivier and Richard Attenborough's outrageous Creakle and Tungay double-act would have brought down the house, closing the bill at the New Cross Empire."

Margaret Hinxman in London *Sunday Telegraph*

"As for the ferocious headmaster, Mr. Creakle, hardly have we seen through another of Sir Laurence Olivier's marvellous disguises before he is gone."

Cecil Wilson in London *Daily Mail*

LONG DAY'S JOURNEY INTO NIGHT   As James Tyrone

1973

LONG DAY'S JOURNEY INTO NIGHT

Directed by Peter Wood; *Produced for ABC Television by* Cecil Clarke; *Based on Britain's* National Theatre *stage production directed by* Michael Blakemore; *TV art direction by* Peter Roden; *Stage scenery and costumes designed by* Michael Annals; *Tape editor:* Alan Pidgen; *Lighting director:* John Rook; *Running Time:* 180 minutes (commercials included).

CAST

Laurence Olivier (*James Tyrone*); Constance Cummings (*Mary Cavan Tyrone*); Denis Quilley (*Jamie, their elder son*); Ronald Pickup (*Edmund, their younger son*); Maureen Lipman (*Cathleen, the maid*).

THE PRODUCTION

Eugene O'Neill termed his four-act autobiographical drama a work "of old sorrow, written in tears and blood." Completed in 1940, but neither published nor produced (according to the author's wishes) until after his death, *Long Day's Journey Into Night* first reached Broadway in 1956. That production, starring Fredric March and Florence Eldridge, won both the Pulitzer Prize and the Drama Critics Circle Award as best play of its year. Sidney Lumet directed its 1962 filming, with Ralph Richardson, Katharine Hepburn, Jason Robards, and Dean Stockwell. This ATV version was based on the 1972 London production, performed with the same cast—with the minor exception of Maureen Lipman, who replaced the National's Jo Maxwell-Muller as the maid Cathleen.

Laurence Olivier's performance won him a 1972–73 Emmy Award (his second) for Outstanding Single Performance by an Actor in a Leading Role. He also introduced the play in a brief dressing-room foreword.

LONG DAY'S JOURNEY INTO NIGHT   With Constance Cummings,
Ronald Pickup, and Denis Quilley

LONG DAY'S JOURNEY INTO NIGHT
With Constance Cummings

CRITICS CIRCLE

"Staged for the National Theatre by Michael Blakemore, *Long Day's Journey* has been directed for television by Peter Wood, and the focus has been brilliantly kept on the play itself. There are no unnecessary visual distractions. . . . With Constance Cummings as Mary Tyrone, Ronald Pickup as Edmund and Denis Quilley as Jamie, the performances maintain a rare level of acting excellence. And with Lord Olivier as James Tyrone, that level rises to the magnificent. With hair slicked down, sporting a theatrical neckerchief and the air of a gentleman-rogue, the former Sir Laurence displays the entire artistic inheritance of his 50 years as an outstanding actor. It is a memorable performance."

John J. O'Connor in *The New York Times*

"It's Olivier who all will tune in to see, and for very good reason. His agonizing performance of James Tyrone, a penny-pinching patriarch, so desperately in love with his wife that his guts are torn from him when she slips back into the drug habit, after a happy hiatus off the needle, is a classic portrayal of a man trying to keep the threads of his life together. . . . The cast is all first-rate, and despite the fact that this is a British company of players, accents do not betray them and not once did we

LONG DAY'S JOURNEY INTO NIGHT   With Constance Cummings

feel we were not in the presence of an Irish immigrant family in America. It's a remarkable, sympathetic, compassionate drama, beautifully acted and produced."

Kay Gardella in New York *Daily News*

"Olivier utilized all of the actor's gifts and techniques at his disposal, especially his great command of the upper registers of his voice, and breathed life into the rather rigid role of the miserly, rusting-out matinee idol. For the skeptics who feel that his reputation as the greatest living actor on the English-language stage is based on what he's done in the past rather than what he's doing now, his mercurial, breath-taking performance of his major scene must surely have been a revelation. Olivier's excellence must give new hope to the cause of TV drama."

Variety

1973

THE WORLD AT WAR

Produced for Thames Television by Jeremy Isaacs; *Chief historical adviser:* Dr. Noble Frankland, DFC, Director of the Imperial War Museum; *Music:* Carl Davis; *Narrator:* Laurence Olivier; 26 fifty-minute episodes.

THE PRODUCTION

This black-and-white history of World War II consisted of archival film footage from both national and private sources, as well as much material that had not previously been screened. In addition, contemporary interviews with statesmen and military leaders of the period were edited in, to considerable acclaim.

CRITICS CIRCLE

"A magnificent undertaking which consistently took a fitting attitude to the violent events of nearly 30 years before, relying on the personal recollections of survivors of all ranks, even when their testimony disagreed with official document-based history."

Philip Purser in *Halliwell's Television Companion*

"The definitive documentary on World War II."

London *Evening Standard*

"Laurence Olivier narrates superbly, of course, and producer Jeremy Isaacs has managed to convey sometimes complex ideas without sacrificing the visual interest of the program."

"Mick." in *Variety*

THE WORLD AT WAR   Recording his narration

THE MERCHANT OF VENICE

Produced and Directed for ABC Television by Jonathan Miller; *Executive Producer:* Cecil Clarke; *An ABC Theatre presentation of Britain's* National Theatre *production of the play by* William Shakespeare; *Running Time:* 150 minutes (commercials included).

CAST

Laurence Olivier *(Shylock)*; Joan Plowright *(Portia)*; Jeremy Brett *(Bassanio)*; Michael Jayston *(Gratiano)*; Louise Purnell *(Jessica)*; Anthony Nicholls *(Antonio)*.

THE PRODUCTION

Olivier and Jonathan Miller originally collaborated on this production for Britain's National Theatre. Deciding to update the play's setting to nineteenth-century Venice enabled Olivier's Shylock to assume the likeness of a Rothschild. And, despite the actor's renowned fondness for false noses, he wisely avoided one in this instance, instead favoring the aid of false front teeth and a gum piece that widened his mouth and altered his outward appearance. As has frequently been the case in modern-day productions of this play, there were protests from Jewish groups. In this case, the telecast was followed by a denunciation of ABC by the Anti-Defamation League of B'nai B'rith, which called the program "a disservice to American unity." In responding to this and the protests of other Jewish organizations, ABC stated that it would stand behind Olivier's preamble to the broadcast, in which he defended this portrayal of Shylock, adding that he would not allow the character to be sentimentalized or caricatured.

CRITICS CIRCLE

"Laurence Olivier is powerful and superb in the role of Shylock, the usurer who demands a pound of flesh if the loan is not repaid on time. And Joan Plowright as Portia strongly challenges the artistic accomplishment of her real-life husband, Lord Laurence. . . . Olivier has very definitely lived up to his avowed commitment neither to sentimentalize nor caricature Shylock. On the contrary, Shylock comes over with great dignity, intellect and human feeling. Even a Christian can feel sympathy for Shylock as portrayed by Olivier."

Val Adams in New York *Daily News*

246

THE MERCHANT OF VENICE   With Joan Plowright

THE MERCHANT OF
VENICE   As Shylock

THE MERCHANT OF VENICE   As Shylock

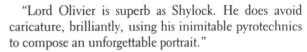

"Lord Olivier is superb as Shylock. He does avoid caricature, brilliantly, using his inimitable pyrotechnics to compose an unforgettable portrait."

John J. O'Connor in *The New York Times*

1975

LOVE AMONG THE RUINS

Directed by George Cukor; *Produced for ABC Theatre by* Allan Davis; *Written by* James Costigan; *Photographed by* Douglas Slocombe; *Editor:* John F. Burnett; *Art Direc-*

THE MERCHANT OF
VENICE   As Shylock

LOVE AMONG THE RUINS   As Sir Arthur Granville-Jones

tor: Carmen Dillon; *Costumes:* Margaret Furse; *Music:* John Barry; *Running Time:* 120 minutes (commercials included).

CAST

Katharine Hepburn *(Jessica Medlicott)*; Laurence Olivier *(Sir Arthur Granville-Jones, K.C.)*; Colin Blakely *(J.F. Devine, K.C.)*; Richard Pearson *(Druce)*; Leigh Lawson *(Alfred Pratt)*; Joan Sims *(Fanny Pratt)*; Gwen Nelson *(Hermione Davis)*; Robert Harris *(The Judge)*.

THE PRODUCTION

This first-ever teaming of two of the screen's older icons, Katharine Hepburn and Laurence Olivier, was—by the actor's later admission—among the happiest collaborations of his career. At that time, *Love Among the Ruins*, which marked the television debut of one of Hepburn's favorite directors, George Cukor, was also the most expensive two-hour film ever made for TV. The production won a raft of Emmys for Hepburn, Olivier (his third), Cukor, and Costigan, as well as for Outstanding Special and Art Direction.

CRITICS CORNER

"*Love Among the Ruins* is a project begging to be irresistible. Unfortunately, it's not. Occasionally, the

LOVE AMONG THE RUINS
With Richard Pearson
and Katharine Hepburn

two-hour romantic comedy, set in 1911, slips from ambitions of charming stylishness into mere silliness. Very occasionally, it becomes a bit of a bore. . . . Ah, but then, there at the center, are Miss Hepburn and Lord Olivier, lovingly overseen by Mr. Cukor. Gorgeously costumed and carefully lighted, they are no doubt capable of making their more fervent admirers believe in not only *Love Among the Ruins* but also Tinker Belle (sic). They are not, however, beyond fault. They fall back on familiar patterns, sometimes toppling into self-parody. Lord Olivier's 'busy' acting touches become a touch too fussy. Miss Hepburn, hidden behind high collars, huge hats and soft focuses, uses tear-filled eyes with the frequency and abandonment of a comic flinging custard pies."

John J. O'Connor in *The New York Times*

"A pair of superb performances, coupled with first-class production values, lifted *Love Among the Ruins* above the unexceptional James Costigan script. Katharine Hepburn and Laurence Olivier did their turns in the romantic comedy with great flair, and the result was amusing, offbeat, high-quality television. . . . Hepburn played a 1911 London widow who turned to barrister Olivier to defend her against a very young man who wormed his way into her affections, then sued her for breach of promise. Hepburn and Olivier had had a torrid three-day affair almost 50 years earlier, which obsessed him but which she had forgotten. . . . The extravagant gifts of Hepburn and Olivier were under the direction of George Cukor, and the three together have more show business experience than the Atlantic has water."

"Mick." in *Variety*

"Writer James Costigan's nostalgic Edwardian romance is just a charming conceit designed to bring Hepburn, 65, and Olivier, 67, together. The director is veteran George Cukor, 75, whose cutting and camera placement impart a subtle tension (and an air of elegant craftsmanship) above and beyond the call of television duty. Indeed, all three conspire to make Costigan seem a much wittier writer than he is. Olivier can get laughs by

LOVE AMONG THE RUINS   With Katharine Hepburn

snuffling or shuffling the pages on his desk. Hepburn in a temper, or just making an entrance or an exit, remains, as always, a great theatrical occasion."

Richard Schickel in *Time* magazine

1976

THE COLLECTION

Directed by Michael Apted; *Produced for Granada Television by* Laurence Olivier and Derek Granger; *Written by* Harold Pinter; *Designed by* Michael Grimes; *Running Time:* 65 minutes.

CAST

Laurence Olivier *(Harry Kane)*; Alan Bates *(James)*; Malcolm McDowell *(Bill)*; Helen Mirren *(Stella)*.

THE PRODUCTION

The first in a series of Olivier-produced plays for Britain's Manchester-based Granada Television, this 1961 Harold Pinter playlet typifies the playwright's terse, enigmatic writing, with a four-character cast weaving in and out of a story of shifting romantic relationships that cleverly blend the satiric with the sinister. The teleplay won a 1977 International Emmy Award in the fiction category.

CRITICS CIRCLE

"The performances, by Alan Bates as the husband, Helen Mirren as the wife, and Malcolm McDowell as her supposed one-night stand on the road, are all excellent as far as they could be as puppet-like Pinter characters in which tone and texture are dominant. Olivier rounds out a curious quadrangle as a man of evident wealth and benefactor of McDowell, with whom he shares his plush townhouse. The part has a certain ambiguity, but the Olivier stamp of authority is, per usual, sharp and compelling. But not overwhelming, which is one of the actor's virtues."

"Pit." in *Variety*

"If you have never really watched a great actor, catch Laurence Olivier in *The Collection*—and have something to tell your grandchildren."

London's *Sunday People*

THE COLLECTION   As Harry Kane

THE COLLECTION   Alan Bates and Malcolm McDowell

251

THE COLLECTION   With Helen Mirren

"Olivier has the smaller role of Harry, and he is perhaps too old for the character described by Pinter as in his forties. But Olivier's every expression and gesture is a model of the actor's art as he moves from petulant bewilderment at a disruption in his routine to apparent mastery of the situation, excoriating Malcolm McDowell's Bill in the play's most scathing speech."

Bob Williams in *New York Post*

1976

CAT ON A HOT TIN ROOF

Directed by Robert Moore; *Produced for Granada Television, in association with NBC-TV, by* Derek Granger and Laurence Olivier; *Written by* Tennessee Williams; *Designer:* Peter Phillips; *Costumes:* James Robinson; *Incidental music:* Derek Hilton; *Running Time:* 120 minutes (commercials included).

CAST

Natalie Wood *(Maggie)*; Robert Wagner *(Brick)*; Laurence Olivier *(Big Daddy)*; Maureen Stapleton *(Big Mama)*; Jack Hedley *(Gooper)*; Mary Peach *(Mae)*; Heidi Rundt *(Dixie)*; Sean Saxon *(Sonny)*; Mark Taylor *(Buster)*; Elizabeth Caparros *(Trixie)*; Jennifer Hughes *(Polly)*; Sam Manseray *(Lacey)*; Gladys Taylor *(Daisy)*; Nadia Catouse *(Brightie)*; George Harris *(Sookey)*; Mel Taylor *(Small)*; David Healy *(Doc Baugh)*.

THE PRODUCTION

Tennessee Williams's 1955 Pulitzer Prize stage play, which starred Barbara Bel Geddes, Ben Gazzara, and Burl Ives, is perhaps best known in its 1958 MGM screen version which starred Elizabeth Taylor, Paul Newman, and—repeating his original role—Ives. This initial TV version (it was later restaged for cable-TV with Jessica Lange, Tommy Lee Jones, and Rip Torn) was produced by Olivier for Granada-Television, which selected the husband-and-wife acting pair of Natalie Wood and Robert Wagner—much to their delighted surprise—to costar with him. Its British airing occurred six days after it premiered in the U.S.

CRITICS CIRCLE

"The production is a disaster. Olivier is a great actor and it is probably impossible for him to give an uninteresting performance, but his Big Daddy refuses to rise above the level of a curious turn. The character isn't convincing for a moment. This is always the distinguished Lord Olivier impersonating a Mississippi bully. The slow Southern drawl refuses to come to terms with the actor's clipped speech patterns. The result sounds more plantation slave than vulgarian owner.

But Olivier's failure is at least not insulting. We sense an unusual intelligence at work. What, then, is to be said of Natalie Wood and Robert Wagner in the roles of Maggie and Brick? Neutral observers can only wonder how and why they got involved in the first place. Miss Wood's acting heights seem to have been scaled in the film *Splendor in the Grass*. And Mr. Wagner has found his most comfortable niche on generally undemanding TV series. In *Cat on a Hot Tin Roof*, it is immediately apparent that they have ventured beyond their modest capabilities."

John J. O'Connor in *The New York Times*

"Lord Olivier himself played the cancer-stricken patriarch, not with the menacing corpulence of Burl Ives, but with a rather puzzling refinement. In his three-piece suit and cigar, Olivier looked like a leering-goat Mark Twain, which is witty but all wrong."

James Wolcott in *The Village Voice*

"Miscast is the only word for Miss Wood and for Bob Wagner. It would be hard to challenge the casting of Maureen Stapleton as Big Mama: she is nothing short of superb. Big Daddy, as played by Laurence Olivier, may not be the actor who would leap to mind for the part, but when he sinks his teeth into the role, he shakes it around as a dog would a bone, and does things to it that never fail to amaze and fascinate. To watch his coarseness flush to

CAT ON A HOT TIN ROOF   As Big Daddy

CAT ON A HOT TIN ROOF With Maureen Stapleton

CAT ON A HOT TIN ROOF   With Robert Wagner and Natalie Wood

the surface when one least expects it, or see his quick flashes of cruelty to Big Mama is like watching a geyser rise and fall."

Kay Gardella in New York *Daily News*

1976

HINDLE WAKES

Produced and Directed for Granada Television by Laurence Olivier and June Howson; *Written for the stage by* Stanley Houghton; *Designed by* Alan Price; *Running Time:* 90 minutes.

HINDLE WAKES   Directing Roy Dotrice (left), Rosemary Leach, and Donald Pleasence

CAST

Jack Hedley (*Christopher Hawthorn*); Rosemary Leach (*Mrs. Hawthorn*); Rosalind Ayres (*Fanny Hawthorn*); Donald Pleasence (*Nathaniel Jeffcote*); Pat Heywood (*Mrs. Jeffcote*); Trevor Eve (*Allan Jeffcote*); Roy Dotrice (*Sir Timothy Farrer*); Judi Bowker (*Beatrice Farrer*).

THE PRODUCTION

Of the plays he produced for Granada TV, this was the only in which Olivier did not also appear. Instead, he directed—with June Howson—Stanley Houghton's 1912 Lancashire drama about small-town lovers whose relationship is broken up when the girl, Fanny, asserts her independence, refusing to marry her boyfriend, Allan, on the grounds that she doesn't wish to "ruin" her life. Feminism before its time!

1977

JESUS OF NAZARETH

Directed by Franco Zeffirelli; *Produced for ITC-RAI Productions by* Vincenzo Labella; *Written by* Anthony Burgess, Suso Cecchi D'Amico, and Franco Zeffirelli, *with additional dialogue by* David Butler; *Photographed by* Armando Nanuzzi and David Watkin; *Editor:* Reginald Mills; *Art Director:* Gianna Quaranta; *Costumes:* Marcel Escoffier and Enrico Sabbatini; *Music:* Maurice Jarre; *TV Running Time:* 360 minutes (commercials included). Released theatrically in Europe.

CAST

Robert Powell (*Jesus Christ*); Anne Bancroft (*Mary Magdalene*); Ernest Borgnine (*Centurion*); Claudia Cardinale (*Adulteress*); Valentina Cortese (*Herodias*); James Farentino (*Simon Peter*); James Earl Jones (*Balthazar*); Stacy Keach (*Barabbas*); Tony LoBianco (*Quintilius*); James Mason (*Joseph of Arimathea*); Ian McShane (*Judas Iscariot*); Laurence Olivier (*Nicodemus*); Donald Pleasence (*Melchior*); Christopher Plummer (*Herod Antipas*); Anthony Quinn (*Caiaphas*); Fernando Rey (*Gaspar*); Ralph Richardson (*Simeon*); Rod Steiger (*Pontius Pilate*); Peter Ustinov (*Herod the Great*); Michael York (*John the Baptist*); Olivia Hussey (*Virgin Mary*); Cyril Cusack (*Yehuda*); Ian Holm (*Zerah*); Yorgo Voyagis (*Joseph*); Ian Bannen (*Amos*); Regina Bianchi (*Ann*); Marina Berti (*Elizabeth*); Oliver Tobias (*Joel*); Maria Carta (*Marta*); Lee Montague (*Habbukuk*); Renato Rascel (*Blind Man*); Norman Bowler (*Saturninus*); Robert Beatty (*Proculus*); John Phillips (*Naso*); Ken Jones (*Jotham*); Nancy Nevinson (*Abigail*); Renato Terra (*Abel*); Roy Holder (*Enoch*); Jonathan Adams (*Adam*); Christopher Reich (*Metelius*); Lorenzo Monet (*Jesus at 12*); Robert Davey (*Daniel*); Oliver Smith (*Saul*); George Camiller (*Hosias*); Murray Salem (*Simon the Zealot*); Tony Vogel (*Rep Player*); Isabel Mestres (*Salome*); Michael Cronin (*Eliphas*); Forbes Collins (*Jonas*); Martin Benson (*Pharisee*).

JESUS OF NAZARETH   As Nicodemus

JESUS OF NAZARETH   Laurence Olivier, Anne Bancroft, James Farentino, Robert Powell (as Jesus), James Mason, Ernest Borgnine, and Ralph Richardson

THE PRODUCTION

Franco Zeffirelli's reverent recounting of the Biblical story was filmed on location in Tunisia, Morocco and Rome, featuring a star-studded cast, many of whom performed little more than cameo roles. When NBC repeated the telecast just prior to Easter 1979, numerous outtakes were edited in, resulting in an eight-hour epic. The CBS/Fox videocassette version of *Jesus of Nazareth* allegedly runs 376 minutes.

CRITICS CIRCLE

"Though slow-paced and a bit *too* reverent, the biopic was visually and dramatically interesting. Without doing violence to the New Testament, writers Anthony Burgess, Suso Cecchi D'Amico and Franco Zeffirelli managed to generate and maintain dramatic tension. The $18,000,000 that Lew Grade—whose ITC coproduced with Italy's RAI—invested was apparent in costuming and locale, and especially in the cast. Robert Powell gained authority in the title role as he built the character, though playing a Deity is obviously an impossibility for a mere human. No humor, nor even any irony, can be allowed to intrude."

"Mick." in *Variety*

"As with all of Zeffirelli's work, from the film *Romeo and Juliet* to his theater and opera stagings, this new production combines minute details with rich visual effects. Olivier and Richardson are superb in their small roles."

John J. O'Connor in *The New York Times*

1977

COME BACK, LITTLE SHEBA

Directed by Silvio G. Narizzano; *Produced for Granada Television by* Derek Granger and Laurence Olivier; *Adapted for television by* William Inge, based on his stage play; *Production designer:* Eugene Ferguson; *Incidental music:* John McCabe; *Running Time:* 120 minutes (commercials included).

CAST

Joanne Woodward *(Lola)*; Laurence Olivier *(Doc Delaney)*; Carrie Fisher *(Marie)*; Patience Collier *(Mrs. Coffman)*; Nicholas Campbell *(Turk)*; Bill Hootkins *(Postman)*; Robert Sherman *(Milkman)*; Sheri-

dan E. Russell *(Telegraph Boy)*; Jay Benedict *(Brice)*; Bruce Boa *(Ed)*; Ed Devereaux *(Elmo)*.

THE PRODUCTION

Olivier was an emergency replacement for Robert Mitchum in the role of alcoholic Doc Delaney, a sensitive man struggling against his addiction and faced with a well-meaning wife who laments both her lost youth and her little, lost dog who once wandered off and never returned. The second in the Granada TV plays to be picked up for presentation in the U.S. by NBC, *Come Back, Little Sheba* was deemed so downbeat an offering that it was, for a time, shelved and forgotten by the network until, as an anonymous spokesman later admitted to the press, "If we didn't show it that night (New Year's Eve, 1977), our option would have run out."

This was, of course, a remake of the William Inge play that had made its mark on Broadway in 1949, starring Shirley Booth and Sidney Blackmer, becoming a motion picture three years later, when it won an Academy Award for Booth.

CRITICS CIRCLE

"The machinery of William Inge's 1949 play creaks rather badly, but the story of a drab marriage in a small Middle Western town is still strangely moving. The project itself, though overseen by Lord Olivier, remains puzzling. It is always interesting to see this superb actor do anything. But perhaps there are some things best left undone as a legacy for mass audiences. If television is going to undertake a rare series of major American plays, is it really necessary that they star Britain's most distinguished actor? Lord Olivier's Middle Western accent is distressingly close to his Southern drawl in the Tennessee Williams play, *Cat on a Hot Tin Roof*. There is much to admire in his performance, but the whole amounts to little more than an odd turn."

John J. O'Connor in *The New York Times*

"Olivier works with an American accent (coached by Bill Hootkins, who plays the postman) and, after the initial viewer adjustment, conveys the anguish of Doc Delaney. His penitent Doc suggests a volcano, and when the eruption and eventual sorrowing occur, Olivier is at his best. Woodward playing at Lola, rather than playing her, misses the character's thrust."

"Tone." in *Variety*

"*Come Back, Little Sheba* is a work that calls for many levels of acting, something Olivier achieves and Miss Woodward does not. Still, perhaps she is not to be

258

COME BACK, LITTLE SHEBA   As Doc Delaney

259

COME BACK, LITTLE SHEBA   With Joanne Woodward

COME BACK, LITTLE SHEBA   With Joanne Woodward

blamed. Since Olivier is the artistic and creative producer of this series, any faults to be found with the telecast should rightfully be laid at his doorstep."

Kay Gardella in New York *Daily News*

"The play itself seems dated and obvious, but Woodward is deeply affecting as the empty-headed beauty grown 'old and sloppy.' Olivier, now 70, is impressive as the alcoholic husband, and Carrie Fisher is charming as the lodger who disrupts their lives."

Judith Crist in *TV Guide*

"Sir Laurence—a last-minute replacement for Robert Mitchum—plays Doc, the MD fallen to chiropractor. He is about as credible as Bob Mitchum would be as King Lear. Joanne Woodward, a lovely, gifted actress, gives an embarrassing performance in the role Shirley Booth played with such divine skill. If you've anything else to do tonight at nine—do it!"

Harriet Van Horne in *New York Post*

DAPHNE LAUREOLA

Directed by Waris Hussein; *Produced for Granada Television by* Derek Granger and Laurence Olivier; *Television adaptation by* Hugh Whitemore, *based on the stage play by* James Bridie; *Designer:* Peter Phillips; *Costumes:* Jane Robinson; *Running Time:* 94 minutes.

CAST

Joan Plowright *(Lady Pitts)*; Arthur Lowe *(Gooch)*; Gregoire Aslan *(George)*; Clive Arrindell *(Ernest)*; Bryan Marshall *(Vincent)*; Laurence Olivier *(Sir Joseph)*; Jan Conrad *(Assistant Waiter)*; Jane Carr *(Maisie)*; Michael Cochrane *(Bill)*; Sara Clee *(Helen)*; David Neville *(Bob)*; Basil

DAPHNE LAUREOLA   With Clive Arrindell

Henson *(Bored Man)*; Moyra Fraser *(Bored Woman)*; Willoughby Goddard *(Mr. Watson)*; Michael Syers *(Manager)*.

THE PRODUCTION

James Bridie's charmingly eccentric little 1949 stage play had proved an excellent vehicle for Dame Edith Evans who, in her early sixties, could (with the aid of stage artifice) still convince her audiences that she could be a woman of about fifty. Olivier's choice of the play as a part of his Granada-TV series was obviously designed as a showcase for the extraordinary talents of his wife, Joan Plowright. Olivier played her eighty-seven-year-old husband, a choice supporting part. Shown in Britain, it did not reach U.S. shores until many years later, when an American cable network picked it up for the edification of PBS-oriented viewers.

CRITICS CIRCLE

"The only trouble was that Miss Plowright robbed it of half its import, simply by being too young and plump, and even more by not bringing extravagant enough a personality to the proceedings. Though the age of the deep-drinking Lady Pitts is indicated somewhere in the text as 48, Bridie wrote the part for Edith Evans, then in her sixties and renowned for playing larger-than-life old ladies. It is also clear from the attitudes of other diners in the restaurant where she is discovered that her ladyship is to be thought distinctly *grand dame.*"

Philip Purser in *Halliwell's Television Guide*

DAPHNE LAUREOLA   With Joan Plowright

261

"Olivier is perfectly unforgivable as the selectively deaf husband."

The Observer

"Joan Plowright was resplendent in the role of the eccentric Lady Pitts, and Larry very delicious as her aged and infinitely understanding husband."

Derek Granger, *Daphne Laureola*'s producer

1978

SATURDAY, SUNDAY, MONDAY

Directed by Alan Bridges; *Produced for Granada Television by* Derek Granger and Laurence Olivier; *Written for the stage by* Keith Waterhouse and Willis Hall; *Adapted from the Italian play by* Eduardo de Filippo; *Designer:* Eugene Ferguson; *Costumes:* Francis Tempest; *Running Time:* 98 minutes.

SATURDAY, SUNDAY, MONDAY   With John Duttine

CAST

Joan Plowright *(Rosa)*; Frank Finlay *(Peppino)*; Edward Woodward *(Luigi)*; Judy Parfitt *(Aunt Meme)*; Caroline Blakiston *(Elena)*; Celia Gregory *(Giulianella)*; Nicholas Clay *(Rocco)*; Clive Francis *(Roberto)*; Gabrielle Lloyd *(Maria)*; Laurence Olivier *(Antonio)*; Maggie Wells *(Virginia)*; John Duttine *(Federico)*; Richard Hope *(Attilio)*; Cyril Shaps *(Catiello)*; Michael Elphick *(Michele)*.

THE PRODUCTION

Britain's National Theatre realized a 1973 hit with the Keith Waterhouse–Willis Hall translation of Eduardo de Filippo's lively Italian farce about a volatile Neapolitan family. Directed by Franco Zeffirelli, it won acclaim in the leading roles for Joan Plowright and Frank Finlay as the imagined-faithless wife and husband, with Olivier judged "brilliant as a zany grandpa on the brink of senility." Many of the National's cast also joined forces for this Granada-TV version which, like its predecessor, *Daphne Laureola*, took a decade to reach American cable audiences.

Saturday, Sunday, Monday marked the end of the Derek Granger–Laurence Olivier TV-play series for Granada.

CRITICS CIRCLE

"Alan Bridges' splendidly operatic production of the play . . . had all the noisy eloquence that anyone could possibly expect from Sunday lunch with a large Neapolitan family. The entire cast rose to the occasion. Frank Finlay was outstandingly superb."

London *Sunday Times*

SATURDAY, SUNDAY, MONDAY   With Joan Plowright

"It was a pleasure to feel again the warmth of Eduardo de Filippo's beautifully constructed human comedy. Laurence Olivier once again transformed himself totally into an ineffectual, pottering old man, and Joan Plowright and Frank Finlay achieved passionate misunderstanding."

London *Daily Telegraph*

"Laurence Olivier, who also produced, drifts through as Grandpa, frail yet feisty; what remains of his mind is concentrated on a new suit with wide-bottomed trousers and big lapels. Joan Plowright plays his daughter, Signora Rosa, queen of the kitchen, who spends most of Act I (Saturday) preparing the ragout that she will serve in Act II (Sunday) and the family will not fully digest until Act III (Monday). Although the adaptation by Waterhouse and Hall and the direction of Alan Bridges keep the pot poppling, the tos and fros and ins and outs that may have seemed so comical in a theater, lose in translation to the television screen. You have to be there."

Walter Goodman in *The New York Times*

1981

BRIDESHEAD REVISITED

Mini-series directed by Charles Sturridge and Michael Lindsay-Hogg; *Produced for Granada Television in association with New York's WNET/13 and NDR Hamburg by* Derek Granger; *Adapted by* John Mortimer *from the novel by* Evelyn Waugh; *Production designer:* Peter Phillips; *Costumes:* Jane Robinson; *Lighting Cameraman:* Ray Goode; *Editor:* Anthony Ham; *Music:* Geoffrey Burgon; *Running Time:* 650 minutes.

CAST

Jeremy Irons *(Charles Ryder)*; Anthony Andrews *(Sebastian Flyte)*; Diana Quick *(Julia Flyte)*; Laurence Olivier *(Lord Marchmain)*; Claire Bloom *(Lady Marchmain)*; Stephane Audran *(Cara)*; Mona Washbourne *(Nanny Hawkins)*; John Le Mesurier *(Father Mowbray)*; John Gielgud *(Edward Ryder)*; Jane Asher *(Celia Ryder)*; Nickolas Grace *(Anthony Blanche)*; John Grillo *(Mr. Samgrass)*; Simon Jones *(Lord Brideshead)*; Charles Keating *(Rex Mottram)*; Phoebe Nicholls *(Cordelia Flyte)*; Jeremy Sinden *(Boy Mulcaster)*; Joseph Brady *(Purser)*; Geoffrey Chater *(British Consul)*; Jonathan Coy *(Kurt)*; Kenneth Cranham *(Sergeant Block)*; Ronald Fraser *(Redhaired Man)*; Michael Gough *(Dr. Grant)*; Stephen Moore *(Jasper)*; John Nettleton *(Commanding Officer)*; Bill Owen *(Lunt)*; Anna Quayle *(Nancy Tallboys)*; Niall Toibin *(Father Mackay)*; Robert Urquhart *(Quartering Commandant)*; John Welsh *(Barber)*.

THE PRODUCTION

Evelyn Waugh's popular 1945 novel had eluded previous efforts to bring it to the motion-picture screen. In the year of its publication, Waugh failed to reach an agreement with MGM, and five years later another deal that would have had Graham Greene as scriptwriter fell through for lack of financing. In 1977, Granada-TV acquired the rights to the book, with the idea of making it a five-part series; it was John Mortimer's eventual adaptation that extended the production to eleven episodes. At a cost of $9.9 million, the most expensive British television project up to that time, *Brideshead Revisited* took four years to reach home screens in the U.K. Filming began in Malta in May 1979, under the direction of Michael Lindsay-Hogg, but was brought to a halt in August, due to an ITV strike. It resumed that October, but Lindsay-Hogg was forced to leave because of other commitments, and Charles Sturridge, a young Waugh specialist, took his place for the remainder of the production, which included locations in Venice, the island of Gozo, and such British locations as Tatton Park in Cheshire and—at Oxford University—Hertford College, Wadham College, and Christ Church. And, of course, standing in for the mythical estate Waugh called Brideshead, is the magnificent Castle Howard in Yorkshire.

Brideshead Revisited, told in flashback form, follows the wealthy and aristocratic Marchmain family of English Catholics from the early 1920s to the close of World War II. It's all recalled through the personage of Charles Ryder (Jeremy Irons), a Protestant school friend of the family's youngest son, the charming but self-destructive Lord Sebastian Flyte (Anthony Andrews).

A tremendous success, of both critical and popular proportions, on both sides of the Atlantic (the series reached U.S. audiences beginning in January 1982), *Brideshead Revisited* won an American Emmy for Laurence Olivier's "guest star" appearance in two substantial segments of the mini-series as Lord Marchmain for "Outstanding Supporting Actor in a Limited Series or Special." Already in his early seventies at the time, Olivier had to range from a man in his late fifties to his middle seventies—and a memorable death scene. Equally deserving of awards were Anthony Andrews as the profligate Sebastian, and Claire Bloom as his coolly self-contained mother, Lady Marchmain.

CRITICS CIRCLE

"Lodged securely in that heady upper region in which *The Forsyte Saga* and *Upstairs, Downstairs* dwell, Waugh's examination of one man's view of an English Catholic family of huge wealth has been splendidly con-

BRIDESHEAD REVISITED With Stephane Audran

BRIDESHEAD REVISITED
With Anthony Andrews and
Jeremy Irons

BRIDESHEAD REVISITED   As the elderly Lord Marchmain

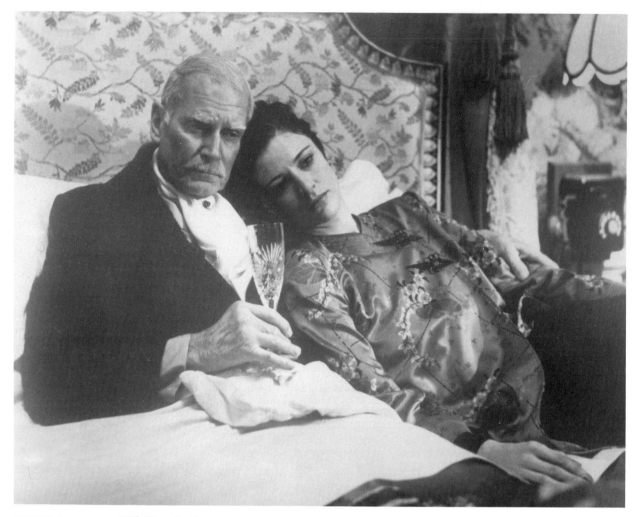

BRIDESHEAD REVISITED   With Diana Quick

verted to vidfare. Directors Charles Sturridge and Michael Lindsay-Hogg elicit remarkable performances from the remarkable cast members, none more so than from Anthony Andrews. John Gielgud's scrupulous depiction of Ryder's father gleams like a shaft of crystal. Laurence Olivier, particularly in the final, two-hour chapter, offers an impeccable performance as the failing marquis. Claire Bloom, playing the gracious, unbending Lady Marchmain, is assured. As Charles Ryder, Jeremy Irons quietly, unassumingly makes the narrator the keystone figure among the eccentric throng. It takes firmness to hold his own among this crowd, and Irons succeeds."

"Tone." in *Variety*

"Evelyn Waugh's 1945 novel *Brideshead Revisited* tellingly captures the *beau monde* of Oxford University during the 1920s, when aesthetic young men lunched on plovers' eggs and champagne. An 11-part adaptation of the novel uses a superb script by John Mortimer and handsome locations to re-create that era. The English aristocracy—whose excesses and eccentricities Waugh both satirized and glorified—is stylishly played by a cast that includes nobility of its own in John Gielgud and Laurence Olivier."

TV Guide

"Jeremy Irons and Anthony Andrews give virtually flawless performances, avoiding excesses while making every nuance blazingly clear. Lord Marchmain is played with cool but imperious disdain by Laurence Olivier. *Brideshead Revisited* is a very special television undertaking, mounted with exceptional care and sensitivity."

John J. O'Connor in *The New York Times*

A VOYAGE ROUND MY FATHER

Directed and Produced by Alvin Rakoff; *Executive Producer for Thames Television:* John Frankau; *Adapted by* John Mortimer *from his stage play; Photographed by* Tony Pierce-Roberts; *Designer:* David Marshall; *Costumes:* Louise Walker; *Editor:* Oscar Webb; *Music:* Marc Wilkinson; *Running Time:* 85 minutes.

CAST

Laurence Olivier *(Father)*; Alan Bates *(Son)*; Jane Asher *(Elizabeth)*; Elizabeth Sellars *(Mother)*; Michael Aldridge *(Headmaster)*; Alan Cox *(Son as a Boy)*; Norman Bird *(Ham)*; Albert Welling *(Japhet)*; James Downer *(Reigate)*; Susan Littler *(Miss Cox)*; Gay Wilde *(Miss Baker)*; Anthony Sharp *(Film Director)*; Ann Davies and Judy Riley *(A.T.S. Girls)*; Jonathan Newth *(Boustead)*; Malcolm Terris *(Thong)*; Jennie Goossens *(Witness)*; Harold Goodwin *(Ringer Lean)*; Patrick Barr *(Doctor)*; Esmond Knight and Raymond Huntley *(Judges)*.

THE PRODUCTION

John Mortimer based his stage play (from which this was adapted) on his father Clifford Mortimer, who was blinded in middle age, yet maintained his life as an eccentric lawyer, family man, and inveterate gardener as though nothing were changed. The story also focuses on young John who, as the years pass, learns to stop trying to understand his parent and settles for loving him.

This bittersweet memory play was filmed in the house and garden where John Mortimer grew up. A *Voyage Round My Father* won a 1984 International Emmy Award.

CRITICS CIRCLE

"A *Voyage Round My Father* seems to have been tailored for television, even though it was originally produced in 1969 as a play for BBC radio and then in the early 1970s, for the British stage. On the London stage, Clifford Mortimer was played by Sir Alec Guinness, who was later succeeded by Michael Redgrave. This TV version stars Laurence Olivier. The role clearly is a magnet for distinguished actors. Clifford Mortimer is not an easy man, and Lord Olivier doesn't seek a smidgen of unearned sympathy for him."

John J. O'Connor in *The New York Times*

"Sir Laurence Olivier's electrifying portrayal of a blind English barrister in John Mortimer's autobiographical A *Voyage Round My Father* is so luminous, finely honed

A VOYAGE ROUND MY FATHER   As Father

A VOYAGE ROUND MY FATHER   With Elizabeth Sellars and Alan Cox

267

and mercurial that one easily envisions a master sculptor at work. It's a performance that wraps around your heart, squeezing out every bit of feeling, and leaves you as lonely and devastated as the author admits he felt when his irascible yet lovable father died in 1960. Watching Olivier stoically tough it out as the elder Mortimer, pretending he isn't blind in the 'stiff upper lip' fashion of the British, is a rare television experience. Olivier's expressive and mobile face, his clever use of his eyes to convey blindness, and his delicious humor as he doles out advice to his son are enthralling."

Kay Gardella in New York *Daily News*

"There's little to respect in the character played by Olivier, but what there is is the ability of the man to command the respect, guardianship and love from those around him despite his growing nastiness. The vidpic has much to say about connections in people's lives and how they can be strengthened through strain. *A Voyage*

Round My Father is premium Olivier, high-class Bates, and fine dramatic stuff."

"Tone." in *Variety*

1983

KING LEAR

Directed by Michael Elliott; *Produced for Granada Television by* David Plowright; *From the play by* William

Shakespeare; *Designer:* Roy Stonehouse; *Costumes:* Tanya Moiseiwitsch; *Music:* Gordon Crosse; *Running Time:* 180 minutes.

CAST

Laurence Olivier *(Lear, King of Britain);* Colin Blakely *(Kent);* John Hurt *(The Fool);* Anna Calder-Marshall *(Cordelia);* Diana Rigg *(Regan);* Dorothy Tutin *(Goneril);* Leo McKern *(Gloucester);* David Threlfall *(Edgar);* Robert Lindsay *(Edmund);* Jeremy Kemp *(Cornwall).*

THE PRODUCTION

Laurence Olivier had first portrayed King Lear in 1946 with the Old Vic. Admittedly an incredibly demanding role of the actor who essays it, Lear is seldom played by someone of an age comparable with the character. In size and scope, it certainly placed cruel demands on the seventy-five-year-old Olivier, especially after his many bouts with life-threatening illness. As he explained in *On Acting:* "Doing *Lear* on television was an exercise of will for me . . . the will to get the right vitality and reality. Physically it was arduous. My frailty suited the old man. I suppose I felt his mood. Loved him. I felt the moods of all my old men." This performance brought Olivier his fourth Emmy Award.

Faye Dunaway, originally scheduled to take the part of Lear's daughter Regan, was forced to bow out; Diana Rigg replaced her.

CRITICS CIRCLE

"Laurence Olivier as King Lear made me cry. I did not expect this. In theory, *Lear* is the most moving play ever

KING LEAR   As the mad King Lear

written, but recent stage productions, trying to be tough, have paid more attention to terror than to pity. So, in my memory, has Olivier, about whom I, like many people under 40, have had something of a block. Unlike Gielgud and Richardson, he has always needed to impersonate. The necessity apparently wrecked his stage Lear of 1946. Well, he was a young man then. His position now, a heroic theatre actor confined to films and television, parallels Lear's after his abdication. A mischievous awareness of this informed his whole performance. And he *was* every inch a king: Leo McKern as Gloucester shuffled towards him with the duty that a very fine actor pays to a great one. Their duet was, literally, breathtaking."

Robert Cushman in *The Observer*

"It will now sit on the visual archive shelves alongside his Henry V, Hamlet, Richard III, Othello and Shylock to give a rounded picture of the greatest actor of our age in his maturity. For this, posterity will surely be grateful."

The Daily Telegraph

"Lord Laurence Olivier's towering portrayal of *King Lear* is the highlight of the finest Shakespearean production ever presented on television and the best Lear this critic has ever seen. Olivier, as an actor, is at the very peak of his powers. Despite reports of illness, this masterful performer whose portrayal soars to heights other actors merely dream of has climbed Mount Everest and triumphed. His Lear is fluent, rich in emotion and detail, as the 80-year-old king swings from childish senility to sharp, lucid moments when his wit cuts through the absurdity of his actions. . . . This is the second Lear of Olivier's career; his first Shakespearean role in eight years, and his very first for television. His commanding performance is petulant, outrageously irrational, touch-

KING LEAR   With Anna Calder-Marshall

271

KING LEAR   Laurence Olivier, Dorothy Tutin, Anna
Calder-Marshall, and Diana Rigg (clockwise)

ing and compelling. His white beard and sensitive face reflect the man Lear once was before sinking slowly into his dotage. Like the bow on a fine Stradivarius, he slips from mood to mood, rage to rage, registering every nuance on his splendid countenance. What makes a great artist is attention to detail, and nobody surpasses Olivier."

Kay Gardella in New York *Daily News*

1983

MR. HALPERN AND MR. JOHNSON

Produced for HBO; *Directed by* Alvin Rakoff; *Written for television by* Lionel Goldstein; *Running Time:* 56 minutes.

CAST

Laurence Olivier *(Joe Halpern)*; Jackie Gleason *(Ernest Johnson)*.

THE PRODUCTION

Produced for HBO in the U.S., this two-character drama marked the unusual teaming of Britain's Olivier with American TV favorite Gleason in a distinct change of pace for both. At his wife's funeral, Halpern meets a fellow mourner—the dapper, elderly Johnson—who's a complete stranger. When they meet again six weeks later, Johnson reveals something Halpern didn't need to know; he and the late Mrs. Halpern had been lovers prior to her marriage—and maintained a platonic friendship thereafter. For Halpern, initial outrage turns to natural jealousy, before mutual revelations turn to poignant memories for both men.

CRITICS CIRCLE

"Any old actor can play against type, but only a great actor can turn type inside out and stand it on its head. In *Mr. Halpern and Mr. Johnson*, Laurence Olivier plays a newly widowed Jewish cardboard-box manufacturer in the Bronx. Forget your preconception of how such a man looks and sounds. Olivier believes he looks and sounds like a fussy hairdresser in one of the drearier suburbs of London. He is helped in this conceit by the script, which says that the character he plays did indeed arrive here from London some 40 years ago. On the other hand, Olivier is such a very great actor that it probably doesn't matter. *Mr. Halpern and Mr. Johnson* is an inspired piece of miscasting. . . . It is inspired because it allows

MR. HALPERN AND MR. JOHNSON   As Joe Halpern

MR. HALPERN AND MR. JOHNSON   With Jackie Gleason

273

Olivier to roll his eyes, thrust his tongue against the inside of his mouth, and fly off into outrageous snits. It is miscasting because it calls on him to play opposite Jackie Gleason. . . . It is wondrous because there is no chemistry between the two actors at all; they seem to occupy separate planets. Mr. Olivier, however, has a lifetime of technique, and the television camera likes his face. Olivier, one suspects, is enjoying himself in much of this, and sometimes he seems to be playing a game with the unaware Mr. Gleason."

John Corry in *The New York Times*

"Mr. Halpern and Mr. Johnson are as unlike as two elderly gentlemen can be. What makes any of this worthy of your attention is the casting: Laurence Olivier and Jackie Gleason play them, and both are splendid."

TV Guide

"Much of the film is a conversation between the two in which their antipodal perceptions of the same woman are meant to be windows into their souls. Unfortunately, the view is obscured by Olivier's peculiarly busy performance. As in *The Jazz Singer*, in which he played the cantor, he seems to have stepped right out of the 'oy vay' school of acting. Although he is not helped by dialogue that circles repetitively over the same terrain, his shrieking and spluttering become dull and annoying; he turns a simple character into a simple-minded one. By contrast, Gleason, the king of comedic excess, is a model of restraint as the spiffy Mr. Johnson. The two men's budding fondness for each other feels forced."

Richard Stengel in *Time* magazine

MR. HALPERN AND MR. JOHNSON   With Jackie Gleason

WAGNER

Mini-series directed by Tony Palmer; *Produced by* Alan Wright and Richard Wagner Film GmbH, in association with Hungarofilm and MTV (Budapest) for London Trust Productions, Ltd.; *Executive Producers:* Derek Brierley, Endre Florian, Agnes C. Havas, and Simon Channing-Williams; *Written by* Charles Wood; *Photographed by* Vittorio Storaro; *Second-Unit Photography:* Nic Knowland; *Designer:* Kenneth Carey; *Costumes:* Shirley Russell; *Editor:* Graham Bunn; Richard Wagner's music *conducted by* Sir Georg Solti, leading the London Philharmonic Orchestra, the Vienna Philharmonic Orchestra and the Budapest Symphony Orchestra; *Running Time:* 561 minutes (Also shown in a 300-minute version.)

CAST

Richard Burton *(Richard Wagner)*; Vanessa Redgrave *(Cosima)*; Gemma Craven *(Minna)*; Laszlo Galffi *(Ludwig II)*; John Gielgud *(Pfistermeister)*; Ralph Richardson *(Pfordten)*; Laurence Olivier *(Pfeuffer)*; Ekkehardt Schall *(Liszt)*; Ronald Pickup *(Nietzsche)*; Miguel Herz-Kestranek *(Hans von Bulow)*; Richard Pasco *(Otto Wesendonck)*; Marthe Keller *(Mathilde Wesendonck)*; Gwyneth Jones *(Malvina von Carolsfeld)*; Peter Hofmann *(Schnorr von Carolsfeld)*; William Walton *(Friedrich August II)*; Sigfrit Steiner *(Ludwig I)*; Bill Fraser *(Mayor of Bayreuth)*; Arthur Lowe *(Meser)*; Lisa Kreuzer *(Friederike Meyer)*; Vernon Dobtcheff *(Meyerbeer)*; Jean-Luc Moreau *(Petipa)*; Barbara Leigh-Hunt *(Queen Mother)*; Andrew Cruickshank *(Minister Bar)*; Stephen Oliver *(Richter)*; Niall Toibin *(Lutz)*; Gabriel Byrne *(Karl Ritter)*; Stephan Paryla *(Rockel)*; John Shrapnel *(Semper)*; Cyril Cusack *(Sulzer)*; Arthur Denberg *(Paul Taxis)*; Jess Thomas *(Albert Niemann)*; Edit Rujsz *(Natalie)*; Laszlo Horvath *(Dr. Hanslick)*; Brook Williams *(Joukowsky)*.

THE PRODUCTION

Richard Burton gave one of his last performances in the title role of this marathon television mini-series by director Tony Palmer, designed to cover the adult life and times of composer Richard Wagner (1813–1883). Three years after its European premiere, it reached U.S. television screens in a four-hour version.

CRITICS CIRCLE

"There's nothing particularly new or revelatory about the new *Wagner*. So the minimal delights of this lengthy biography come from the overblown and absurd ele-

WAGNER   Vanessa Redgrave and Richard Burton

ments of this film. However, director Tony Palmer certainly lacks the finesse of Ken Russell when it comes to mixing the outrageous and historical. The most curious aspect of the film is that one might have anticipated a warmer homage. As embodied in script and performance, Wagner is a loutish, insensitive, manipulating bigot. And, while the film is handsomely mounted, very little is seen of the actual operas, which might have at least justified some of the composer's mania for money. Burton's performance as Wagner presents an almost entirely unsympathetic picture. Vanessa Redgrave and Gemma Craven as Wagner's wives have largely thankless roles. For buffs, the film's biggest draw is watching England's acting knights—Olivier, Gielgud, Richardson—working together for the first time on screen. Gielgud, who also narrates much of the film, has the largest and most satisfying role. Conversely, Olivier mugs outrageously, winding up the loser of the three."

"Klad." in *Variety*

"Gielgud, Richardson and Olivier—in their only screen appearance together—make a wonderfully comic ensemble as King Ludwig's ministers."

David Patrick Stearns in *USA Today*

"I have just exhausted four hours of my life watching the miniseries of *Wagner*, and I would willingly have them returned to me. This pedestrian, even plodding, video excursion into Wagnerian biography and hagiography is a disaster—not least in Richard Burton's almost disinterested account of the composer. But how about, you may ask, Burton's formidable co-stars in the movie, so well-featured in the publicity, Sir Ralph Richardson, Sir John Gielgud and Sir Laurence Olivier. In the third episode all three of them, together on the same screen for the first and last time, contrive to give some conspiratorial fun to the dreary proceedings."

Clive Barnes in *New York Post*

"Separating the silly man from the gifted artist requires delicacy of the highest order. *Wagner* is about as delicate as a 300-pound Brünnhilde. . . . In the relatively small roles of Ludwig's advisers are John Gielgud, Ralph Richardson and Laurence Olivier, appearing for the last time in a film scene together. Twittering and twitching away like three slightly dotty old dears, they do a hilarious turn trying to upstage one another."

John J. O'Connor in *The New York Times*

WAGNER   Ralph Richardson, Laurence Olivier, and John Gielgud

A TALENT FOR MURDER With Angela Lansbury

A TALENT FOR MURDER With Angela Lansbury

A TALENT FOR MURDER

Directed by Alvin Rakoff; *Produced for the British Broadcasting Corporation by* James Rich, Jr., and Cedric Messina. *Written by* Jerome Chodorov and Norman Panama, *based on their stage play; Camera supervisor:* Jim Atkinson; *Editor:* Phil Southby; *Designer:* Alan Anson; *Costumes:* Juanita Waterson; *Music:* William Goldstein; *Visual Effects:* Stuart Brisdon; *Running Time:* 80 minutes.

CAST

Angela Lansbury *(Anne Royce McClain)*; Laurence Olivier *(Dr. Anthony Wainwright)*; Charles Keating *(Laurence McClain)*; Hildegard Neil *(Sheila McClain)*; Garrick Hagon *(Mark Harris)*; Tracey Childs *(Pamela Harris)*; Tariq Yunus *(Rashi)*.

THE PRODUCTION

Based on the Broadway comedy-mystery that ran for a modest seventy-seven performances in 1981 with Claudette Colbert and Jean-Pierre Aumont, this BBC-TV adaptation changed the French Dr. Paul Marchand to the English Dr. Anthony Wainwright, while—oddly enough—retaining the play's American, Berkshire Hills setting. This, despite an all-British cast for television. Perhaps foreshadowing her ongoing *Murder, She Wrote* television series, in which she plays mystery novelist Jessica Fletcher, Angela Lansbury is cast here as the elderly, ever-tippling, wheelchair-bound "queen" of crime fiction, Anne Royce McClain. Lansbury later admitted that the whole production was "a rush job," but indicated that her main reason for doing A *Talent for Murder* was the opportunity to team with Laurence Olivier.

CRITICS CIRCLE

"In A *Talent for Murder,* a somewhat rickety but totally amusing mystery, the effervescent Angela Lansbury does her very best to keep the comedy bubbling to the end. Unfortunately, it fizzles before she does. Granted it's not the best comedy around, but watching pros perform, no matter what the vehicle, has its rewards. Olivier plays Dr. Anthony Wainwright, the live-in lover of wealthy Anne Royce McClain (Lansbury), the world's foremost mystery writer. He is deliciously attentive, underplaying his role beautifully to give his leading lady full range. Unfortunately, it's not suspenseful enough to make you care who killed the murder victim (her daughter-in-law is done away with), which completely undermines the last half of the comedy. It would have made a great one-acter."

Kay Gardella in New York *Daily News*

"Two incandescent stage presences, Laurence Olivier and Angela Lansbury, glow in each other's light in the delightfully impish whodunit, *A Talent for Murder.*"

Stanley Marcus in *TV Guide*

"A *Talent for Murder* was clearly designed as a 'vehicle' for Laurence Olivier and Angela Lansbury, although they could hardly have expected that they would be forced to get out and push it. It was an effort for everyone concerned, but especially for those of us who watched until the end. It was a 'mystery' story, although the only real mystery was why it was televised in the first place.... Angela Lansbury was not so much made-up as embalmed—but since she was playing the part of a lady thriller-writer, that was perhaps just as well. Lord Olivier had decided to use his high, quavering voice and on the many occasions when he exclaimed 'My daaaarling' he sounded as if he were standing at the Wailing Wall. Sometimes actors seem to believe that they can rise above a bad or nonsensical play by being grand or excessively theatrical—it is called being an 'old trouper'—but this ploy does not work on television, where even the most talented performers can be reduced to the sum of their mannerisms."

Peter Ackroyd in *The Times* of London

1984

THE EBONY TOWER

Directed by Robert Knights; *Produced for Granada Television by* Roy Roberts; *Adapted by* John Mortimer, *from the short novel by* John Fowles; *Photographed by* Ken Morgan; *Designer:* Peter Phillips; *Costumes:* Charlotte Haldich; *Editor:* Anthony Ham; *Music:* Richard Rodney Bennett; *Running Time:* 80 minutes.

CAST

Laurence Olivier (*Henry Breasley*); Roger Rees (*David Williams*); Greta Scacchi (*Diana/"The Mouse"*); Toyah Wilcox (*Anne/"The*

Freak"); Georgina Melville (*Beth Williams*); Yves Brainville (*Jean-Pierre*); Denise Bailly (*Mathilde*).

THE PRODUCTION

In his final, full-length leading role, Laurence Olivier proved that he was still in full command of his powers as an actor in John Mortimer's intriguing adaptation of a John Fowles novella, shot mostly on locations in France, near Limoges. The main setting is a spacious old farmhouse in the sunny French countryside, where a famed British painter (of the representational school) lives in retirement, sharing his home in a bizarre ménage à trois with a pair of nubile young art students. Into this unconventional surroundings comes a young English critic and avant-garde artist, intent on interviewing the old man, but soon at loggerheads with him over theories of art and life.

CRITICS CIRCLE

"If you like beautiful naked women, high-level conversations about art and the natural green beauty of the French countryside, then *The Ebony Tower* is your ticket to paradise. *The Ebony Tower* is John Fowles' shortest novel. In the hands of John Mortimer, who also adapted *Brideshead Revisited* for television, it becomes thought-provoking fun.... Sir Laurence Olivier captures all sides of aging artist Henry Breasley: the imp and the intellectual, the drunk and the dirty old man. Roger Rees is sufficiently wimpy and confused as the academic David. Greta Scacchi and Toyah Wilcox are natural in their roles as the often-nude nymphets."

Ricardo Hunter Garcia in *New York Post*

"Mr. Fowles does not lend himself easily to screen adaptation, as was clear with *The French Lieutenant's Woman.* And even the gifted Mr. Mortimer has had difficulty illuminating the dark, dense corners of *The Ebony Tower.* The one consistent delight is Lord Olivier, at his most devilishly charming, oohing, aahing and clucking with a glint in his eye that is never less than wicked."

John J. O'Connor in *The New York Times*

"On film and on television we have watched Sir Laurence Olivier handle every which role. Even in movies as unworthy as *The Betsy*, he seems never to be slumming and always to enjoy the exercise; patronizing an audience may be the one trick he can't manage. How does he do it? It seems to be selflessness and sympathetic magic, as though he identified the crucial quirk of any character, the animating madness, and opened himself up to it, like

THE EBONY TOWER   With Toyah Wilcox, Roger Rees, and Greta
Scacchi

THE EBONY TOWER   As Henry Breasley

a shaman, or an exorcist letting in the Devil. And then he edits the Devil. He knows more about the character he plays than he lets us see. He holds something in reserve, to keep us guessing; we want a peek at his hole card.

"He is admirable in *The Ebony Tower*, an adaptation of John Fowles' novel for television by the busy John Mortimer. What an opportunity for Olivier to show off, to play a randy old Yeats or a paranoid Stravinsky or a cunning Picasso, to pile on the ever-popular nineteenth-century life force. And to be sure, he chews some scenery. But even when he's chewing scenery, Sir Laurence never steals scenes; everybody around him is allowed to breathe. . . . *The Ebony Tower* is literate entertainment, and who on earth will play these roles when Olivier is gone? There is nobody else."

John Leonard in *New York* magazine

1984

THE LAST DAYS OF POMPEII

Mini-series directed by Peter Hunt; *Produced for David Gerber Productions, Centerpoint Productions, Columbia Pictures Television, and RAI by* Richard Irving and William Hill; *Adapted by* Carmen Culver *from the novel* *by* Edward Bulwer-Lytton; *Photographed by* Jack Cardiff; *Editors:* Richard Marden and Michael Ellis; *Production designer:* Michael Stringer; *Art directors:* Fred Carter and John Roberts; *Music:* Trevor Jones; *Performed by the* London Symphony Orchestra, Marcus Dods conducting; *Costume designer:* Anthony Mendelson; *Running Time:* 420 minutes (commercials included).

CAST

Duncan Regehr *(Lydon)*; Linda Purl *(Nydia)*; Franco Nero *(Arbaces)*; Nicholas Clay *(Glaucus)*; Olivia Hussey *(Ione)*; Ned Beatty *(Diomed)*; Brian Blessed *(Olinthus)*; Ernest Borgnine *(Marcus)*; Lesley-Ann Down *(Chloe)*; Siobhan McKenna *(Fortunata)*; Anthony Quayle *(Quintus)*; Laurence Olivier *(Gaius)*; Benedict Taylor *(Antonius)*; Gerry Sundquist *(Clodius)*; Catriona MacColl *(Julia)*; Malcolm Jamieson *(Petrus)*; Tony Anholt *(Lepidus)*; David Robb *(Sallust)*; Stephen Greif *(Sporus)*; Peter Cellier *(Calenus)*; Barry Stokes *(Gar)*; Howard Lang *(Medon)*; Joyce Blair *(Lucretia)*; Marilu Tolo *(Xenia)*; Francesca Romana Coluzzi *(Stratonice)*; Brian Coucher *(Melior)*; George Claydon *(Philos)*; Brian Coburn *(Burbo)*; Michael Quill *(Catus)*.

THE LAST DAYS OF POMPEII   As Gaius

THE PRODUCTION

This was a three-part TV adaptation of Sir Edward Bulwer-Lytton's epic 1834 novel, which had first reached the screen in the form of silent Italian spectacles in 1913 and 1925, followed by a 1935 American production starring Preston Foster and an Italian-made vehicle for bodybuilder Steve Reeves in 1960.

CRITICS CIRCLE

"*The Last Days of Pompeii* is an unintentionally amusing seven-hour mini-series chronicling fictionalized events leading up to Mount Vesuvius' revenge on rampant Roman empire corruption, circa 79 A.D. With its name-studded international cast, its elaborate final-episode special effects, its assiduous attention to historic accuracy and its authentic venues, *Pompeii* is one of the most self-important examples of epic high camp ever conceived for TV. . . . Generally, *Pompeii* is a stilted pastiche of soap-operaish melodrama, anachronistic sitcom humor and disaster-flick banality, cloaked in historic docudrama pomposity. . . . In supporting roles, Laurence Olivier, Siobhan McKenna, Anthony Quayle and Brian Blessed register valiantly at points."

Gail Williams in *The Hollywood Reporter*

"More like a Roman circus than a respectful adaptation of Edward Bulwer-Lytton's 1834 warhorse, *The Last Days of Pompeii* gives kitsch a bad name. Filmed in Italy and London (with miniatures looking like they were filmed in someone's garage), the seven-hour telefilm gallops along with acting styles ranging from Laurence Olivier's fragile nobleman to Ned Beatty's low-comedy used-car-dealer type. No one distinguishes himself in the vidpic, and Trevor Jones' score has been poured like syrup over the production. *Last Days of Pompeii* takes too long to explode in its final hour—and even that's a disappointment."

"Tone." in *Variety*

"Five years in the planning, costing $19 million, featuring an international cast that includes Laurence Olivier, partly filmed in the ruins of Italy's Pompeii, the production is colossal in many ways. But basically, it is a colossal failure, or, at the very least, the kind of colossal hoot that will be treasured by entertainment buffs. The destruction of the Styrofoam sets consumes at least a half-hour of the finale. It couldn't come a moment too soon."

John J. O'Connor in *The New York Times*

1986

PETER THE GREAT

Mini-series directed by Marvin J. Chomsky and Lawrence Schiller; *Produced for NBC Television by* Marvin J. Chomsky, Lawrence Schiller, and Konstantin Thoeren; *Adapted by* Edward Anhalt *from the book by* Robert K. Massie; *Photographed by* Vittorio Storaro; *Editors:* James T. Heckert and Bill Parker. *Production designers:* Alexander Popov and John Blezard; *Costumes:* Ella Maklakova and Sibylle Ulasmer; *Music:* Laurence Rosenthal; *Running Time:* 480 minutes (commercials included).

CAST

Maximilian Schell *(Peter the Great)*; Vanessa Redgrave *(Sophia)*; Omar Sharif *(Prince Feodor Romodanovsky)*; Trevor Howard *(Sir Isaac Newton)*; Laurence Olivier *(King William III)*; Helmut Griem *(Alexander Menshikov)*; Jan Niklas *(Peter as a Young Man)*; Elke Sommer *(Charlotte)*; Renee Soutendijk *(Anna Mons)*; Ursula Andress *(Athalie)*; Mel Ferrer *(Frederick)*; Hanna Schygulla *(Catharine Skevronskaya)*; Lilli Palmer *(Natalya)*; Mike Gwilym *(Shafirov)*; Gunther-Maria Halmer *(Peter Tolstoy)*; Jan Malmsjö *(Patriarch)*; Geoffrey Whitehead *(Prince Vasily Golitsyn)*; Jeremy Kemp *(Col. Patrick Gordon)*; Boris Plotnikov *(Alexis)*; Roman Filippov *(Danilo Menshikov)*; Vsevolod Larionov *(Prince Sukhorukov)*; Algis Arlauskas *(Father Theodosius)*; Walter Buschoff *(Silvestre Mons)*; Christoph Eichhorn *(King Charles XII)*; Lyubov Ghermanova *(Afrosina)*; Burkhard Heyl *(Count Piper)*; Natalya Andreichenko *(Eudoxia)*; Graham McGrath *(Peter as a Boy)*; Nicolai Lazerev *(Ivan)*; Ulli Philipp *(Louise)*; Tolly Thwaites *(Alexis as a Boy)*; Denis DeMarne *(Peter as an Older Man)*.

PETER THE GREAT   Maximilian Schell as the mature Peter

THE PRODUCTION

Among the more ambitious and costly productions ever attempted for American network television, *Peter the Great* was the first to be produced in the Soviet Union, where many months of filming were complicated by behind-the-scenes problems, during which the man who conceived the project and began directing it, Lawrence Schiller, was dismissed and replaced by Marvin J. Chomsky. Later, illness forced star Maximilian Schell to return home to Switzerland—and then to a previous directorial commitment—while another actor stood in for him (under necessarily shadowy photographic circumstances).

Peter the Great was an Emmy winner as Outstanding Mini-series, credit for which (after official arbitration) went to Chomsky, Schiller and Konstantin Thoeren. Laurence Rosenthal's evocative score also won an Emmy, while nominations went to actress Vanessa Redgrave, cinematographer Vittorio Storaro and those responsible for costume and production design, as well as the sound editors.

CRITICS CIRCLE

"NBC's momentous, Fabergé-looking account of the life of Peter the Great cuts the 6 ft., 7-in. czar down to TV size, but does a solid job of making him entertaining. . . . Stockier, more mature than the czar actually was, Schell still conveys the savagery and anger of the mighty barbarian. Because of a contractual obligation, Schell was replaced in part by Denis DeMarne, but Schell's voice-over and dubbing make the switch all but undiscernible. . . . Vanessa Redgrave projects a cool, commanding half-sister of Peter, assuredly drawing to herself every scene she is in. The late Lilli Palmer as her stepmother and Peter's mother delivers a strong, persuasive finale. Such major performers as Omar Sharif, Laurence Olivier (as the English king), Mel Ferrer, Elke Sommer and Ursula Andress make courtesy calls in the huge drama.

"Tone." in *Variety*

"Filmed on location in the Soviet Union (an American TV first), Austria and West Germany, it's a rugged, occasionally dull journey into Russia's past, but one well worth taking. Emerging as an outstanding actor in the international cast is Jan Niklas, whose captivating performance as the young czar is achieved with style and flair.

PETER THE GREAT   With Maximilian Schell

He has the energy, vigor, excitement and physical grace of the late Errol Flynn, and unquestionably walks away with the series laurels, making Maximilian Schell—who plays him in his later years—look leaden by comparison. . . . Much of the grandeur in the lavish production is lost on the small screen. As filmed in Suzdal, Moscow, Leningrad and the monastery at Zagorsk, it cries out for wide-screen treatment. But this critic is still grateful that the story of Peter, based on Robert Massie's Pulitzer Prize-winning book, was attempted, despite the many liberties taken."

Kay Gardella in New York *Daily News*

LOST EMPIRES   As Harry Burrard

1986

LOST EMPIRES

Mini-series directed by Alan Grint; *Produced for Granada Television by* June Howson; *Adapted by* Ian Curteis *from the novel by* J.B. Priestley; *Photographed by* Mike Popley; *Designed by* Roy Stonehouse and David Buxton; *Running Time:* 320 minutes.

CAST

Colin Firth (*Richard Herncastle*); Carmen Du Sautoy (*Julie Blane*); Beatie Edney (*Nancy Ellis*); John Castle (*Uncle Nick*); Brian Glover (*Tommy Beamish*); Laurence Olivier (*Harry Burrard*); Gillian Bevan (*Cissie Mapes*); Patricia Quinn (*Doris Tingley*); Weston Gavin (*Bill Jennings*); Kenneth Nelson (*Hank Johnson*); Pamela Stephenson (*Lily Farris*); Alfred Marks (*Otto Mergen*); Rachel Gurney (*Agnes Foster-Jones*); Lila Kaye (*Rose Bentwood*); Patricia Heneghan (*Varvara Wall*); Roy Barraclough (*Alfred Bentwood*); Wanda Ventham (*Muriel Dirks*).

THE PRODUCTION

Laurence Olivier gave here his final dramatic performance for television, accorded special billing in the meaty supporting role of Harry Burrard, an elderly variety artist past his prime—and very much an older edition of Olivier's Archie Rice in *The Entertainer*. The mini-series aired in the U.S. beginning in January of 1987, as part of PBS's *Masterpiece Theatre* series. Reportedly, *Lost Empires* took over ten months to film, as well as months of pre- and post-production, at a cost of between four and five million British pounds.

CRITICS CIRCLE

"This seven-part romance about life upon the wicked stage is adapted from J.B. Priestley's 1965 novel. The title refers not to the British Empire, but to the music hall palaces (or empires) whose hold on the public imagination waned in World War I. It's your basic coming-of-age story, in which a sensitive lad (Colin Firth) falls under the spell of his eccentric uncle (John Castle), a music-hall magician, and encounters wine, women and woe upon the path to manhood and soldierhood. Set in 1913–14, as Europe prepares for the barbaric world war, this evocative mini-series enchants with its randy, bustling backstage atmosphere and the entertainers' rather frank passions and perversions. . . . Luckily, the peripheral characters are intriguingly drawn. In the two-hour opener, Laurence Olivier is fascinating in his hammy way as a pathetic and obviously doomed has-been comic. Made up in ghastly little-boy togs, Olivier minces and grimaces his way through an act that's met nightly with catcalls and abuse."

Matt Roush in *USA Today*

"*Lost Empires* is a stunning, accurate evocation of a vanished age; a nostalgic look at life in the British Music

Hall before WWI. It's an elegant, richly mounted seven-part series, and boasts outstanding performances by Colin Firth and John Castle. As Harry Burrard, a pathetic comic whose style of comedy is out of favor, you'll have to look closely beneath the comic makeup to find Sir Laurence Olivier, looking like an older Archie Rice. A frightened, nervous fellow, his big fear is being given 'the bird' (fired). . . . Rife with songs and patriotism, the war ultimately brought down the curtain on not only the Empire theatres, but the British Empire—hence the title of the Priestley work. As for the production, taping it to watch in one sitting works best; only then can you appreciate how meticulously this era has been evoked."

Kay Gardella in New York *Daily News*

"*Lost Empires* is a safe, reassuring series, lovely to look at and well acted, but it stretches the viewer's patience more than his mind. It does not have the philosophical breadth, geographical range, or dramatic depth to justify seven hours on the box. The pace is too plodding, the plot too predictable, and it goes soft in the middle. . . . Whatever the limits of plot, the acting throughout is superb, from relatively unknown talents in top roles to star billing in the lesser parts. Sir Laurence Olivier, for example, appears as an aging Archie Rice type whose style of vaudeville is fast losing favor. He commits suicide early in the series."

"Guid." in *Variety*

THE PROFESSIONAL THEATRE OF LAURENCE OLIVIER

1924—Professional debut as The Suliot Officer in *Byron*, by Henry Oscar; Century Theatre, London.

1925—Policeman in *The Ghost Train*, by Arnold Ridley; Hippodrome, Brighton.

Lennox in *Macbeth*, by William Shakespeare; St. Christopher Theatre, Letchworth.

Flavius in *Julius Caesar*, by William Shakespeare; Lena Ashwell Players, Century Theatre, London.

Orsino's Servant in *The Cenci*, by Percy Bysshe Shelley; Empire Theatre, London.

Thomas of Clarence and Master Snare in *Henry IV, Part 2*, by William Shakespeare; Regent Theatre, London.

1926—Birmingham Repertory Company:

Minstrel in *The Marvelous History of St. Bernard*, by Henri Gheon.

Bit part in *The Barber and the Cow*, by D.T. Davies.

Richard Coaker in *The Farmer's Wife*, by Eden Phillpotts.

Matt Simon in *The Well of the Saints*, by J.M. Synge.

Walk-on in *The Comedian*, by Henri Gheon.

Tom Hardcastle in *The Third Finger*, by R.R. Whittaker.

Guy Sydney in *Something to Talk About*, by Eden Phillpotts.

1927—Vanya in *Uncle Vanya*, by Anton Chekhov.

Parolles in *All's Well That Ends Well*, by William Shakespeare.

Tony Lumpkin in *She Stoops to Conquer*, by Oliver Goldsmith.

Young Man in *The Pleasure Garden*, by Beatrice Mayor.

Ensign Blades in *Quality Street*, by J.M. Barrie.

Gerald Arnwood in *Bird in Hand*, by John Drinkwater.

Mervyn Jones in *Advertising April*, by Herbert Farjeon and Horace Horsnell.

Jack Barthwick in *The Silver Box*, by John Galsworthy.

Ben Hawley in *Aren't Women Wonderful?*, by Harris Dean.

Mr. Milford in *The Road to Ruin*, by Thomas Holcroft.

1928—Birmingham Repertory Company, Royal Court Theatre, London:

Young Man in *The Adding Machine*, by Elmer Rice.

Malcolm in *Macbeth*.

Title role in *Harold*, by Alfred Lord Tennyson.

A Lord in *The Taming of the Shrew*, by William Shakespeare.

Martellus in *Back to Methuselah*, by George Bernard Shaw.

Gerald Arnwood in *Bird in Hand*; Royalty Theatre, London.

Captain Stanhope in *Journey's End*, by R.C. Sherriff; Apollo Theatre, London.

Graham Birley in *The Dark Path*, by Evan John; Royalty Theatre, London.

1929—Title role in *Beau Geste*, by Basil Dean; Her Majesty's Theatre, London.

Prince Pao in *The Circle of Chalk*, by Klabund; New York Theatre, London.

Richard Parish in *Paris Bound*, by Philip Barry; Lyric Theatre, London.

John Hardy in *The Stranger Within*, by Crane Wilbur; Garrick Theatre, London.

Hugh Bromilow in *Murder on the Second Floor*, by Frank Vosper; Eltinge Theatre, New York.

Jerry Warrender in *The Last Enemy*, by Frank Harvey; Fortune Theatre, London.

Ralph in *After All*, by John Van Druten; Arts Theatre, London.

1930—Victor Prynne in *Private Lives*, by Noël Coward; Phoenix Theatre, London.

1931—Victor Prynne in *Private Lives*, Times Square Theatre, New York.

1933—Stevan Beringer in *The Rats of Norway*, by Keith Winter; Playhouse Theatre, London.

Julian Dulcimer in *The Green Bay Tree*, by Mordaunt Shairp; Cort Theater, New York.

1934—Richard Kurt in *Biography*, by S.N. Behrman; Globe

Theatre, London.

Bothwell in *Queen of Scots*, by Gordon Daviot; New Theatre, London.

Tony Cavendish in *Theatre Royal*, by Edna Ferber and George S. Kaufman; Lyric Theatre, London.

1935—Peter Hammond in *The Ringmaster*, by Keith Winter; Shaftesbury Theatre, London.

Richard Harben in *Golden Arrow*, by Sylvia Thompson and Victor Cunard; Whitehall Theatre, London.

Romeo and Mercutio (exchanging roles with John Gielgud) in *Romeo and Juliet*; by William Shakespeare; New Theatre, London.

1936—Bob Patch in *Bees on the Boatdeck*, by J.B. Priestley; Lyric Theatre, London.

1937—Old Vic Company at the Old Vic Theatre, London:

Title role in *Hamlet*, by William Shakespeare.

Sir Toby Belch in *Twelfth Night*, by William Shakespeare.

Title role in *Henry V*, by William Shakespeare.

Title role in *Macbeth*.

Title role in *Hamlet*. (Kronborg Castle, Elsinore, Denmark.)

1938—Iago in *Othello*, by William Shakespeare.

Vivaldi in *The King of Nowhere*, by James Bridie.

Title role in *Coriolanus*, by William Shakespeare.

1939—Gaylord Easterbrook in *No Time for Comedy*, by S.N. Behrman; Ethel Barrymore Theater, New York.

1940—Romeo in *Romeo and Juliet*; San Francisco, Chicago, and the 51st Street Theater, New York.

1944—Old Vic Company:

Sergius in *Arms and the Man*, by George Bernard Shaw; New Theatre, London.

Button Moulder in *Peer Gynt*, by Henrik Ibsen; New Theatre, London.

Title role in *Richard III*, by William Shakespeare; New Theatre, London.

1945—Directed *The Skin of Our Teeth*, by Thornton Wilder; Phoenix Theatre, London.

Old Vic Company, New Theatre, London:

Astrov in *Uncle Vanya*.

Justice Shallow in *Henry IV, Part 2*.

Title role in *Oedipus*, by Sophocles.

Mr. Puff in *The Critic*, by Richard Brinsley Sheridan.

Arms and the Man, Peer Gynt, Richard III (tour of Belgium, Holland, Germany and France).

1946—*Henry IV, Parts 1 and 2; Oedipus; The Critic; Uncle Vanya*; Century Theater, New York.

Title role in *King Lear*, by William Shakespeare; New Theatre, London.

1947—Presented and directed *Born Yesterday*, by Garson Kanin; Garrick Theatre, London.

1948—Australian tour, Old Vic Company:

Sir Peter Teazle in *The School for Scandal*, by Richard Brinsley Sheridan, also directed.

Mr. Antrobus in *The Skin of Our Teeth*, by Thornton Wilder, also directed.

Title role in *Richard III*.

1949—Old Vic Company, New Theatre, London:

Sir Peter Teazle in *The School for Scandal*.

Chorus in *Antigone*, by Jean Anouilh, also directed.

Directed *The Proposal*, by Anton Chekhov.

Title role in *Richard III*.

Directed *A Streetcar Named Desire*, by Tennessee Williams; Aldwych Theatre, London.

1950—Actor-Manager at St. James's Theatre, London:

Duke of Altair in *Venus Observed*, by Christopher Fry, also directed.

1951—Caesar in *Caesar and Cleopatra*, by George Bernard Shaw.

Antony in *Antony and Cleopatra*, by William Shakespeare.

Caesar and Cleopatra and *Antony and Cleopatra*; Ziegfeld Theater, New York.

1952—Directed *Venus Observed*; New Century Theatre, New York.

1953—Grand Duke in *The Sleeping Prince*, by Terence Rattigan, also directed.

1955—Shakespeare Memorial Theatre, Stratford-on-Avon:

Malvolio in *Twelfth Night*.

Title role in *Macbeth*.

Title role in *Titus Andronicus*, by William Shakespeare.

1957—Archie Rice in *The Entertainer*, by John Osborne; Royal Court Theatre, London.

Titus Andronicus; tour of Paris, Venice, Belgrade, Zagreb, Vienna, Warsaw, and Stoll Theatre, London.

The Entertainer; Palace Theatre, London.

1958—*The Entertainer*; Royale Theater, New York.

1959—Title role in *Coriolanus*, by William Shakespeare; Shakespeare Memorial Theatre, Stratford-on-Avon.

1960—Berenger in *Rhinoceros*, by Eugene Ionesco; Royal Court Theatre, London.

Title role in *Becket*, by Jean Anouilh; St. James Theater, New York.

Directed *The Tumbler*, by Benn W. Levy; Helen Hayes Theater, New York.

1961—Toured the U.S. as Henry II in *Becket*; and Hudson Theater, New York.

1962—Director of Chichester Festival Theatre:

Directed *The Chances*, by John Fletcher.

Prologue and Bassanes in *The Broken Heart*, by John Ford, also directed.

Astrov in *Uncle Vanya*, also directed.

Fred Midway in *Semi-Detached*, by David Turner; Saville Theatre, London.

1963—Director of National Theatre, at the Old Vic:

Directed *Hamlet*.

Astrov in *Uncle Vanya*, also directed.

Captain Brazen in *The Recruiting Officer*, by George Farquhar.

1964—Title role in *Othello*.

Solness in *The Master Builder*, by Henrik Ibsen.

1965—Directed *The Crucible*, by Arthur Miller.

Tattle in *Love for Love*, by William Congreve.

Othello (National Theatre Company tour, Berlin and Moscow).

1966—Directed *Juno and the Paycock*, by Sean O'Casey.

1967—Edgar in *The Dance of Death*, by August Strindberg.

Plucheux in *A Flea in Her Ear*, by Georges Feydeaux (National Theatre Company tour, Canada).

1968—Directed *Love's Labours Lost*, by William Shakespeare.

Co-directed with Donald MacKechnie *The Advertisement*, by Natalia Ginsburg.

1970—Shylock in *The Merchant of Venice*, by William Shakespeare.

1971—Directed *Amphitryon 38*, by Jean Giraudoux; New Theatre, London.

James Tyrone in *Long Day's Journey into Night*, by Eugene O'Neill; New Theatre, London.

1972—*Long Day's Journey Into Night*; Old Vic.

1973—Antonio in *Saturday, Sunday, Monday*, by Eduardo de Filippo; Old Vic.

John Tagg in *The Party*, by Trevor Griffiths; Old Vic.

1974—Directed *Eden End*, by J.B. Priestley.

1980—Directed *Filumena*, by Eduardo de Filippo; St. James Theater, New York.

1986—Akash (a "portrayal" in hologram form) in the musical *Time*; Dominion Theatre, London.

FREE!

Citadel Film Series Catalog

From James Stewart to Moe Howard and The Three Stooges, Woody Allen to John Wayne, The Citadel Film Series is America's largest film book library.

Now with more than 125 titles in print, books in the series make perfect gifts—for a loved one, a friend, or yourself!

We'd like to send you, free of charge, our latest full-color catalog describing the Citadel Film Series in depth. To receive the catalog, call 1-800-447-BOOK or send your name and address to:

Citadel Film Series/Carol Publishing Group
Distribution Center B
120 Enterprise Avenue
Secaucus, New Jersey 07094

The titles you'll find in the catalog include:
The Films Of...

Alan Ladd
Alfred Hitchcock
All Talking! All Singing!
   All Dancing!
Anthony Quinn
The Bad Guys
Barbara Stanwyck
Barbra Streisand:
   The First Decade
Barbra Streisand:
   The Second Decade
Bela Lugosi
Bette Davis
Bing Crosby
Black Hollywood
Boris Karloff
Bowery Boys
Brigitte Bardot
Burt Reynolds
Carole Lombard
Cary Grant
Cecil B. DeMille
Character People
Charles Bronson
Charlie Chaplin
Charlton Heston
Chevalier
Clark Gable
Classics of the Gangster
   Film
Classics of the Horror Film
Classics of the Silent Screen
Cliffhanger
Clint Eastwood
Curly: Biography of a
   Superstooge
Detective in Film
Dick Tracy
Dustin Hoffman
Early Classics of the
   Foreign Film

Elizabeth Taylor
Elvis Presley
Errol Flynn
Federico Fellini
The Fifties
The Forties
Forgotten Films
   to Remember
Frank Sinatra
Fredric March
Gary Cooper
Gene Kelly
Gina Lollobrigida
Ginger Rogers
Gloria Swanson
Great Adventure Films
Great British Films
Great French Films
Great German Films
Great Romantic Films
Great Science Fiction Films
Great Spy Films
Gregory Peck
Greta Garbo
Harry Warren and the
   Hollywood Musical
Hedy Lamarr
Hello! My Real Name Is
Henry Fonda
Hollywood Cheesecake:
   60 Years of Leg Art
Hollywood's Hollywood
Howard Hughes in Hollywood
Humphrey Bogart
Ingrid Bergman
Jack Lemmon
Jack Nicholson
James Cagney
James Stewart
Jane Fonda
Jayne Mansfield

Jeanette MacDonald and
   Nelson Eddy
Jewish Image in American
   Films
Joan Crawford
John Garfield
John Huston
John Wayne
John Wayne Reference
   Book
John Wayne Scrapbook
Judy Garland
Katharine Hepburn
Kirk Douglas
Lana Turner
Laurel and Hardy
Lauren Bacall
Laurence Olivier
Lost Films of the
   Fifties
Love in the Film
Mae West
Marilyn Monroe
Marlon Brando
Moe Howard and The
   Three Stooges
Montgomery Clift
More Character People
More Classics of the
   Horror Film
More Films of the '30s
Myrna Loy
Non-Western Films of
   John Ford
Norma Shearer
Olivia de Havilland
Paul Newman
Paul Robeson
Peter Lorre
Pictorial History of Science
   Fiction Films

Pictorial History of Sex
   in Films
Pictorial History of War
   Films
Pictorial History of the
   Western Film
Rebels: The Rebel Hero
   in Films
Rita Hayworth
Robert Redford
Robert Taylor
Ronald Reagan
The Seventies
Sex in the Movies
Sci-Fi 2
Sherlock Holmes
Shirley MacLaine
Shirley Temple
The Sixties
Sophia Loren
Spencer Tracy
Steve McQueen
Susan Hayward
Tarzan of the Movies
They Had Faces Then
The Thirties
Those Glorious Glamour Years
Three Stooges Book of Scripts
Three Stooges Book of Scripts,
   Vol. 2
The Twenties
20th Century Fox
Warren Beatty
W. C. Fields
Western Films of John Ford
West That Never Was
William Holden
William Powell
Woody Allen
World War II